URBAN SPRAWL

Determinants | Consequences | Sustainability

A study of urban expansion in Karachi, Pakistan

URBAN SPRAWL

Determinants | Consequences | Sustainability

A study of urban expansion in Karachi, Pakistan

Dr. Akhtar Hussain

EXCELLER BOOKS®
A GLOBAL PRESS

URBAN SPRAWL

Determinants | Consequences | Sustainability

A study of urban expansion in Karachi, Pakistan

Cover by Exceller Books using resources from Pixabay.com

ISBN: 978-81-19524-31-0

First published in India in 2025 by Exceller Books,
An imprint of GE Group
Address: G1, Dream Apartment, Degree College Road, Belgharia,
Kolkata, 700056, India
www.excellerbooks.com

EXCELLER BOOKS®
A GLOBAL PRESS

Dedication

This book is the result of long and sustained hours of hard work and sheer dedication. This journey is dedicated to everyone, be it family, friends, peers, and supervisors, who made all their efforts to create this masterpiece. This book is also dedicated to my readers, who will find interest in the chapters in the future.

Acknowledgements

I am very pleased and delighted to submit this dissertation after a long journey. The doctoral study really touched my patience, and I had to work very hard to reach this milestone. I am thankful to Almighty Allah for giving me the right direction throughout this journey, without which I could not have reached this far. I am grateful to my friends, relatives and acquaintances, who kept motivating me to complete this study. I am really obliged to my supervisor, Dr. Noman Ahmad, whose guidance kept me on track to improve my studies and finally conclude them. I am thankful to Dr. Riaz Sheikh, Dean of Social Sciences at SZABIST, who was always kind and helpful to me, whenever I needed any support. I am especially thankful to Saif Ullah, a doctoral candidate, and Dr. Irshad for providing their expertise whenever I required it. I would like to take this opportunity to show my gratitude to the management and support staff of SZABIST, who always treated me with utmost respect and provided all necessary logistics during the course of my study. I hope my study will provide further impetus in the field of Urban Studies and will be useful in academia. I am looking forward to your prayers and best wishes.

Abstract

Urban sprawl is a global phenomenon of the present era and is mostly taking place in developing countries. The prompt expansion in the urbanized world includes the enlargement of cities and towns with an increase in population. Often, urban sprawling would require settlement and resettlement for a large portion of the population. There is a consistent and vibrant trend among people in developing countries to agglomerate in megacities and large urban centers. This phenomenon has gained the attention of researchers in the fields of urban geography, environmental studies and city and regional planning. This dissertation traces the spatial growth of Karachi and its impact on the urban ecosystem. The literature shows that without careful investment and planning, megacities will be overwhelmed by burgeoning negative impacts on the environment, natural resources, human health, and a host of social and economic issues. Moreover, the study aims to fill the gap by analyzing the impact of increasing urban sprawl on the city and what other effects it can bring towards the sustainability and development of Karachi. Most of the previous studies focused on the urban trajectories of Karachi and concentrated on the technical issues of image processing and classification. Furthermore, many pieces of research merely focused on baseline projections, failing to determine and explore the phenomenon of urban sprawl holistically for developing cities such as Karachi. The previous studies related to Karachi failed to adopt the monocentric city model and other related theories to quantify the causative factors of suburbanization.

This study can contribute to understanding urban sprawl, causative factors, consequences and development trends in Karachi. The aim of this study is to contextualize urban growth and sprawl experienced in the coastal city of Karachi in southern Pakistan. For this purpose, remote sensing tools and mixed methods were employed to identify and determine the causative factors respectively in Karachi from 1975 to 2016. The study was based on the Monocentric Model and extended further, as demonstrated in the literature, to frame the hypothesis and evaluate the determinants of sprawl in Karachi. This thesis integrates Remote Sensing (RS) and Geographic Information System (GIS) technology for deriving LULC classification, analyzing LULC changes and using a statistical analysis approach to measure urban sprawl. The study uses a mixed methods approach by employing qualitative and quantitative tools to find out the determinants and consequences of urban sprawl and enrich theoretical and empirical urban research.

The data and information of the study were collected through primary and secondary sources that include satellite images, historical maps, time series data, documents, private stakeholders and public participants. The study revealed that from 1975 to 2016, LULC changed drastically; major agricultural lands were converted into built-up lands. This study pinpoints random expansion at the urban fringe, strip development along or between highways, scattered development of industrial land, and leapfrog development of urban residence and industrial areas, showing a multi-directional nature in Karachi. The findings reveal that migration, population growth, non-implementation of master plans, economic prosperity, weaker governance, political patronage and land encroachment are major forces contributing towards urban growth. The research highlights the non-provision of essential civic and municipal services and ecological challenges caused by the unending physical expansion of Karachi in numerous directions. This dissertation proposes urban vision and policy changes to control the undesired sprawl and stimulate sustainable urban development. This study can be essential for urban planners, policymakers and social scientists to frame appropriate policies for the sustainable development of the cities.

Keywords: *Land use change, urban sprawl, spatial growth, remote sensing, periphery, mixed methods, sustainability, Karachi (Pakistan)*

List of Tables

List of Figures

Table of Contents

Chapter 1| Introduction

The trend of urban development can be gauged from the fact that around 75% of the population of developed countries live in urban areas, whereas 45% live in developing countries (Leichencko & Solecki, 2005). The growth in urban population is positively correlated with economic activities by overlooking negative consequences for urban residents and for society at large (World Bank, 2006). Urban growth is strongly linked with economic growth, but at the same time, cities of developing countries lack the capacity to deal with a growing urban population (White, 1998). The policy failures may lead to urban slums, shortages of residential units, excessive pressure on urban infrastructure, an unhealthy environment, bad aesthetics, overcrowding, and social problems (Luck & Wu, 2002).

"Cities" are complex systems and policies related to urban density and form that significantly affect the functionality, economics, and sustainability of cities (Newton, 1997). Urbanization, globally, has led to a general perception that cities are becoming more dense and overcrowded places (Araya & Cabral, 2010). Why do cities keep growing even after countries are already highly urbanized, and why do some cities grow faster than others? The first thing is that the population growth of cities is economically important in itself. Urban economics has proposed a number of theories to explain the population size of cities. Over several decades, many other theories have emerged around urban sprawl. These theories were brought by geographers, planners, economists, and transportation engineers.

The formal modelling of urban spatial structure originated in the monocentric city model by Alonso (1964). The model was extended to include production, transportation and housing by Mills (1967; 1972) and Muth (1969). The theory assumes the city is monocentric; that is, all production activities within a city are supposed to take place in a point representing the central business district (CBD), and all workers living in the surrounding area are supposed to commute to the CBD. The study of Mieszkowski and Mills (1993) labels the causal factors included in Brucekner and Fansler's (1983) study as making up the "natural evolution" theory of suburbanization. Gordon and Richardson (2000) also write about the natural economic factors that generated the greater dispersion that has been observed in urban areas of America over the last 50 years.

The "flight from blight" theory is another important theory for the increased suburbanization. It looks beyond the natural forces that increase the footprint of an urban area and decrease population density, seeking a further explanation for urban decentralization based on the desire to avoid the real and perceived blight of more centralized locations. The theoretical effect of "fiscalization of land use theory" on the size of an urban area is still ambiguous under general assumptions. Using a specific form of an individual preference function, Song and Zenou (2006) derive the theoretical effect that greater reliance on local property taxation results in urban areas that use less land. The "spatial mismatch hypothesis" (SMH) argues that low-skilled minorities residing in US inner cities experience poor labour market outcomes because they are disconnected from suburban job opportunities.

'Urban sprawl' refers to the extent of urbanization, which is a global phenomenon mainly driven by population growth and large-scale migration (Langley et al., 2001). Urban sprawl is often labeled as an outward spreading of a city and its suburbs to exurbs, to low-density and often auto-dependent development on rural land in the outskirts of the cities (Gillham, 2002). For example, the study carried out by Rubiera et al. (2016) on Madrid confirms how its metropolitan area tends to expand towards the periphery before the pressure on land use in the areas closest to the centre forces it to do so. In other words, the most remote municipalities are the ones that are growing the most, although there is abundant space for urban growth in the closest municipalities.

According to Dieleman and Wegener (2004), the development which gets out of control is called urban sprawl. Classically, urban sprawl is a USA phenomenon associated with the rapid low-density outward expansion of US cities, stemming back to the early part of the 20th century (Ke et al., 2009). It is fueled by the rapid growth of private car ownership and the preference for detached houses with gardens (Cabral et al., 2016). With a few exceptions, urban growth management policies and plans are designed with the aim of limiting the growth of cities challenged further by failure or limitations (Millward, 2006). The process of urban sprawl dates back to the era of the 1950s when the USA's urbanization, in the form of residence and commercial areas, encroached on the surrounding farmlands and forest areas (Jiang et al., 2007).

In recent years, most recent research has paid attention to the complexity of mobility in dispersed cities in emerging countries in Latin America (Coq & Asian, 2019) and in Asia (Xu et al., 2019). In general, the conclusion of these works is that city models can provide true solutions to urban mobility problems. Compact cities facilitate the use of public transport by having a high population density that is combined with strong centres that act as a point of interaction and interconnection.

The extent of urbanization or its growth drives the change in land use and cover pattern, which might create adverse impacts on the ecology of the area, especially the greenness (Herold *et al.*, 2003; Liu & Lathrop Jr., 2002; Grimm *et al.*, 2000). The other main environmental aspect around which the greatest scientific studies have been carried out in recent years is related to the exploration and analysis of the relationship between urban sprawl and energy efficiency from a residential perspective. The study by Navamuel et al. (2018), carried out in 17 regions of Spain, determined the effects of urban sprawl on electricity demand via quantile regression, reaching similar conclusions for the Spanish case. This residential model increases the energy costs as more kilometres of pipelines or power lines at a higher cost and greater loss of the resource during transport to be borne. The studies conducted by Hatab et al. (2019) and Vicenzotti et al. (2018) demonstrate the immediate environmental impact of the extension of a city and the soil predation produced by its dispersion and show how dispersion aggressively invades landscapes and damages natural environments.

The study by Gruebner et al. (2017) highlights the relationship between social isolation and discrimination, as well as poverty in the neighbourhood, which contribute to the mental health burden and the built environment. The negative impacts of density are also linked to competition for space that displaces street life in the absence of urban planning.

The urban movement, which originated in advanced Western countries, including the USA and Europe, is being replicated in the cities of developing countries (Cowherd & Heikkila, 2002). Urban population in developing countries grew by 40% between 1900 and 1975 (Balogun et al., 2011). The study conducted by Arnfield (2003) observed that by the year 2000, almost 45% of the world population was living in urban areas, and projected half of the world living in urban areas by 2007. The latest projections indicate that 60% of the global world population will live in cities (UNPF, 1999).

The study by UNFPA (2007) confirms that the cities in developing countries, mainly in Asian and African countries, are growing at a rapid pace, and by 2025, half of the population living in developing countries will be urban. The study further elaborates that the urban population is expanding so fast due to the advances and breakthroughs in the fields of agriculture, nutrition, and medicine. The study by UNPD (2006) states that 3.3 billion people are already living in urban cities across the world, and by 2030, that number will have risen to almost 5 billion. The total population is increasing by 280.000 people per day, whereas 95% of the annual population increase between

1994 and 2004 occurred in less developed regions. It is evident that developing countries are now in the midst of urban growth, resulting in dis-urbanization and sub-urbanization caused by a high rate of motorization combined with prosperity and the development of traffic and communication infrastructure.

Urban areas have significantly increased in this era of globalization hailed by many scholars as an indicator of progress (Njoh, 2003). In his study, Scott (2002) argues that big cities in developing countries, being the hub of commercial and economic activities, are the driving forces for the integration of their national economies into the global economy. Rapid urban growth in Asian developing countries has led to large urban agglomerations called "megacities." The study of Rustiadi et al. (2021) mentions that Jakarta megacity keeps growing and has extended along a corridor linking Jakarta to the Bandung metropolitan area. The continuation of this urban expansion, which converts strategic rice fields, seems unstoppable, regardless of its adverse impacts. The study by Deuskar et al. (2015) points out that Manila's urban spaces — defined as areas where the built environment covered more than 50 per cent of the landscape in a given pixel — had expanded from 1,800 square kilometres to 2,300 square kilometres (2.4 per cent per year) between 2000 and 2010. The expansion was the sixth highest in Asia in both absolute and proportional terms.

The city of Bangkok has shown rapid urban growth in recent times due to increasing population, causing the city to grow physically on all sides, including the adjacent provinces, resulting in colossal loss of agricultural land in the surroundings (Perera et al., 2007). Rapid urban growth in Mumbai urbanization has resulted in dispersed growth in peri-urban pockets due to socio-economic aspects with the burgeoning population of the city, and consequently, there has been an uneven growth pattern apart from expanding slums in and around the city (Ramachandra et al., 2014). Dhaka is another stellar example mentioned in Pramanik and Stathakis (2016), as its physical characteristics are gradually changing due to plots and open spaces being transformed into built-up areas, open squares into car parks, and low land and water bodies into reclaimed built-up lands. The cities of developing countries are predominantly destinations of transhipment, hubs of export-oriented industries and regional bases of multinational corporations for their offshore operations (Davis, 2005).

Many economists and researchers believe that urbanization is the main consequence of economic prosperity. However, some empirical studies suggested that they have not found evidence that urbanization affects the economic growth rate (Bloom, Canning & Fink, 2008). They argued that a rapid increase in the urban population is also strongly associated with growing barriers to productivity and environmental degradation. The accelerating pace of urban growth should be the primary concern for planners as it leads towards sprawl, an undesirable urban expansion. Urban development in the form of sprawl is characterized as non-compact growth, low-density suburban development, scattered, leapfrog or ribbon structure (Ewing, 2008).

The sprawl adversely affects city centers due to unsustainable energy consumption, extensive mobility through automobiles, reduced public transportation in the suburbs and the fragmentation of urban development (CEC, 2006; Walsh, 2012). The reduction in sprawling phenomenon simply brings sustainability and better functioning of the cities, as there is an argument that sprawl brings a better quality of life away from the city center and close to nature at the urban fringe (Frenkel & Ashkenazi, 2008). The empirical literature on the consequences of urban sprawl in the case of developing countries, particularly in Pakistan, is rare. However, the phenomenon of urban sprawl is more intense (ADB, 2012). There are study gaps in areas of exploring urban trends, their manifestations, forms, causes and consequences for the sustainability of the cities (United Nations, 2010). In this context, the current study is an attempt to explore the concept of urban sprawl and its determinants and consequences in Karachi, Pakistan.

Karachi is the country's premier financial, economic, industrial, service and marine hub, generating 12–15 percent of Pakistan's gross domestic product (GDP) and is a powerhouse of manufacturing employment in the country. The city's economy has been robust, and it can be checked from World Bank staff estimates that it is the least poor district in Sindh province and the third least poor in Pakistan. However, due to the large population, there are a fair amount of wealth variations and inequalities within different segments of the population. It is a cosmopolitan city inhabited by people with culturally enriched backgrounds and a sense of social commitment. With its enormous potential to serve the country, Karachi is now emerging as a globalized complex in competition with other regional centers of a similar order. Since 1923, five master plans were formulated, but none of them was backed with legal cover, resulting in urban sprawl, widespread *katchi abadis*/slums and gross deficiencies of required infrastructure/utilities, limiting the potential opportunities of Karachi.

The city's population has witnessed a massive surge on the back of rapid urban growth due to large-scale industrialization. The city's population, which was a mere 1.068 million in the 1951 census, jumped 16 times by 2017, presenting all sorts of challenges to urban planners. The city's urban growth and population growth have been relatively higher than those of the rest of the urban centres in the country. The city's inner core is abandoned on varying grounds and replaced by new developments at the edge of the city in Malir and West districts because of land abundance and low density. The city's physical expansion is taking place on the outer edge of the city due to large-scale residential and industrial activities, while poor and vulnerable communities have become denser in the existing informal settlements in the inner core of the city. The perennial housing shortage in the city also continues to worsen, with at least 50 percent of the population living in informal settlements of varying quality (Hasan et al., 2017).

1.1. Background of the Study

According to Ishrat (2014), no country can attain middle-income level status without industrialization, urbanization, and vibrancy of its cities. The high incomes supported by strong urban growth rates and economies of scale backed by urban management are prerequisites for such progress to materialize (Yang et al., 2011). In their study, Kiran and Joshi (2012) indicated that cities are being flooded with people on the back of massive urbanization, flourishing economy and industrial base, creating pressure on land use planning. The exceeding physical limits of cities in the modern era have compelled social scientists to ask some fundamental questions (Birch, Wachter 2011): Who are these new dwellers? Where will they live? How can services for them best be financed and supplied? Urban sprawl is directly linked with socio-economic information and unexpected population growth, resulting in uncontrolled sprawl with poor infrastructure facilities and poor economic performance as demonstrated by Sarvestani et al. (2011), Jieli et al. (2010) and Kiran & Joshi (2012).

Successful urban centers must facilitate provision of jobs, quality education and health care, cleaner neighborhoods, effective transportation, and welcoming spaces for all residents (Inman, 2009). The cities of the modern era require innovative solutions to address the urban sprawl (Simmie, 2001). Urban sprawl is a worldwide phenomenon but is the latest in terms of developing countries with varying characteristics and features. Urban sprawl is labeled as unending development, increasing congestion, reduction in green spaces, exorbitant property prices, infrastructure woes and class segregation. Most of the academic literature is in accord with the view of sprawl as 'the lack of continuity in expansion' (Mills, 1981), as adopted from Clawson (1962). According to the findings of Ewing (1997), sprawl leads to fundamental changes in the city landscape by overburdening the public utilities, creating mobility issues, severely impacting the vegetative land and resulting in psychic costs.

Urban sprawling is also related to an increase in pollution, traffic and energy. In addition, an increase in sprawl might increase the destruction of wildlife and harm natural areas. Studies by Czech et al. (2000), Johnson (2001) and Robinson et al. (2005) have clearly pointed out the grave environmental concerns linked to urban sprawl as large sizes of vegetative land are encroached upon to meet the sprawling demands. In contrast, Hasse and Lathrop (2003) have documented the social costs of increasing the burden on the provision of public services due to expanding cities. The study by Sinha (2017) concludes that urban sprawl is an unsustainable form of urban growth because of the negative externalities associated with it. Sprawl exhibits poor planning, low-density development, encroachment into agricultural and forest areas, and unlimited outward expansion in the form of leapfrog, radial and ribbon development fuelled by growth in automobiles.

Urban sprawl brings with it various negative consequences like green space consumption, densification of land and stress on existing infrastructure (Punia & Singh, 2011). The official figures suggest that the city of Karachi is witnessing an unprecedented population growth rate at 7% per annum coupled with unplanned and haphazard developmental activities leading towards sprawl, causing tremendous pressure on the provision of required infrastructure and delivery of social services at a reasonable cost. Urban sprawl has aroused wide social focus because it is possible to impede regional sustainable development.

The increase in population numbers and spatial growth of Karachi has been greatly witnessed from 2000 to 2010 because of persistent migration and expanding suburbs (Kotkin & Cox, 2013). It is projected that by 2025, almost half of the country's population will reside in urban centers, overburdening Karachi at the same time. Ewing (1997), Malpezzi (1999) and Galster et al. (2001), in their studies, observed that it is essential to separate the causes, characteristics, and effects of sprawl to reach a consensus on what sprawl is. The current study attempts to identify and quantify sprawl, and then efforts have been made to look for its spatial characteristics. What does sprawl look like on the ground? What characteristics should one look for in the landscape to declare a city sprawled or sprawling?

1.2. Problem Statement

The objective of the study is to evaluate and determine the factors of urban sprawl and their impact on the urban eco-system of Karachi. Moreover, the problem area and field study of this research will be Karachi. It also aims to explore the factors and characteristics of urban sprawling and their impact. Moreover, the study presents varied problems currently being faced by Karachi, the largest urban agglomeration in the country. Pakistan is already one of the most urbanized and largest countries in South Asia, with around 36.4% of its population living in cities according to the recent census of 2017, and it is estimated that more than 60% of the country's population will be urban by 2050. The urban population of the country stands at 75.58 million and is increasing day by day due to accelerated economic activities in urban centers. The province of Sindh is the most urbanized province, with 52.02% of the population living in urban areas, whereas 68% of the population is concentrated in three major cities – Karachi, Hyderabad and Sukkur.

The study aims to look into sprawling trends of the city over the years, the major determinant factors leading to physical and haphazard growth and challenges that have resulted in the form of socio-economic development, quality and sustainability of the infrastructure and the main consequences for the people living in a megacity like Karachi. All cities need high-quality infrastructure to facilitate the movement of people and goods and the delivery of basic services with a better environment to live in. It is imperative to assess and address the bottlenecks related to key issues like urban transport, water supply and sanitation, and municipal solid waste by containing the urban sprawl through policy mechanisms and effective enforcement. This dissertation aims to explore policy tools and recommendations to provide a necessary mechanism to other urban centers of the country, which are witnessing similar patterns of urban growth along with complexities of the issues like Karachi, as exhibited in this study.

1.3. Research Objectives

The main objective of this research is to investigate the dynamics responsible for causing urban sprawl so that this knowledge will support managing and mitigating urban sprawl with the larger objective of framing policies that can lead towards the sustainability of the urban eco-system in Karachi. A key requirement to understand these dynamics is to identify the sprawl through appropriate metrics or indicators. Subsequently, this paper aims to analyze the urban growth process and spatial patterns in Karachi, Pakistan, from 1975 to 2016 by employing GIS and remote sensing technologies. Moreover, this study will capture and evaluate the dynamics of causal factors through investigations that are accelerating the sprawling process in Karachi. This would aid as a policy tool and aid in management for mitigating the impacts of urban sprawl. In order to realize this, the specific objectives are:

To undertake an extensive review of the literature for a better understanding of the sprawl and the features, determinants, characteristics, patterns, theories, debates, costs and alternatives associated with it.

- To acquire and analyze medium spatial resolution satellite data from the Landsat platform at different intervals along with the population census data to map urban expansion and peri-urban land cover change in Karachi.
- To develop a better understanding of the collection and utilization of qualitative data and gain insights from participants' experiences and observations regarding urban sprawl in Karachi.
- To determine the different drivers and causal factors responsible for sprawl and establish the linkages

through a quantitative method by basing the Monocentric City Model for Karachi.

- To evaluate, compute, and examine the responses of citizens through a quantitative survey regarding urban infrastructure, municipal services, utilities, and other related factors and draw consequences about the effects of urban expansion in Karachi.
- To propose solutions to control, check and monitor the spatial growth for the sustainability of sprawl in Karachi.

1.4. Research Questions

The aim of this doctoral study is to highlight the extent of outgrowth (or the sprawl) that is factored by the process of land-use change and pinpoint the causative factors that are driving this whole process. The following questions need to be addressed:

- What are the determinants of urban sprawling in Karachi?
- What are the features, patterns and characteristics associated with sprawling cities?
- What are the methods of sprawl identification in the city of Karachi?
- What are the sustainable policy options for managing urban sprawl?

1.5. Significance of the Study

Governments have started to seek solutions to address the complex urban structures in cities. Recently, the negative impacts of urban sprawl have been widely discussed in the academic world. Many scholars have also proposed policy suggestions for the growth management of the cities (Liu, 2002; Song, 2005). However, in the case of Karachi, to the best of the authors' knowledge, there is no single study to quantify the sprawl and its determinants. This study adds to the extended literature by identifying the sprawl, its causative factors and its consequences on the urban structure of Karachi. The information regarding the extent of urban growth has great significance for the municipalities of growing urban and suburban areas for multiple purposes. The key indicators in this context would include water and land resource management, urban planning, service allocation, marketing analysis, etc. Development authorities need to give more time and attention and accelerate their efforts for proper management of land and other resources to accommodate the expanding population.

The study aims to thoroughly quantify the sprawling environment of Karachi, pointing out its reasons and structure and finding out its trends, outcomes and future direction. The consolidation or containment of the sprawl around the urban fringe should be supported by strong institutional mechanisms, the provision of essential facilities, and reaching out to the marginalized communities of urban society, thus reducing the economic gaps.

This study has threefold significance:

- First, how extensive the urban growth was between 1975 and 2017.
- Secondly, to model the urban growth to make predictions in the future.
- Thirdly, it proposes sustainable solutions for the betterment of communities living in the city of Karachi.

The contribution of this research in urban growth modeling aspires to provide a useful tool in urban planning and support appropriate decision- making initiatives. Cities across the globe have experienced a major wave of urban sprawl and its consequences, so it is of prime interest to comprehensively examine the sprawling process, determinants, results, and policy issues related to Karachi. This study is an effort to contribute to the ever-expanding field of urbanization, urban planning, urban development and urban economics. The study is directed to academia, research scholars, urban professionals, think tanks, policy-makers, NGOs, civil society, freelance researchers, and government institutions that include municipalities and provincial and federal authorities.

1.6. Boundaries of the Study

Besides being the capital of the Sindh province, Pakistan, Karachi is the premier financial and industrial hub. It is spread over 3527 km^2 (Lu et al., 2019) with significant urban coverage area mostly comprised of flat or rolling plains with hills on the western and northern boundaries of the urban sprawl. Karachi is the most cosmopolitan city in the country, with a major transportation hub and the distinctive advantage of the two largest seaports: Port Karachi and Port Bin Qasim. Its international airport acts as the major aviation hub of the country. The two rivers, Malir and Lyari, flow through the city. Karachi comprises 07 districts, as shown in figure 1.1. It is projected that by 2025, almost half of the country's population will reside in urban centers, overburdening Karachi at the same time.

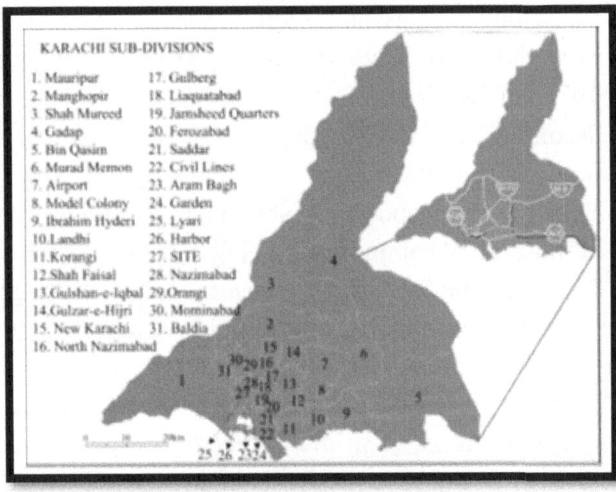

Figure 1.1: Study Area: Karachi, The Capital City of Sindh Province
Source: Fahad et.al (2021)

1.7. Structure of the Dissertation

The dissertation consists of four parts:

1.7.1. Discussion and Statement of Problem

This part mainly covers chapter 1, which entails discussing the introduction of the topic, the background of the studies, narrating the research problems, setting the objectives, defining the research methodology, and stating its significance for the academic world.

1.7.2. Background, Theory and Methods

This part of the dissertation highlights chapters 2 to 4. The discussions in this section come under the purview of the nature of the literature review. The discussions under chapter 2 cover the range of theoretical perspectives about urban sprawl, its relevance to the modern world, and its significance and socio-economic implications on citizens across the world. Chapter 2 presents an overview of urban growth dynamics in Karachi. The study presents further deliberations in chapter 4 by discussing the methodology of the study at length.

1.7.3. Analysis and Findings

This is the main body of the dissertation, which consists of chapters 5 and 6. The RS and GIS approach adopted in this chapter is all about the identification of sprawl in Karachi metropolitan. The study applies a mixed method approach to find out the determinants and causes of sprawl by presenting qualitative and quantitative data. In the end, the household survey portrays citizens' perceptions of the delivery of different services in Karachi.

1.7.4. Conclusion and Recommendations

The study is completed in the form of chapters 7 and 8, which have major policy implications. An effort has been made to recommend policy measures for countering the sprawl and ensure sustainable development. This part also covers the scenarios of future research and clearly mentions the limitations encountered during the course of the study.

In order to do this, the study was designed in the following way:

- Firstly, the literature was carefully reviewed;
- Secondly, the study was continued with research design and mixed methods;
- Thirdly, the methodology was framed, followed by data analysis and discussion of results, and
- Lastly, conclusions and recommendations were put forward for the target audience.

The illustration is explained in figure 1.2.

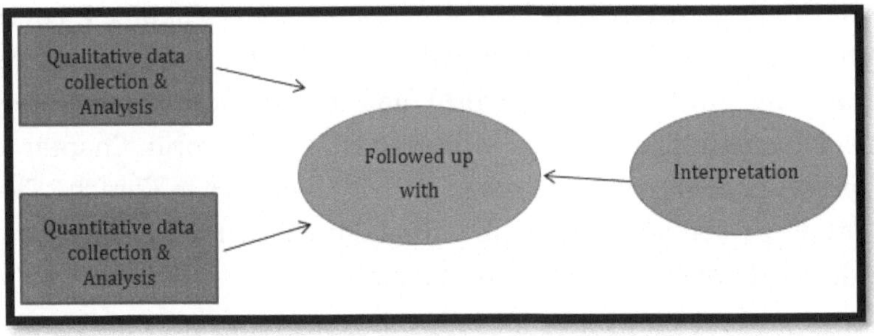

Figure 1.2: Convergent Mixed Methods Design (Creswell, 2012)

1.8. Hypotheses

- H1: Population is significantly correlated with urban sprawl in Karachi
- H2: Household income contributes significantly to the urban sprawling
- H3: Transport cost has a negative and significant effect on sprawl in Karachi
- H4: KMC revenue is positively associated with the sprawl in Karachi
- H5: Vacant plot tax is negatively related to the sprawl in Karachi

- H6: Interest rate has a negative influence on sprawl in Karachi
- H7: Employment opportunities promote sprawl in Karachi
- H8: Average monthly wages are significantly related to the sprawl in Karachi
- H9: Health facilities (Person Per Doctor) have a positive impact on sprawl in Karachi
- H10: Education facilities (School Enrolment) are positively attributed to the sprawling in Karachi
- H11: Electricity consumption promotes sprawling in Karachi
- H12: Increase in private transportation leads to sprawling in Karachi

1.9. Limitations of the Study

The study is limited to a time frame (doctoral thesis) to meet the requirements and objectives of the research. All sections were construed to meet expected deadlines. The limitation of the time creates threats to the internal and external validity of the research. However, all necessary measures have been undertaken to address the problematic areas of the research in a timely manner. The mixed method approach adopted in this study had to have lengthy deliberations as one has to triangulate the results and reach a logical conclusion. This approach might have missed some important models and conceptual frameworks, which, otherwise, may have complemented this study.

1.9.1. Literature Limitations

This study was conducted to check and evaluate the causative factors of urban sprawl with respect to Karachi. The extent literature mainly covered the sprawling trends in technologically advanced countries because urban sprawl as a phenomenon has been mainly discussed and narrated from the advanced countries' perspective. However, recently, academics have undertaken numerous studies covering patterns, forms, and constituents of urban sprawl in developing countries. It is possible that trends, forms, manifestations and constituents of urban sprawl in developing countries may be compared and related to those advanced countries, or there could be a probability of deviation arising in developing countries as it has been found that cities in developing countries are overcrowded, congested and less urban.

1.9.2. Resource Limitations

The resources linked with this thesis were limited, and every effort was made to use them adequately. The major constraints were time, budget, personnel and other related limitations. Finding data was very hard as the acquisition avenues were very difficult and, at the time, very expensive. The interviews were conducted by people who mostly belonged to the private sector, academia, and urban planning, leaving them short of government representation due to their reluctance and shortage of time. The lack of government input may result in missing their work in the field of urban planning in the city of Karachi. The household survey was conducted in the midst of limited time and budget and the outbreak of COVID-19. The survey sample of around 150 people conducted from different areas may not necessarily reflect the perceptions of the whole population universe living across the city. All efforts were made to frame the scientific questionnaire and form an appropriate sampling method to present more reliable, valid, and generalizable results and substantiate the claims of the research study.

1.9.3. Technological Limitations

Fulfilling technological requirements was a challenging part of the study as it required extensive software, tech applications, and other related tools. The study would not have been completed and possible without technological assistance, which was sought from tech-savvy personnel whenever required during the course of this study.

1.9.4. Geographic Limitations

The undertaken study is case-based and applies to the geographic limitations of Karachi. The study has only been conducted in the sprawling context of Karachi, and it can derive different meanings and results if applied to other sprawling cities of the country. The other sprawling cities may have their own trends, patterns and dimensions, making them distinguished from Karachi. The methodology applied in this study may not be appropriate and significant if applied to other cities. Other cities may have their own determinants and consequences in sprawling scenarios.

1.10. Knowledge Gaps

The characteristics and urbanism of Karachi have been discussed and debated in several studies. The study by Hashmi (1965) attempted to present an analysis of data on the demographic characteristics of the population of Karachi from a historical point of view. In this monograph, an attempt was made to present the analysis of some data on the demographic characteristics of the population of Karachi. The increase in migration in the post-independence scenario, growth patterns of the city, increasing density due to a large influx of people and fast pace of urbanization have somehow pressurized the government as well as policy-makers to design policies looking at socio-political conditions in Karachi (Hassan, 1999).

The study by Akhtar and Dhanani (2013) thoroughly investigated the decline in central density and peripheral growth of the population and found out that the population density gradient of Karachi has developed a gentle slope. The study by Afshan, Mujeeb and Gill (2016) focused extensively on spatial expansion and enormous increase in a short span of time and, secondly, the bizarre appearance of informal settlement and their amalgamation in the urban areas. The research by Qureshi et al. (2010) underlined the sensitivity of Karachi as a challenge for environmental and urban planning and an acute opportunity for research, where the discussion embarks on the requirement of a thorough trans-disciplinary approach to study such urban systems.

The increased urbanization has brought several issues, such as management challenges, enhanced demographic density, resource deficiency and ecological pressures, due to the uncontrolled spreading of the city in the form of urban sprawl (Hasan, Arsalan, & Fatima, 2015). The key question is whether researchers have scientifically proven and established any link of sprawl with these outcomes. Moreover, minimal studies have quantified the drivers of sprawl by employing a base model of the Monocentric City Model and engaging with urban experts to understand this complex phenomenon, particularly in Karachi.

Massive suburbanization and motorization generally contribute to urban land use and transportation systems that are socially, economically, and environmentally unsustainable (Qureshi & Lu, 2007). The continuous extension of roads and low interest rates are driving the exponential growth of vehicles, which has an immense impact on extending the urban footprints of Karachi. Moreover, studies are required to check the impact of voluminous growth in vehicles with spatial growth in Karachi, as these need to be carefully studied for better urban planning in Karachi. The cost of commuting is strongly related to the suburbanization of cities. This study checks the impact of commuting costs on the sprawling of Karachi.

The need to manage urban sprawl also arises from the global concerns of achieving sustainable urbanization. Sustainable urbanization is a dynamic, multi-dimensional process that covers environmental, social, economic, and political institutional sustainability (UNDP, 2012). The phenomenon of urban sprawl is potentially observed as a threat to achieving sustainable urban development.

The outgrowth beyond the municipal limits is also aided by minimal or no restrictions on building guidelines. Thus, the outgrowths are marked by the process of land-use changes. However, it is important to characterize these outgrowths and forecast them so that local governments can systematically ensure the delivery of services and attempt planned development in these regions. It is essential that an effective understanding of the phenomenon of urban sprawl, especially from the perspective of a developing country, should be gained. This would eventually aid in evolving any policy and management options for effectively addressing the problem of urban sprawl.

Chapter 2| Literature Review

The cities of the ancient past were primarily used as a tool for sheltering and military defence, mainly focusing on agricultural activities. Before the advent of the Renaissance, cities used heritage-based urban transformation as an initial strategy on an urban scale (Jokilehto, 1986). The study conducted by Mumford (1961) narrates that from the Renaissance until the tail end of the 18th century, the urban transformation featured geometric urban patterns, monumental architecture, and wider streetscapes. The study by Rykwert (1976) pinpoints that the 19th century triggered a wave of urbanization in pre-modern industrial cities, a dominant paradigm that instigated urban formation and urban growth. The studies by Elkin et al. (1991) and Arbury (2005) confirm that urban areas formed after the Industrial Revolution were never witnessed before in human history.

The advent of the 20th century conceived debates and challenges evolving from capitalism, industrialism and liberalism (Hillier & Healey, 2010). The cities adopted a paradigm shift in urban processes from modern industrial cities to post-modern and post-industrial global cities (Freestone, 2000) in the theory and practice of urban planning (Ward, 2004) at organizational and spatial levels. The era of the 21st century has enforced the process of urban regeneration as a dominating paradigm in urban studies by turning global cities into sustainable ones, knowledge hubs, and competitive regions, as well as concentrating on the ecological and historical protection of the urban environment in the planning paradigm of the 2000s (Gülersoy & Ayrancı, 2011). The land and property markets have turned into instrumental players in urban design, urban policies, and economics in the planning agenda (Tasan-Kok & Beaten,

2011), making way for market-driven spatial planning and the emergence of profit-driven land usage.

The changing land dynamics have manifested the upward growth of cities, resulting in the mass expansion of their boundaries (Habibia & Asadib, 2011; Daramola & Ibem, 2010). This phenomenon of land transformation has been labeled as urban sprawl (Bhatta, 2010; Sudhira, 2008; Arbury, 2005). The study of urban sprawl has enthused researchers, planners and policy-makers in the USA, Australia, Canada, and some industrialized European countries since World War II (Gill, 2008). Urban sprawl is labeled as unending development, increasing congestion, reduction in green spaces, exorbitant property prices, infrastructure woes and class segregation (Weng, 2001).

2.1. Determinants of Urban Sprawling

Urban sprawl is a global phenomenon but with varying characteristics and features. Patacchini et al. (2009) stated the non-availability of standard definitions for defining the urban areas across Europe. Sprawl is mostly termed a process in which a large portion of the available land is utilized to earmark the urban areas. According to Dieleman and Wegener (2004), the development which gets out of control is urban sprawl. The study by Gordon and Richardson (1997) concludes that sprawl results from free market decisions made by households and firms; it maximizes the overall welfare of society.

The study by Galster et al. (2001) has defined sprawl by a combination of its causes (zoning and poor planning), carrying out characteristics of (low density and leap-frogging) and producing negative effects (traffic congestion and air pollution). The study by Burgess (1998) defined sprawl as a process in which spatial growth exceeds population growth, causing physical development in cities with lower densities. Lee et al. (1998) mention inefficient land use, leap-frogging, and low density as essential attributes of urban sprawl that take place at the urban fringe.

Brueckner (2000) defined urban sprawl as the excessive spatial growth of cities, dissecting places of work, education, recreation, and commercial activities, thus requiring cars to move between places. Ewing (1997) argued that poor accessibility due to separate land uses, besides the lack of functional open spaces, are the primary hallmarks of sprawl. Urban sprawl is very much noted and opined by many researchers (Harvey & Clark, 1971; Snyder & Bird, 1998; Persky et al., 2000; Knaap, 1998; Pendall, 1999; Shen, 1996; Feitelson, 1993; Levine, 1999). In the case of sprawling cities, if undesirable outcomes are more than desirable, as many planners believe, it would be essential to design policy tools for the containment of the sprawl.

The related studies have focused on the features, causes, pitfalls, and factors that subsequently led to the sprawl and discussed at length the impacts, consequences, and challenges set forth by urban sprawl and countermeasures to contain this phenomenon. Before the Industrial Revolution, there was a fraction of people who used to live in urban areas. From the late 1700s onwards, on the back of technological advances and massive industrialization, people started migrating from rural to urban areas (Elkin et al., 1991). The study by Newman et al. (1992) highlighted that traditionally cities were small, consisted of dense environment, often walled and never exceeded five kilometers. The design of European cities and older cities in North America and Australia is indicative of such structures. Gillham (2002) links the contemporary version of suburbs and sprawl to the Industrial Revolution of the 19th century, which led to the foundation of advancement in modern communication and transportation triggered by automobile technology in post-WWII.

Classically, urban sprawl is a USA phenomenon associated with the rapid low-density outward expansion of USA cities, stemming back to the early part of the 20th century, fuelled by the rapid growth of private car ownership and the preference for detached houses with gardens. The process of urban sprawl dates back to the era of the 50s when the USA's urbanization in the form of residences and commercial areas encroached on the farmlands and forest areas (Jiang et al., 2007). In the historical context, since the events of the great depression in the USA, real estate projects and development patterns have mostly favoured low-density development (Jackson, 1987). The North American sprawling plans can predominantly be seen in the period after 2nd World War with the visuals of dependence on automobiles, outer development, leap-frogging and above all, the changing development preferences of developers preferring outskirts instead of competing for remaining infill sites due to stringent statutory requirements (Williams & Shiels, 2000).

According to the studies, urban sprawl has caused major drawbacks to large cities and towns. However, the historical study conducted by Buttenheim and Cornick (1938) observed the unrestricted and disorderly expansion of cities into rural areas, enhanced built-up activities, and expansion at the urban fringe in American and European cities during the 1930s. The study conducted by Rodwin (1945) presents slums, indeterminate zoning, and traffic congestion as byproducts of sprawl in the greater London region during the late 1930s to early 1940s.

The study undertaken by Zhang (2002) highlights that the suburbanization of the late 50s in American cities triggered the process of urban sprawl, redefining the urban boundaries by encroaching large tracts of farmland and forests. The study by Burchfield et al. (2006) mentions that sprawl in the USA between 1976 and 1992 resulted from groundwater availability, temperate climate, rugged terrain, decentralized employment, early public transport infrastructure, and low impact of public service financing on local taxpayers. The 20th-century urban development presents sprawl as the primary form of urban development, disregarding its socio-economic and environmental implications.

2.2. Urban Sprawl in Developed and Developing Countries

The studies in the extent of academic literature focused on the trends of sprawl in North America and Europe (Christiansen & Loftsgarden, 2011; EEA, 2006). The urban sprawl in developed countries is related to consumer preferences for new lifestyles and new strategies of capital accumulation in cities through real estate development (Muñiz, Calatayud & Dobana, 2013). In North America and Europe, urban development mostly consists of areas with low densities, outward expansion, far from the central district, and leap-frog development (Couch et al., 2007). In the North American and Australian cultures, sprawling communities in the form of exclusive neighborhoods, spacious homes and multiple automobiles are considered status symbols and signs of success (Farkisch et al., 2011). The cities in developing countries are growing faster than developed countries, but resource utilization in developed cities is unsustainable and far ahead of developing cities (Kumar et al., 2007). The empirical literature on Europe usually focuses on particular regions. The UNDP (2012) report mentions that 73% of the European population living in cities is projected to reach 82% by 2050, posing a threat to sustainability and causing land use conflicts.

The natural growth of the population induces sprawl, as confirmed by the census data for the period 1970-90 of the hundred largest urbanized areas in the USA, accounting for (50.90%) of the sprawl (Kolankiewicz & Beck, 2001). The study further confirms immigration as a major cause as it has been on the rise, especially after World War II and appears as a major contributor to overall sprawl caused by population growth. Most of the recent literature highlights that sprawl in the developed world does not take place in isolation; in fact, it is linked to some benefits among city dwellers because of lower housing costs, larger homes with ample space, neighborhoods with marginal crime rates, desire for better educational facilities and subsequent influence on local governments, some of the reasons for suburban settlements (Knaap et al., 2000; Brueckner, 2003).

The study by Batty et al. (1999) features income and racial segregation as important components of sprawl in the developed world. The rich elite and white households move to peripheries to avoid social problems associated with city centres (Audirac et al., 1990; Glaeser & Kahn, 2003; Glaeser et al., 2004), helped by improved connectivity and modern transportation. This fastens the urban decay and segregation of the urban poor as they cannot afford expensive cars and are forced to live in the city centers (Gin & Sonstelie, 1992; Glaeser & Kahn, 2003). The assertion is well supported by Glaeser et al. (2001) that poverty rates tend to increase in locations close to transit stops and public transportation. Glaeser and Sacerdote (1999) point out that sprawl in developed countries leads towards lesser social interactions as people living in big houses are less likely to interact with their neighbors than people residing in the city centers.

In comparison and contrast to other countries like those in Europe, sprawl has altered land uses as data from 2000 to 2006 suggest that the continent has lost 1120 km2 on average per year of natural and semi-natural areas to urban development (EEA, 2011b). The study by Seto et al. (2012) shows probabilistic computations that 77500 km2 of the European continent will be or have been converted to urban areas between 2000 and 2030. The urban built-up has continued even in regions (e.g. eastern Germany) with declining populations (Grobmann et al., 2013; Rienow et al., 2014), pointing out other contributory factors for this expansion. Numerous studies (Couch et al., 2007; Siedentop & Fina, 2012) have addressed urban sprawl in Europe.

The urban movement, which originated from the advanced Western countries, including the USA and Europe, is being replicated in the cities of developing countries (Cowherd & Heikkila, 2002; Leichencko & Solecki, 2005). The study of urban sprawl is less explored in developing countries, considering this phenomenon is more intense and that there are study gaps in areas of exploring urban trends, its manifestations, forms, causes and consequences for the sustainability of the cities (Maktav & Erbek, 2005; Sarvestani et al., 2011).

Critically compared to developed and industrialized countries, urban growth in developing countries is increasing rapidly and will continue to increase in the next decades (Punia & Singh, 2011). The highest growth will mainly occur in the cities of Asia and Africa, in areas that are now more than two-thirds rural and by 2025 will be half urban (Arabani & Amani, 2007). A number of empirical studies, notably those of the Globalization and World Cities Group (GAWC), have categorized many large developing country cities as global/world cities based on their economic function and the presence of global headquarters and producer service firms (Mirmoghtadaee, 2012).

Cities in developing countries considerably enjoy the position of command and control system because they are the hubs of manufacturing production for the global market, exporting a large array of products and services (Masoumi, 2014). However, once the sprawl expanded beyond the USA, urban planners in developing countries began to contribute to the literature on sprawl, such as Israel (Frenkel & Ashkenazi, 2008), South Korea (Sohn & Choi, 2008), India (Sudhira et al., 2004). The study by Twumasi-Ankrah (1995) considers rural-urban migration as a main factor of population growth in urban regions of Ghanaian cities due to the urban primacy nature of cities, where a few cities are developed at the cost of others with adequate infrastructure turning out to be attractive destinations for the people residing into rural areas. The research by McKinsey Global Institute (2011) articulates that 136 new cities from developing countries, mainly belonging to Indonesia, China, India, Nigeria and Pakistan, will make way on the list of the top 600 cities in terms of GDP, requiring a lot of resources to compensate the continuous growth.

The study by Scott (2002) elaborates that big cities in developing countries are the hubs of commercial and economic activities. These activities lead to the integration of their national economies into the global economy. Examples of cities like

Manila, Jakarta, Bangkok, Mumbai, Dhaka and Karachi can be quoted as they have emerged as major destinations of transshipment, export-oriented industries, service sector and regional base of multinational corporations for their offshore operations. The determinants of urban sprawl in the public sector in industrialized and least developing countries are impacted differently. Public infrastructure in developing countries is considered relatively poor (Niemeier, Bai, & Handy, 2011). The roads are broken, public transport is outdated, and power supplies break very often (Bjorwatn, 1999). Urban centers around the world, particularly in developing countries, are facing challenges of aging and obsolete infrastructure (Sinha, 2017). The infrastructure deficiency, coupled with the growing population, is creating a suffocating environment (Tyagi, 2015). Engineers in cities are facing mounting challenges in rehabilitating the infrastructure and keeping pace with the development of new infrastructure (Zhang, 2004).

Urban migration in developing countries is increasing faster than in other regions of the world, contributing to the augmentation of existing problems (Patrov et al., 2009). The developing countries, despite being deficient in basic amenities and infrastructure, are attracting people from surrounding areas because of human agglomerations (Allmendinger, 2002). Urban agglomerations, along with the explosive growth of population in developing countries, create messy urbanization and threaten the social, economic and ecological environment (Birabi, 2007). Menon (2004) considers the lack of space in the inner core of a city in developing countries as a major factor for people moving into suburban areas because the failure of the government to manage and predict urban population growth effectively results in the formation of slums at the urban core, paving the way for new developments at the peripheries.

Exporting labor is an important commodity produced by world cities (McGrath, 2005). Recently, there has been growing interest in international migration. According to data released by the United Nations, in 2013, there were 232 million international migrants, who accounted for 3.2% of the world population, representing an increase from 175 million in 2010 and 154 million in 1990 (Yoshino et al., 2017). The number of labor migrants is also increasing. It is estimated that developing countries received a staggering $125 billion in inward remittances from their overseas workers in 2004 (Maimbo & Ratha, 2005) and it is estimated to have reached $436 billion in 2014 (Wickramasekara, 2016). In many countries, the inward remittances have far exceeded the foreign direct investment (Mohammadi, Zarabi, & Mobaraki, 2012). In the case of the Philippines, remittances were comparatively seven times higher than foreign direct investment in recent years (Maimbo & Ratha, 2005). The study by Tyner (2000) observed that urban centers in developing countries are the largest supplier of migrant workers mainly because of superior facilities.

The dearth of planning leads towards a gloomy situation and creates a chaotic situation in the cities (Poormohamadi & Jamekasra, 2011). Experts agree that the major problems faced by urban residents in the cities of developing countries are: traffic congestion, economic segregation, growing poverty, water-related crises, natural disasters, and other negative social and environmental effects (Shaalan, 2013). The 3 billion people expected to be added to the global population between 2005 and 2050 will mainly be in Asian and African cities (McLaren, Coleman, & Mayunga, 2005). Owusu-Ansah and O'Connor (2010), in their study by Kumasi (Ghana), ascribed the proliferation of nuclear families, complexities in the land administration system and incremental housing as the reasons for urban development.

2.3. Urban Sprawl Models & Theories

The pioneer theory in urban economics related to Suburbanization is the Monocentric City Model (Alonso, 1964; Mills, 1981; Muth, 1961; Wheaton, 1974). The model narrates that all employment takes place within the jurisdiction of the single Central Business District (CBD). So many studies have tested the empirical validity of the monocentric city model, such as Deng et al. (2008) and Shanzi (2009), which can be referred to in terms of developing countries as they applied the monocentric city model to Chinese cities. The study conducted by Deng et al. (2008) pointed out that the wave of industrialization, service sector growth, and upward economic growth were major determinants of Chinese urban sprawl.

Many mathematical, engineering and theoretical models have been used to attempt to develop an understanding of some aspects of urban structure, transportation and socio-economic relationships (Cheng & Masser, 2003; Fragkias & Seto, 2007; Jiang et al., 2007). It is stated that sprawl virtuously results from an orderly market and not from microeconomics or land speculation (market). Over several decades, many other theories have emerged around urban sprawl. The dissertation attributes and discusses selected theories of urban sprawl. These theories offer useful guidance for conducting empirical work on urban growth by providing us with specifications and highlighting the number of identification pitfalls.

2.4. Monocentric City Model

The pioneer theory in urban studies related to Suburbanization is the Monocentric City Model. This urban spatial structure model was conceived by Alonso (1964) and further extended after the inclusion of production, transportation and housing by Mills (1967, 1972) and Muth (1969) and formalized by Wheaton (1974), with its parameters set to match broad features of a stylized city. The model narrates that all employment takes place within the jurisdiction of the single Central Business District (CBD). The model operates on the assumption that the city has a fixed population level, and with the given income level and with the notion that people travel into the city centre for work, and hence, commuting is costly and increases with distance from the CBD, households would choose to live closer to the city centre. The study, therefore, looks at these models to apply and look at the benefits and shortcomings of urban sprawling.

The CBD is surrounded by higher-density dwellings and taller buildings, but it distinctively changes its morphology as it gets closer to the outer urban fringe, turning out to be the least denser and horizontal development. However, the physical structure and composition of the city totally depends on the size of the population, the cost of transport and the value of land in alternative uses, such as agriculture. A large amount of literature has been dedicated to the focus on the importance of location for intra-city commutation because it is a key determinant of land use land classification (LULC) and the development of housing infrastructure in cities. In turn, the ease of commuting, the availability of housing, and earnings determine the population size of cities.

The model's simplicity helps focus on fundamental forces that are likely to matter for all large cities, as observed by Brueckner (1987). This simple yet powerful model explains the main observed regularities of the urban structure. Numeral studies have tested the empirical validity of the Monocentric City Model. These theories offer useful guidance for conducting empirical work on urban growth by providing us with specifications and highlighting a number of identification pitfalls. The studies by Deng et al. (2008) and Shanzi (2009) can be referred to in terms of developing countries as they applied the Monocentric City Model to Chinese cities.

2.5. Natural Evolution Theory

The natural evolution theory related to suburbanization is another theory favored by urban theorists and transportation experts (Mieszkowski & Mills, 1993). The theory states that when employment is concentrated at the center of a city, the pattern of residential development takes place from the inside out, paving the way for minimizing the commuting costs for work trips to the Central Business District (CBD). The infilling of land in the center of the city gains momentum, ensuring fast-paced development leading towards scarcity of the land in the CBD and providing ground to realtors and developers for initiating new residential units on open tracts of land in the suburbs. The series of new developments at the urban fringe provides a compelling ground for high-income earners to settle because of spacious homes, lush gardens, ample parking, and modern housing. The older homes previously built in the CBD on the basis of lower real incomes conveniently move to lower strata of society, leading towards income-stratified neighbourhoods and fragmentation. The theory emphasizes that the middle class prefers larger single-family lots in the suburbs to denser multi-family residences in the central city.

The revolutionary changes in the mode of transportation in the form of streetcars, commuters, railroads, and finally, the automobile have improved the prospects of decentralization in the outer urban rings, thus significantly increasing the size of the urban area, the decreased residential densities and spatial growth of metropolitan cities in all directions. The larger firms, at the behest of enhanced connectivity, lower land costs, lower wages and customer-centric approach, preferred re-location at the urban fringe. This process was self-reinforcing: as large employers became suburbanized, their employees followed them. Separate literature on lifecycle effects has provided empirical evidence that supports Rossi's (1955) lifecycle hypothesis argument that changes in household size, age of household members, and marriage status force households to change their housing preferences (Clark & Onaka, 1983; Kendig, 1984).

The natural evolution theory focuses on the rising income levels of urban households, their desire and preference to locate at lower densities and the adaptability of modern means of transportation. Thus, cities easily transform into sprawling zones, laying the foundation for haphazard growth. The growth of the city in multiple directions forms the basis of polycentric cities with numerous central business districts.

2.6. Flight from Blight Theory

As compared to the monocentric city model and natural evolution theory, this theory of suburbanization stresses that old neighborhoods and city centers have their own social and fiscal issues in the form of high taxes, degraded schools, low-quality environment, congestion and racial tensions forcing affluent residents to flee and migrate to suburbs, which presumably present better life prospects. This migration of affluent classes often leads towards fragmentation and ghettoization of the communities as these migrants prefer to reside among individuals of similar income, education, race, and ethnicity. The homogeneity of the individuals tends to enhance the quality of education, as evidence suggests that peer-group effects are crucial for producing educational excellence. In the good olden days, people of English backgrounds moved away from the influx of low-income European immigrants to improve their academic credentials. American suburbanization is often driven by the flight of middle-class residents from the center of the city by the fact that low-income blacks commit a disproportionate share of crime.

The fiscal-social problems approach is mainly driven by the well-known Tiebout (1956) model. Although he did not mention land use controls, they have clearly been an important part of the suburban homogenization process, at least since World War II. Land use controls have become increasingly stringent in the 1970s and 1980s, and residential segregation now works increasingly by income and somewhat less by race and ethnicity. The study by South and Crowder (1997) provides evidence that suburbanization is backed by a desire to relocate to affluent areas to segregate from lower-class households.

The adherence to this theory led towards the establishment of well-financed and high-achieving schools, which further fueled suburbanization and attracted other households that placed a high value on education, furthering their quality and reputation. The "flight from blight" theory implies that important externalities are involved between income groups: positive externalities from the affluent to the poor and negative externalities running the other way. Scholars have provided evidence of urban poverty and its role in inducing outward movement among more affluent households (Adams et al., 1996; Bradford & Kelejian, 1973). The uneven distribution of private and public amenities, particularly the facilities available in the center of cities compared to suburbs, is viewed as the main determinants of suburbanization.

2.7. Fiscalization of Land Use Theory

The fiscalization of land use — the use of land use planning and development to encourage revenue production as a first-order goal became important in the United States anti-tax environment of the 1980s. At the most basic level, planners may not understand the state and local context that determines revenues and costs and how they affect land use and economic development. Some local governments have established policies in their Municipal Codes that new development should be "fiscally neutral" or should result in a net zero or net positive impact on the city budget. This is particularly common for annexation applications, where the city has not completed any long-term land use planning.

Land use decisions become "fiscalized" when influenced by the local fiscal surplus, as concluded by Ladd (1998), who concluded that gaining fiscal space has been a local planning tool in the USA since the 1940s. Misczynski (1986), Brunori (2004), and Pagano (2003) have demonstrated in their studies that local fiscal impact analysis is getting traction in the states with limited property tax collection, pushing fiscal impact analysis to the forefront of many local officials' criteria for choosing among alternative land uses. The studies by Ladd (1998) and Lewis (2001) point out that a few empirical studies have tried to isolate fiscal considerations from other influences on urban land use outcomes.

Local governments across the world are driven by financial considerations, causing the likelihood of dispersion and degree of urban sprawl observed in the urban areas. The local governments holding large tracts of undeveloped land are likely to use revenue considerations in choices related to land use. The study by Brueckner and Kim (2003) points out that the expected influence of a property tax on land improvements is a reduction in the intensity of land development, a subsequent decrease in population density, and an increase in the spatial size of an urban area.

Land use fiscalization became necessary for financing services and public capital because public infrastructure in the form of roads, highways, airports, ports, sewers, water lines, and grids are instrumental for economic development, as reported by Bougheas, Demetriades & Manuneas (2000). The accumulation of infrastructure is important for productivity gains, as supported by Agenor & Moreno-Dodson (2006). Public infrastructure can affect economic growth through several means, including indirectly enhancing labor productivity, facilitating the adjustment costs and mobility associated with the formation of private capital, and enhancing the durability of private capital.

2.8. Spatial Mismatch Hypothesis

The research work by two sociologists, Kasarda (1985, 1988, 1989) and Wilson (1987), has contributed to a renewed interest in the so-called "Spatial Mismatch Hypothesis" in the United States. These studies have stressed the existence of a black underclass in inner-city ghettos and termed it the reason behind the dismissal performance of Black Americans in the number of entry-level jobs located in inner cities. The idea of Spatial Mismatch was first discussed by Kain (1968) in a seminal paper that residential and work locations may be detrimental to ethnic or racial minorities. He argued that inner-city ghettoization and the availability of jobs in suburban areas were major sources of unemployment for blacks in American cities. The hypothesis presented by Kain, better known as the "Spatial Mismatch Hypothesis" (SMH), can be summarized as, "The availability of limited residential choices and dispersion of jobs from central cities are main reasons for low employment and low earnings of Afro-American workers."

In the USA, suburbanization has two major patterns: the emergence of suburban job centres and the development of edge cities at the periphery of large metropolitan areas (Garreau, 1992; Henderson & Mitra, 1996; Fujita, Thisse & Zenou, 1997; McMillen & McDonald, 1998). Despite the emergence of employment sub-centers, employment suburbanization can be said to remain rather diffused (Glaeser & Kahn, 2000). Edge cities, contrary to sub-centers, can be defined as real towns located near transport nodes, which are typically group service industries they export (Bogart, 1998).

Continuous job suburbanization has posed some challenges to commuting, as stipulated by SMH, which states that inner-city residents are physically disconnected from their jobs. This disconnection may be perceived through commuting patterns. The higher cost of travelling may just deter the minority races from actively participating in job markets and offering their services with whatever skills they possess. This is unlike rich suburbanites who commuted to the CBD, where they held jobs. It can be safely argued that high unemployment and low incomes of inner-city dwellers are the sources of intense poverty in central cities, thus widening the discrepancies between central cities and suburbs and well supported by the evidence from urban labour markets of USA cities that low-skilled central-city residents face lower local wages, higher local unemployment rate and have a higher exposure to poverty than those residing in the suburbs.

Urban sprawl has evoked many debates because of excessive usage of open spaces, green belts and continuous emissions (Jaeger et al., 2010). The extent to which the literature on sprawl seeks causes and traces cost-benefit analysis of this phenomenon (Burchfield et al., 2006). Leapfrog development is an important part of sprawl (Glaeser, Edward, & Kahn, 2003). Developers believe that working with a vast empty land at the city's periphery rather than working in older neighbourhoods makes sense (Jarvis, Lambie & Berkeley, 2009). Putnam (2000) argued that the low-density suburban lifestyle associated with sprawl reduces social capital, leading to a less healthy society.

It is a common argument among urban planners that decreasing densities results in a sharp increase in development costs (Kelly, 1993; Knaap & Nelson, 1992; Nelson & Duncan, 1995; Porter, 1997) because it will take huge investments on the part of the government to extend roadways, transmit basic infrastructure in the form of sewerage lines, public utilities for the utility of few people (Carruthers, 2002). The debate on urban sprawl internationally often has as its focus on the wasteful use of land and infrastructure caused by dispersed residential development at the expanse of predominantly low-intensity and single-use development due to poor and non-existent planning (Peiser & Chang, 1999). The sprawl is criticized principally on the grounds that it hampers the provision of cost-effective public services (Gordon & Richardson, 2000). The theorists maintain that urban development directly shapes the overall landscape of the city, its infrastructure, socio-economic culture and ambiance of the city (Farkisch et al., 2012). Planning is a major driver responsible for shaping cities into what they 'ought' to be, but there are very few rigorous criteria for justifying one outcome over another (Talen & Ellis, 2002). Other theorists view financial loss as an important aspect of urban sprawl. It is stated in the literature review that more development in cities can cause economic loss in the long term.

Historically, the growth of cities has been driven by increasing urban population (Birkmann, 2006). A deeper understanding of the relationships between the trends that drive urban sprawl and the specific national, regional, and local considerations that fashion the development of the cities is essential to redress the adverse effects of sprawl (Roshan, Rousta, & Ramesh, 2009). Since the period of 1960s, the exodus of jobs and businesses from CBD has been stark and universal (Lagro & James, 1994). The cities, which were the epicenter of manufacturing facilities, began to transform as the centers of administration, information exchange and higher-order service provision (Heilburn, 1987). Urban economists submit that businesses moving away from the CBD have created a loss of jobs, a lack of job opportunities, and an increase in poverty (Saraei, 2007). The resultant poverty causes high crime rates, the seeking of unemployment benefits, the formation of slums and excessive usage of drugs (Yanich, 2001).

The sprawl is viewed positively by individuals, as confirmed by Surveys of Americans by Time Magazine (Dokko et al., 1999) and National Association of Home Builders (NAH, 2002) that people have a high likelihood towards owning spacious homes with ample access to automobile parking and other allied facilities regardless of the fact that localities are distanced away but this is never feasible at city or regional level. Burchell and Mukherji (2003), in their study, explain that urban sprawl has resulted in nuclear families, enabling individuals to live away from urban centers rife with crime and poverty along with a network of well-planned highways helping them to use their automobiles according to their travel needs.

People living in the urban fringe are oblivious to any negative effects caused by sprawl as they benefit from large residences and socially homogenous neighborhoods (Zohry, 2009). The study by Gordon and Richardson (1997) has linked sprawl with the preferences of the consumers as it is their choice to make living decisions. The theorists maintain that individual maximization is not societal maximization, and in the short run, individual maximization involves bearable negative social costs (Tali & Murthy, 2012).

The literature also shows that the global city model is criticized on three specific grounds. The first questions the narrowness of the focus on "certain stylish sectors of the global economy," related to production, service and high-tech industries, as the leading sectors altering the course of contemporary urban development (Robinson, 2002). The second set of critics argues that global city literature is tinged with ethnocentrism by assuming that cities will follow the suit of New York and London, but realistically stating these cities have been shaped by capitalist ideology, spending culture and polarized social structure (White, 1998; Hill & Kim, 2000; Hill, 2004). A third group of critics point out that much of the global city literature is historical and is directed towards the cities of economically advanced countries and that recent changes in the context of globalization have not been accounted for (Davis, 2005).

However, there are strong advocates of the global city model arguing that "the gains of global cities have far outweighed the losses" (Taylor et al., 2002). Gordon and Richardson (1997), in their study, expressed strong support for urban sprawl, calling it a 'natural' process in an environment of growing population and termed any countermeasure as a futile exercise because of impediment to economic growth and impairing free choices. The extensive studies conducted by Galea, Freudenberg and Vlahov (2005), Berry (2007), and Moudon (2009) posit sprawl as an alternative to noisy cities, overcrowded streets and crammed public transport. This huge influx of people to the urban fringe is to avoid multiple stresses and to experience the restorative effects of nature (Hartig et al., 1991; Grahn & Stigsdotter, 2003). The natural spaces in the urban fringe are important for the physical education of children, providing impetus for the parents to leave an inner core and create an enabling environment for the upbringing of their children.

Ingram (1998) concludes that companies, most of the time, resort to the outskirts of cities to occupy more space and connect their operations with a wider transport system, thereby reducing air pollution and traffic congestion. Haber (2007) critically examined the sprawl, and warned forcefully that land and fertile soil are disappearing at an alarming pace because of residential, industrial, commercial, and recreational activities at the urban fringe and any inaction in this regard would invite stiff competition in land, food and energy leading towards ecological trap. He emphasized adopting corrective measures based on ecological science and urban planning.

2.8.1. Characteristics & Features of Urban Sprawl

Urban sprawl, better known as urban decentralization, is a topic of utmost importance for academic intelligentsia, urban planners and the general public in the contemporary world as it is related to most of the undesirable outcomes in metropolitan areas: increased motorization leading towards congestion, lack of spaces, elevated pollution levels, reduction in farmland, duplication of the infrastructure, urban inequalities, racial segregation, ghettoization and fragmentation (Ewing, 1997; Club, 1998; Downs, 1999; Wasserman, 2000). The advocates of urban decentralization present choice of preferential housing, enhanced lifestyle, and the development of new suburban local governments likely to have reduced crime rates and better infrastructure (Siegel, 1999; Burchell et al., 2000; Goto, 2000; Gordon & Richardson, 2000; Glaeser & Kahn, 2003).

Related studies have consequently come out, covering the features, causes, impact of sprawl, and countermeasures. Urban sprawl refers to the physical extension of the cities, which is a global phenomenon mainly driven by population growth and other causative factors (Hill & Kim, 2000). Planners consider sprawl to be inevitable, harmless, or even positive (Hill, 2004). Early uses of the term 'sprawl' suggest that it consumes excessive space in an uncontrolled, disorderly manner, leading to loss and poor distribution of open spaces, excessive demand for transportation, and social separation (Davis, 2005). Urban sprawl, most of the time, leads towards less dense cities, resulting in environmental and socio-economic issues (Christens, 2004).

Torrens and Alberti (2000) characterize sprawl as a wasteful method of urbanization based on low-density development extending along the fringes of metropolitan areas within no time. Sprawl primarily initiates with encroaching agricultural land and is often developed in a fragmented and piecemeal fashion. Kumar et al. (2007) and Tyagi (2015) have described sprawl as an unplanned, haphazard development beyond municipal limits. Sinha (2017) has listed a number of characteristics of urban sprawl in Indian cities.

Burgess (1998) characterized sprawl as a spatial growth exceeding population growth in metropolitan regions. Lee et al. (1998) featured low density, leapfrogging and inefficient land utilization as important characteristics of sprawl. The Club (1998) found the requirement of cars for the purposes of movement between different zones as an essential tool for sprawl. Brueckner (2000) defined urban sprawl as an excessive spatial growth of cities. Ewing (1997) argued that poor accessibility, difficulty in moving among widely separated land uses, and a lack of functional, public open spaces are the primary hallmarks of sprawl.

The study by El Nasser and Overberg (2001) demonstrated that density is a common measure followed by comparisons between the rate at which land is urbanized and the rate of population growth. Richardson (1987), in his famous work, presented empirical work on Bangladesh, Egypt, Pakistan and Indonesia, which showed that the social investment cost of absorbing one extra family in a large urban area was three times more than in a rural area, causing physical extension of the city. Sinha (2018) carried out a comparative analysis of characteristics of urban sprawl in developing and developed world cities and found significant differences in sprawl between the cities of developing and developed world. He revealed that cities in the developed world are characterized by being widely spaced with small built-up areas along with huge open spaces, whereas on the other hand, densities in the cities of the developing world are much higher with compact housing, small living space, and thinner distances between houses. He also demonstrated social segregation as another feature of urban sprawl. He mentioned that poor people in the developing world are left out in the city compared to the rich, who can afford a new house in sprawling areas and commute on private transport. He found stark social contrast in the developing world as class segregation on the basis of religion, language and culture is more visible in the sprawling environment of the cities.

The characteristics of Asian urbanization have been addressed extensively in the literature. McGee (1991) and Yokohari et al. (2000) in their studies have demonstrated that messy urbanization in Asian cities led to the emergence of a new complex landscape in urban fringe areas and further emphasized the establishment of sound policies to address the unique local needs. The extent to which urban literature sums up different features is presented in table 2.1 below.

Characteristic Description	Selected Citations
High/inefficient land, low population density	Black, 1996; Downs, 1999
Consumption, population density, high levels of urbanized development	Freeman, 2001
Fringe Development away from city center	Besl, 2000
Rapid development of open spaces	Katz & Bradley, 1999
Lack of connectivity, Arterial street systems	Duany & Plater-Zyberk, 1998
Leapfrogging, scattered development that skips over empty land	Clawson, 1962; Mills, 1981
Separation of different land uses	Brown et al., 1998
Beyond the edge of employment and retail services	Zyberk, 1998
Lack of residential development in city center	Galster et al., 2001
Aesthetics and Architecture, Big-box retail, strip malls, no sidewalks	Gore, 1998
Excessively wide roads	Koffman, 1999

Table 2.1: Spatial Characteristics of Sprawl Found in the Literature
Source: Hess et al. (2001)

Scholars have discussed different spatial forms that characterize urban sprawl (Harvey & Clark, 1973; Gillham, 2002). These points will be discussed in the following section.

2.9. Different Spatial Forms of Urban Sprawl

The extended academic literature presents various forms of urban sprawl, as it is widely used in academic literature to indicate inefficient urban expansion (Wu et al., 2013). The expansion mainly covers vegetative lands, green cover lands, and the development at the urban fringe by taking over nearby villages (Youssef et al., 2011). There are mainly three spatial forms of urban sprawl: leapfrog development sprawl, ribbon sprawl and low density continuous sprawl (Barnes et al., 2010). However, Gillham (2002) points out another form of sprawl, which is single-use development.

2.10. Leapfrog Development

The development that takes place outside the city center and is often discontinuous is regarded as leapfrog development (Araya & Cabral, 2010). The new development is carried out outside the existing urban area (Saraei, 2010). The leapfrog development exists in the form of new development zones and semi-urbanized villages (Jiang et al., 2007). The study conducted by Holcombe et al. (1999) reveals that developers tend to prefer cheaper land away from existing urban areas rather than planning on existing urban areas.

The development zones are specialized forms of leapfrog development at the macro level (Heng, Wayne & Nigel, 2007). These are areas that may not have low density but would be planned on discontinuous lands further away from the city center (Acioly & Davidson, 1996). One spatial consequence of large-scale development zones is that many cities now look like 'twin cities' with an old city and a new development zone miles away (Deng et al., 2010). These new emerging developments lead towards the formation of cities that cannot be separated from the old cities socially, politically and economically (Deka et al., 2011). These types of cities can best be described as dual-centric cities. They create strain on commutation and, at the same time, overburden the physical infrastructure (Müller,

Steinmeier & Küchler, 2010). Meanwhile, semi-urbanized villages constitute another type of leapfrog development and are prevalent in developing countries (Kumar et al., 2007). Their distinctive feature is low (construction) density and lack of urban infrastructure (Saravanan & Ilangovan, 2010). The constraints put by political institutions are the motivating factors behind the development across the semi-urbanized villages as they do not necessarily reflect the preferences of the people compared to the sprawl in the developed countries that are people-driven (Osman, Arima & Divigalpitiya, 2016).

The leapfrog development as a basis of sprawl leads to extra costs and longer trips between destinations, eventually becoming a source of traffic congestion (Holcombe, Pope & Bast, 1999).

2.11. Strip or Ribbon Development

Ribbon sprawl is characterized and manifested by outward development along with major transportation arteries (Shahraki et al., 2011). The development is carried out in the adjacent lands leading up to the major roads in the form of office complexes, shopping centers, fast food restaurants, gas stations, parking lots and others (Gillham, 2002). In his study, Arbury (2005) concludes that this form of sprawl shapes low-density development and is mainly car-dependent, with a chain of retail outlets surrounded by spacious parking lots, thus reducing pedestrian accessibility. This form of spatial development integrates various business chains and creates economic activity (Halbert, Henneberry & Mouzakis, 2014). In their study, Holcombe, Pope and Bast (1999) argue that barring a few exceptions, this type of sprawl is "spread out" in nature and tends to create congestion in the roads of main arteries because of the continuous movement of customers and employees on automobiles, completely bypassing the rights of the pedestrian customers.

2.12. Low-Density Development

The academic literature is consistent with the fact that urban sprawl is mainly a low-density development (Saleh & Rawashdeh, 2007). Over the past few decades, sprawled low-density suburban development (often referred to as 'conventional' development) has become standard in North American and Australian cities, particularly on the urban fringe (Lang, 2005). The buildings mainly consist of one-storey dwellings with ample open spaces replicated in the same form in developing countries (Loibl & Toetzer, 2003). According to Elkin et al. (1991), low-density results from an increase in population in any urban area of 25 people per hectare, mostly in North American and Australian cities. However, the phenomenon is different in European and Asian cities where a density of 50 to 100 people per hectare can easily be found. Low-density development is distinguished from alternative development due to the poor accessibility of related land uses to one another (Ewing, 2008). The increased distances make it difficult for pedestrians and cyclists to reach their destinations as part of their routine (Falconer, 2008). Low-density development is pivotal for increasing car dependency as the provision of frequent public transportation becomes unviable (Giles-Corti, 2010).

2.13. Single Use Development

Another form of sprawl, which is called Euclidean zoning, is used as a tool in modern urban planning to control the different types of land uses in a city (Sabry & Talaat, 2015). Elliott (2012), in his study, argued that this phenomenon is mostly observed in all large American cities to regulate land use but termed it redundant, obsolete, complex and dysfunctional and called for its overhaul. Euclidean zoning uses mechanistic principles to conceive the city as a fixed machine, contrary to the argument espoused by the German urbanist Hans Reichow that cities continuously evolve and operate on the basis of changing dynamics (Hillier & Healey, 2008). Hall (2006), in his study, criticized single-use development by stating that zoning often leads to municipal infrastructure and social capital and causes poverty and underfunding in certain neighborhoods. Silbaugh (2007) also criticized zoning as a form of urban development as it makes work-family balance difficult to achieve because greater miles need to be commuted to integrate the different domains of life.

Urban academicians argue and consider sprawl as a form of development that causes expansion and change in land dynamics (Bhatta et al., 2010). It may be difficult to determine what factor has the greatest influence on urban sprawl, as urban sprawl is affected by many factors (Peijun et al., 2010). Different driving forces are responsible for urban sprawl; these forces vary between cities and countries (Lawrence, 2005). The following is a summary of the leading causative factors behind urban sprawl.

2.13.1. Urban Expansion and Population Growth

The uptick in population growth is the main reason behind the haphazard expansion of the cities (Polyzos, Minetos & Niavis, 2013). Bhatta et al. (2010) and Günay (2007), in their respective studies, pointed out that rapid expansion of the cities is predominated by two essential factors: Natural population growth and migration to urban areas. Natural population growth is an excess of births over deaths, whereas internal migration within the country and international migration from exterior borders contribute immensely to the expansion of the cities (Pirotte & Madre, 2011). In internal migration, people mostly migrate from rural areas to urban areas because of pull and push factors, whereas international migration, being another type, includes labor migration, refugees and undocumented migrants (Paulsen, 2012). Both internal and international migrations significantly contribute towards the expansion of the cities (Oueslati, Alvanides & Garrod, 2013).

The greater influx of population in urban centers raises density and available space for maneuvering because cities, being the engine of economic growth, are perceived as better places to attain higher wages, secure a good lifestyle and have a better quality of life (Jingnan et al., 2007). Thus, seeking better economic prospects compels individuals to migrate from rural areas towards urban areas as cities provide numerous opportunities for social mobility because businesses that generate jobs and capital are located in the cities (Gabriel et al., 2006). This is the transition from a pre-industrial society to an industrial one and is quite rampant in developing countries as developed countries have already passed through this phase (Lopez & Hynes, 2006).

Education, health, and entertainment facilities also play a pivotal role in attracting migrants from rural areas, as cities enjoy better infrastructure of schools, hospitals, and recreation to improve their quality of life and bring them up to par with the rest of city dwellers (Hassan, 2011).

The UNFPA (2007) report states that globally, the urban population will touch 4.9 billion by 2030, and at the same time, the world's rural population is projected to decrease by some 28 million by 2030. At the universal level, all numbers indicate explosive population growth, mainly in towns and cities, with most of the growth taking place in developing countries. The report further mentions that the urban population of Africa and Asia is expected to double in 2030 compared to 2000.

The explosion in urban population will lead towards uncontrolled urban growth, resulting in sprawl (Engelen et al., 2016). The massive growth of population will not only alter the land uses and landscapes of urban areas but will seriously overburden the existing infrastructure of municipalities, public services and allied services, leading towards the degradation of the physical environment (Gaston et al., 2013). The urban problems will be further compounded in the form of traffic congestion, overcrowding, air pollution, noise pollution and crime (Bhatta et al., 2010).

Moreover, looking at the role of urban sprawling, the preferences of consumers have played a major role in the outward expansion of the city along with various factors such as household incomes and changing lifestyles, which compel individual households to move to the urban fringe of the city (Velibeyoglu, 2004) and lead their lives in a safe and secure environment. In his study, Gunay (2007) stated that grave environmental issues and worsening crime situations within the city centers force individuals to move to safer suburbs. Langorgen (2007), in his study, stated that economic growth has always remained a pull factor for people migrating to the cities because large metropolitan cities operate as engines of growth and provide numerous opportunities for people to productively uplift their lives and make a difference.

The metropolitan areas mainly comprise large-scale industries located within suburban and exurban areas to lower costs and achieve economies of scale (Heimlich & Anderson, 2001). The industry structure always affects density and centralization, as cities tend to be denser if they specialize in sectors where employment is unified (Mobaraki, Mohammadi & Zarabi, 2012). The business and industrial sectors are examples of such sectors because they are chiefly dependent on good communication (Bhatta, 2009). Increased investments in infrastructure and increased availability of land may contribute to new areas that become attractive spaces for residential and industrial purposes and cause urban sprawl (Law & Zhao, 2009).

Economic expansion backed by new technologies in the cities leads to higher wages and an increase in the number of employed persons, resulting in more demand for new housing and space for households (Boyce, 1963; Giuliano, 1989). Technology-driven growth has widened the scope of economies in metropolitan areas, and there is a continuous demand for a skilled and diversified workforce (Solon, 2009). In order to meet the residential requirements of the potential workforce, rapid construction of new houses is carried out by developers, resulting in a messy development and a lack of co-ordination amongst developers, governments and proponents of these schemes (Cirtautas, 2013).

2.13.2. Infrastructure and Transportation

The availability of infrastructure constitutes an integral part of urban sprawl. The extent literature gives evidence that the organic direction of city development can easily be predicted through its different phases of development (Jaeger & Schwick, 2014). Roads are commonly considered in modelling and forecasting urban sprawl (Cheng & Masser, 2003; Yang & Lo, 2002) because they are a major catalyst of sprawl.

The study by Knaap et al. (2000) pointed out that the government's investment in physical infrastructure is a major cause of urban sprawl in the USA, overlooking its effects on urban forms and zoning (Pendall, 1999; Shen, 1996; Feitelson, 1993; Levine, 1999). The USA is poised to invest around $927 billion during the period 2000-2025 to provide necessary road infrastructure to meet the demands of its citizens (Burchell & Mukherji, 2003). Bhatta (2010), in his study, mentioned that the transportation facilities of a particular place play a crucial role in inward and outward trips to be carried out by its residents and surrounding neighborhoods. The phenomenon of sprawl first takes place along the transportation routes because of connectivity and accessibility to the best services to meet the needs of the exploding population (Masoumi, 2013). The lands, along with these transit routes, attract investment from the developers, followed by a huge influx of the population (Ebrahimpour-Masoumi, 2014). The demand for municipal services, physical infrastructure in the form of schools and hospitals, commercial strips and recreational facilities attract a greater deal of investment to serve the customers at doorsteps and to take benefit of the labor force living nearby (Heimlich & Anderson, 2001).

The non-availability of efficient public transport leads to car dependency and increased motorization due to faster travel than public transport (Nielsen, 2001). On the other hand, overcrowded public transport is considered a sign of weak urban planning, not a feature of a dense city; for example, Copenhagen, being a dense city, has a great ambience with lush green gardens, parks and green infrastructure. Also, when it comes to land development, municipalities have different goals and concerns about attracting new residents. Surrounding municipalities can offer large areas and low-density development (Lewis, 2001). The idea is that people will settle in the surrounding areas because of their preference for larger homes and outdoor areas (McGrath, 2005). Dosch (2009), in his study, explained that local governments want to attract residents and businesses to generate tax revenues; therefore, municipalities ease taxes in new areas to increase demand from households and related concerns.

Brueckner and Kim (2003), in their study, pinpointed that the land at the peripheries is allotted to the developers at many reduced rates, and only a fraction of the cost related to community and pubic-related infrastructure is demanded, which favors the economic model of the developers and hence urban expansion is carried out at the expense of taxpayers. In their study, Brueckner and Pereira (1997) mentioned that ideally, development at the urban fringe is costly and merits high taxes but is generally lower than the core city; hence, such decision-making promotes the spatial growth of the cities. The existence of multiple local government tiers within an urban jurisdiction creates competition for enhancing the property tax base, resulting in the expansion of the city, which is otherwise undesired. In their study, Dye and McGuire (2000) pointed out that there is a strong relationship between sprawl and local governments in an urban area. The greater number of local authorities creates confusion and lack of proper planning and enforcement because of the problems that arise in coordinating policies across a large number of jurisdictions, thus paving the way for urban sprawl (Mann, 2009). However, a high demand for housing may contribute to urban sprawl (Williams & Shiels, 2000).

The city center and core city are in the highest demand, and the prices are high in these localities; therefore, the lower prices at the urban fringe force buyers to seek new homes in these areas (Salvati & Carlucci, 2014). High land prices in the city center can act as a driving force behind the phenomenon of people moving to areas with lower prices, resulting in an unplanned expansion of the city (Paulsen, 2013). The urban fringe also attracts new migrants to settle in the adjoining areas because of the affordability and proximity to workstations (Nechyba & Walsh, 2004). In developing countries, it has been observed that the unaffordability of formal houses leads to the formation of informal settlements in the form of *katchi abadis* and judges on state land (Rahman et al., 2010). In their study, Dieleman and Wegner (2004) mentioned that economic growth coupled with high paychecks has increased the disposable income of households that seek better lifestyles by possessing cars and better housing. Glaeser and Kahn (2003) also believed that economic growth can be a driving force behind urban sprawl.

A survey carried out by Couch et al. (2005) in Liverpool showed in more detail the reasons people gave for moving toward suburban or peripheral areas. Those who moved to suburban areas stated that most had a craving to trade up, alterations in household size and small housing units in the city (Serra et al., 2014). High demand for housing may contribute to urban sprawl (Williams & Shiels, 2000). In the USA, high and affluent households move to suburban areas, desiring large tracts of land for their families at bargain prices, fuelling the sprawl in the peripheries (Gordon & Richardson, 1997; Fuguitt & Brown, 1990; Sullivan III, 1994). The household's demand for housing can be classified in the following forms: In his classic study, Clawson (1962) pointed out that outlook about future growth prospects, economic liberalization, and provision of facilities may fuel speculation in the land prices by channelizing the investment in the real estate without proper planning. The political manifestos also set the course for speculation, enabling individuals to predict the growth scenario and magnitude of future growth (Borsdorf & Hidalgo, 2008).

The expectations of land appreciation at the urban fringe form the basis of sprawl by withholding land for development, thus shaping the discontinuous pattern of development (Lessinger, 1962; Ottensmann, 1977). The expectations of higher growth rates in metropolitan areas build the expectations of land appreciation, encouraging speculators and investors to withhold more land for future development (Wissen et al., 2010). The study carried out by Harvey and Clark (1965) pointed out that institutions and even individuals desire land ownership, but often, these lands remain vacant within the core city area and are just subjugated to nominal vacancy tax, thus making infill policies unsuccessful. The land on the edge of the urban fringe, due to a lesser cost, attracts the developers, institutions and individuals to accumulate more land, and as a result, the city grows outward, leaving the undeveloped land portions within the city laying vacant (Lin & Fuller, 2013).

The booming population, increased literacy rates, and improving incomes have manifested huge demand for the provision of housing to single families across the globe generally and in urban areas particularly, thus exploding the cities outward, causing urban sprawl and increasing per capita consumption of the land (Pili et al., 2017). Langorgen (2007), in his study, differentiated urban and rural living by stating that off-localities or suburban areas have minimal environmental degradation, the occurrence of low crime, an abundance of green belts and peaceful vicinities. These factors are essential drivers to motivate individuals to pursue their second homes away from the core city, leading towards the horizontal expansion of the city (Kumar et al., 2011).

In the case of developing countries, the inner city lacks sufficient living space; thus, countryside development is encouraged to produce more living space for the residents (Gupta & Sen, 2008). The property and land prices in the countryside are way lower than in the inner core of the city, paving the way for the increased use of automobiles (Gabriel et al., 2006). The car dependency factor plays a pivotal role in claiming more space in the outskirts as miles travelled are traded as opportunity costs for less stress, good ambience, and a clean and green environment (Hu & Huapu, 2007). However, it is pertinent to note that unregulated, unplanned, messy, and low-density development will pave the way for a spatial form of sprawl (Yang & Gakenheimer, 2007). Cities in the least developed countries are comparatively three times denser than the cities in advanced countries (Acioly & Davidson, 1996). Therefore, better utilization of consumption per capita would yield better results within the confines of compact urban growth (Travisi et al., 2010).

2.13.3. Poor Planning & Regulatory Framework

Planning plays a very pivotal role in the sustainable and continuous development of any city, but a lack of well-documented master plans may cause urban sprawl (Savini & Aalbers, 2016). Planning without enforcement and implementation does not necessarily produce results, as demonstrated by Gunay (2007) that cities under local governments often lack proper mechanisms and instruments, mostly in the case of developing countries, to contain the expansion in the form of population growth and hence people's tendencies to move around the suburbs get accelerated and turns into sprawl. The enforcement in developing countries is not only resource-constraint but also corrupt, politically compromised and professionally incompetent, which is why expansion in the cities goes unchecked and unaccounted for (Tratalos et al., 2007).

Tennoy (2012) characterizes spatial planning as a complex challenge and states that all stakeholders should be put on board, whether public or private, to mitigate the risks of ill-conceived planning because public interests need to be safeguarded against vested interests. Loftsgarden and Christiansen (2011) found indications that local authorities, due to a lack of knowledge and understanding, pave the way for the haphazard development of the city. The policy challenges, development regulations and quality of urban services amongst neighboring municipalities may change the urban discourse towards cities, which are favorably leaned towards development or are less able to prevent or control it (Barnes et al., 2001).

2.14. Consequences of Urban Growth and Sprawl

Urban sprawl has been under discussion for its positive and negative effects on cities and its pitfalls on the long-term sustainability of the cities. Burchell (1998) has termed sprawl as "development based on low-density, automobile-driven, non-continuous development, carried with conversion and consumption of agricultural lands and forests land." Scholars and academicians have carried out extensive debates and discussions and framed their opinion that its negative effects outweigh the positive implications (Gunay, 2007).

The positive aspects of the sprawl are attributed to higher economic production, better employment opportunities, better lifestyles and better services (Kline, 2000). Urban growth, barring a few improved services in the form of water, sewer, educational and health facilities, leads to sprawl (Deka et al., 2011). In their studies related to sprawl, Fan et al. (2005) argued that sprawl is linked to a wide array of socio-economic and environmental costs. During the nineteenth and early twentieth centuries, the developed countries witnessed a massive wave of urbanization because of industrialization, due to which surplus and cheap labor for the factories were provided, resulting in the mass movement of the population from villages towards cities (Becker & Heller, 2009).

The developing countries, at the behest of globalization and liberalization of economies, are facing a similar influx of people in the cities with massive concentrations of capital and investments (Shahraki et al., 2012). Investors in developed countries are diverting their investments to developing countries due to economies of scale and lower costs of production (Weber, 2010). City dwellers in the developing world have a distinguished lifestyle from those living in developed cities as a substantial number of people in the developing world lead their lives within the city or urban fringe with abject poverty and degraded environment (Kraus, 2006). The settlements are mostly dense, lacking urban municipal services and related infrastructure, further compounding the miseries, but cities have enormous opportunities for the transformation of lives compared to rural areas (Van Loon, 2016).

Urban sprawl poses a serious challenge across the globe as it completely transforms the physical environment and spatial structure of the cities (Pohanka & Fitzgerald, 2004). The poorly planned urban development is taking a serious toll on public health and quality of life (Heinrichs et al., 2009), and its consequences need to be evaluated on the basis of socio-economic and environmental impacts. The consequences are explained as follows:

2.14.1. Environmental Costs

Evidence of the environmental impacts of sprawl continues to mount, as reported by Kirtland et al. (1994), that the impact of urban land on environmental quality is much larger than its spatial extent would imply. There is growing evidence that sprawl is inflicting huge environmental costs on the cities, further confirmed by the studies by Guiliano & Narayan (2003), Garcia & Riera (2003), and Anderson et al., 1996) and that it is an attractive phenomenon for the real estate developers, investors, rich elite and speculators at the expense of environmental degradation and state resources. Haughton and Hunter (1994) have done Maths and come up with the statistics that, on average, a city of one million people consumes 625,000 tonnes of water, 2000 tonnes of food and 9500 tonnes of fuel and generates 500,000 tonnes of wastewater, 2000 tonnes of waste solids and 950 tonnes of air pollutants on a daily basis. The environmental costs are further declassified as follows:

2.14.1.1. Energy Inefficiency

The studies undertaken by Ewing (1997) and Burchell (1998) demonstrate that sprawling cities have a greater dependency on automobiles, which causes an increase in the demand for fossil fuels. Moreover, higher densities mean shorter trips but more congestion. The nature of sprawl is such that it requires more distances to be covered from suburbia to the central city, thus, more fuel consumption, which is also one of the main reasons behind traffic congestion (Newman & Kenworthy, 1989). The study further mentions that low density and linear development have profound effects on environmental pollution as inefficient fuel usage, along with transport mobility, becomes a source of persistent emissions. The study conducted by Nuissl, Rink and Steuer (2005) assessed and concluded that sprawl led to:

- Over-exploitation of the resources to substantiate the demand for more construction activity to build houses, industries, and commercial strips.
- The higher household consumption of energy (electricity, fuel) adds extra costs for extending and maintaining the service delivery system.
- The system also bears unaccounted losses during the delivery of essential commodities, which overburdens scarce resources.
- More resources and high levels of energy are needed to ascertain the needs of the people living in the sprawling areas.
- The high-level need for transportation is met by personalizing vehicles, which means burning more fuel and pollution.

2.14.1.2. Land Consumption

The effects of land consumption are already stated in the introduction of the study, which states that urban sprawl has significantly contributed to higher development costs and economic value. Urbanization, generally, and sprawl, in particular, contribute to the loss of farmlands and open spaces to allocate the lands for housing, industries, recreation and infrastructure (Berry & Plaut, 1978; Fischel, 1985; Nelson, 1990; Zhang et al., 2010). Even in the developed world, as in the case of the USA, urban growth is predicted to consume 7 million acres of farmland, 7 million acres of environmentally sensitive land, and 5 million acres of other lands from 2000–2025 (Burchell et al., 2005). Since the start of the 20th century, authorities in developed countries have encouraged single-family homes, subdivisions linked with business centers and recreational points through main arteries and expressways (Newburn & Berck, 2011). This pattern of urban development consumes excessive land and enhances car dependency even for shorter routes, which is not a positive sign for the general well-being of city dwellers (Benfield, 1999; Oge, 1995).

The following important points have been discussed by Burchell et al. (1998):

- Low-density residential development requires higher consumption of land for parking and other purposes.
- Development pressure on the adjacent agricultural lands increases significantly after initial projects.
- Those large tracts of land are assembled by the farmers and speculators to fetch higher prices in the future.

Green spaces are adversely affected at the cost of outward growth, considering that green belts have a tremendous role to play by providing opportunities for outdoor recreation and fresh oxygen and keeping a balancing act on the physical environment (Stephenson, 1999; Stoel, 1999).

2.14.1.3. Loss of Farmland

The loss of farmland is the by-product of sprawl as depressing prices of agricultural output propel farmers to sell their lands to the developers and speculators combined with the irrational land-use policies of the local government authorities (Irvine et al., 2013). The loss of agricultural activity around the metropolitan areas not only reduces food security and raises the prices of essential commodities for urban dwellers but also deprives households of their hard-earned money by paying extra costs (Ferrara et al., 2014). It has been observed that inflationary trends in essential food items badly affect the urban poor as their income levels cannot compete with the rising prices, thus creating income inequalities (Kelly et al., 2015).

The loss of agricultural land has also caused changes in the lifestyle of rural people as rural residential development contributes to the loss of thousands of hectares of productive agricultural land annually (Shalaby, 2012). The loss of agricultural land in the sprawling cities is not only the loss of local food resources but also the loss of habitat and other species (Goldberg, 1999). The presence of farms on the rural landscape provides benefits such as green space, rural economic stability, and preservation of the traditional rural lifestyle (Shahraki et al., 2012).

2.14.1.4. Air Pollution & Loss of Heritage Sites

Urban sprawling is a leading cause of worsening air pollution, as it contributes to poorer air quality by encouraging a car-dependent lifestyle, thereby adding carbon emissions, nitrates and microscopic particles (Frumkin, 2002). In 1998, Houston's toxic air emissions equaled 90 per cent of the total gas emitted by the whole state of California, while in 1999, its smog exceeded federal standards in 52 days (Nozzi, 2003). These pollutants are the main reason behind smog, global warming and public health issues (Stone, 2008). Kahn and Schwartz (2008) emphasized that despite better living conditions led by low-density urban growth, there is sufficient evidence to believe that air pollution in urban environment progresses, due to which temperature rises, and so does the demand for cooling appliances in the form of fans, air coolers, air conditioners, requiring more power output. The power generation mix led by thermal energy burns fossil fuels, particularly in summer, and generates carbon dioxide and air toxics (Colantoni et al., 2015). Meanwhile, Frumkin (2002) states that air pollution has detrimental effects on human health, working capacity, and learning abilities. The air pollutants wreak havoc on the health of different age groups, including the elderly and the young, in the form of respiratory problems leading towards asthma, choking, coughing, wheezing and tearing in the eyes (Benfield et al., 1999; Office of Air & Radiation, 1995; Office of Mobile Source, 1993).

The growth of the cities inevitably threatens buildings of historical importance, archaeological sites, cultural sites and monuments (Fan et al., 2005). Sprawl dampens the revitalization prospects of historically older city structures due to the existence of regulations and policy barriers besides the concentration of extreme poverty in the immediate vicinity of older structures, leading towards consumption and disappearance of the sites altogether (Burchell et al., 1998).

2.14.1.5. Water Pollution

The increase in built-up areas has damaged the water aquifers in urban areas as rainwater and snowmelt are unable to soak into the ground due to pavements, roads, parking lots and houses. Gurin (2003) has mentioned two sources of water pollution:

- Point source: The discharges from sewage treatment plants and factories directly flow into rivers, seas, lakes and streams.
- Non-point source: The discharges caused by runoff (rainfall or snowmelt) water, picking up pollutants and depositing them into watersheds, lakes, rivers, seas, wetlands and marshes (Moriondo et al., 2008).

Urban sprawl can affect the quality of water in many ways. The prominent one is "point source", where discharges from industries, factories or treatment plants flow directly into water bodies such as rivers, streams, lakes or reservoirs (Roshan et al., 2010). According to Gurin (2003), another one is a "non-point source", which is caused by runoff (rainfall or snowmelt) across the land surface, picking up pollutants and sediments and depositing them into watersheds, lakes, rivers, wetlands and marshes (Jones & Kammen, 2014).

The "non-point source" is considered a major threat to water supplies (Frumkin, 2001) because any extra rain can easily flow into wetlands and rivers, destroying vegetation and damaging habitats along the riverbanks. The extra flowing water can also turn into urban flooding, resulting in inundation and erosion (Jacquin et al., 2008). So urban areas located in flood-prone areas are exposed to increased flood hazards, including inundation and erosion (Jacquin et al., 2008). The flooding situation in urban areas is a point of major concern to the public, planners, government and insurance companies as more claims and damages will be filed (Wisner et al., 2004; Jacquin et al., 2008).

Dispersed development in cities and towns can incapacitate the drainage and sewerage systems combined during heavy thunderstorms (Wasserman, 2000). Water pollutants can enter human bodies by consuming contaminated fish from affected waterbodies and drinking contaminated surface water or groundwater sources (Lassila, 1999).

2.14.1.6. Biodiversity & Climatic Conditions

The planet Earth consists of diverse species and habitats performing their own functions and providing the delicate balance necessary for living a healthy life. Because of unending development, the animals and plant species have been endangered, and many are on the verge of extinction (Baillie & Groombridge, 1996). The sprawl poses a threat to biodiversity and global species because it increases human interaction and activities in the larger landscape (Forys & Allen, 2005). The increase in built-up area around the metropolitan cities restricts the movement of migratory species and their dispersal patterns (Fahrig et al., 1995; Forman, 2002). The lack of connectivity may result in a loss of genetic variation and population viability (Lande & Shannon, 1996; Hale et al., 2001). The natural ecosystem is facing serious challenges due to excessive human activities, which do not bode well for an integrated and cohesive environment (Simberloff, 1981; Rejmánek, 1989).

There is a positive correlation between land surface temperature and impervious surface, clearly indicating temperature increase in the sprawled area (Wang et al., 2012). On warm days, urban areas can be 6–8 ∘ F (3.5–4.5 ∘ C) warmer than surrounding areas, an effect known as an urban heat island (Frumkin, 2002) caused by the following two factors:

- Dark surfaces in built-up areas absorb heat from sunlight and radiate it.
- Urban areas, due to the shortage of trees, are unable to cool the air through evapotranspiration.

The continuous expansion of the city aggravates the urban heat island if the pattern of development features extensive tree-cutting and road construction (Pauleit et al., 2005). As cities sprawl outward, the heat island effect expands, both in geographic extent and in intensity, particularly if the pattern of development features extensive tree-cutting and road construction as more distances would be covered by automobiles, thus more fuel combustion (Wilson & Chakraborty, 2013). The metropolitan cities, due to the large number of inhabitants and morphology, contribute extensively to greenhouse emissions resulting from increased driving (Shao et al., 2008).

2.14.2. Economic Costs of Urban Sprawl

Sprawl is blamed due to its economic cost because it is costly to the residents and society (Buiton, 1994). The main economic concern is low-density, rapid and uncoordinated development (Goldberg, 1999). The studies by Burchell et al. (1998), Downs (2017) and Schafer (1975) have featured the following economic costs related to sprawl:

2.14.2.1. Higher Infrastructure Costs

Urban academicians and researchers are consistent with the argument that developing infrastructure in the form of roads, schools, hospitals, and installation of sewer lines are more costly in sprawled areas compared to compact development (Frank,

1989; Duncan et al., 1989; Archer, 1973; Duensing, 1977). The infrastructure primarily covers public projects carried out under the domain of "state, county, provinces or local government such as roads, highways, utility system, schools, and sometimes the private sector carries out the development of utility systems and roads for private purposes" (Burchell et al., 1998). The expansion of cities does not augur well for the economies as there is a perpetual need for the development of new infrastructure, upgradation and maintenance of existing services, such as schools, hospitals, water services, police stations, and sewers in the countryside (Barnes et al., 2001) because more wires and pipes would be required to connect with central stations than the compact development. Municipal services such as waste collection, street cleaning and postal services are costlier in low-density developments, whereas efficient public transit systems cannot operate efficiently in dispersed localities (Pedersen et al., 1999).

Also, the infrastructure costs, if financed by developers and passed out to end consumers, may achieve economic efficiency as it is less likely to burden public finances (Brueckner, 2000; Heimlich & Anderson, 2001). However, it will lead towards inefficiency if taxpayer's money is used to finance the provision of community infrastructure, its operation and maintenance (Wasserman, 2000), and it would further escalate with spatial segregation of different types of land, leading towards fragmentation.

2.14.2.2. High Housing Costs and Land Costs

In urban localities, sprawl can push construction costs upwards because of larger layout and spatial planning (Schafer, 1975). Single-family dwellings are the most sought-after residential units on the edge of the urban fringe as nuclear families are looking out for spacious places away from the hue and cry of the inner city (Burchell et al., 1998). Similarly, non-residential land uses in the form of commercial and industrial lands have also excessively spread out on large tracts of land, making this whole process more expensive (Seidel, 1978). The study by Burchell (1992) found that development costs for residential and non-residential purposes are affected by two factors:

- The zoned land for new development with respect to zoning regulations and
- The lengthy permitting process underlined in the local land-use laws.

The more suburban development escalates the prices of the adjoining lands, the more demand from developers skyrockets the land prices, and in the end, consumers pay inflated prices, basically a pattern of development which incurs never-ending upward costs (Burchell et al., 2005; Wassmer & Bass, 2004). The authorities have worked on the physical and infrastructure-related costs of the sprawl, but the extent of research in recent times concludes that sprawl, due to other associated costs, comes with a high-level price tag (Osman et al., 2008).

2.14.2.3. Disparity in Wealth

Sprawl has caused a host of economic issues and unevenness in the communities living at the edge of the urban fringe and in the quality of life in suburbia (Wilson et al., 2003). The higher cost of physical infrastructure on financial and technical grounds inflicts huge costs on the earnings of the households living in the suburban areas, and often, it is difficult to establish a concrete mass transit system for efficient transportation connecting peripheral areas with central city (Benfield et al., 1999; Kunstler, 1993; Mitchell, 2001; Stoel, 1999).

2.14.3. Social Costs

The sprawling cities have produced negative connotations to the social fabric, and they have invited broad-based discussions from scholars and officials to discuss the social impact of sprawl in recent years (Bengston et al., 2005). Urban growth promotes social segregation, fragmentation, and ghettoization and adversely impacts the public health of the citizens (Gillham,

2002; Hillman, 1996; Deal & Schunk, 2004; Sturm & Cohen, 2004; Song & Knaap, 2004; Duany et al., 2001).

2.14.3.1. Public Health

Public health is one of the major problems allied with sprawl (Randolph, 2004). The long commute hours between working and living places because of the large distances between automobiles generate multiple health hazards (Chen et al., 2014). The statistical analysis conducted by Koslowsky et al. (1996) found a correlation between "commuting time, stress, and workers' attitudes toward their jobs." Vincent et al. (1994) and Novaco et al. (1990) found evidence that long commuting increases stress levels. The study by Frumkin (2002) states that the effects of adopting a suburban lifestyle can give the feeling of peaceful refuge and benefit physical and mental health as people are closer to nature here than in denser areas. Savitch (2003) concluded that existing living choices have resulted in reduced physical activity, higher accidents and an increase in pollution levels.

Urban citizens tend to spend more time on crowded roads, inflicting huge psychological stress and reducing the time available for work, family and leisure (Wilson et al., 2003). Automobile dependency means greater exposure to the roads, leading to more accidents and crashes and filling individuals with a feeling of "Road Rage" scenario in which an angry or impatient driver tries to kill or injure another driver after a traffic dispute (Rathbone & Huckabee, 1999). Breathing and skin-related health issues are common outcomes of sprawl (Putnam, 2000).

Community health is also compromised as individuals cannot walk or cycle freely, an essential component of public health, due to long distances between intersections or crosswalks and roadways lined with large commercial establishments and apartment blocks (Brueckner, 2000; Ewing, 1997). Heat in urban areas is another health hazard, causing fainting, swelling, cramps, heat exhaustion, vomiting, and heat stroke due to the presence of pollutants and carbon emissions (Wasserman, 2000).

2.14.3.2. Weakened Sense of Community

The studies by Burchell et al. (1998) and Ewing (1997) have concluded that sprawl has led to declining social capital and personal neighborhood ties between residents in the following forms: Weak connections of households on the neighborhood level and then on the metropolis community level. The social linkages are compromised due to a lack of accessibility and connectivity because of low residential density and car dependency (Yanos, 2007; Sturm & Cohen, 2004). The households in metropolitan areas lack bondage and commonality because of different economic and ethnic backgrounds, thus weakening communal harmony (Burchell et al., 1998; Goetz, 2002).

2.14.3.3. Spatial Mismatch

Spatial mismatch theory, driven by the work of sociologists Kasarda (1990) and Wilson (1987), investigates the mismatch theory with respect to the conformity of black Americans in the USA. The theory can be characterized as:

- Employers have moved out from the inner city to far-out locations, causing joblessness.
- Young blacks and low-skilled are not informed about the job opportunities existing in the urban periphery.
- Informed blacks do not have adequate resources to access those remote locations, causing inequalities based on color and race.

2.14.3.4. Residential Segregation

Sprawl contributes to residential segregation on the basis of income and race, creating permanent divisions among the communities living in the cities (Blakely & Snyder, 1997). The residents' interests have been overlooked by the prevention of construction of affordable housing for low and middle-income households by putting zoning restrictions (Freilich & Bruce, 1997) and by maintaining real estate fees as high as possible without weighing the costs to be incurred for installing the public infrastructure and provision of other services (Fischel, 1985). The spatial distribution in the form of a "gated community" is another undesirable outcome of sprawl as it leads towards social exclusion, individualism, fragmentation and loss of communities, resulting in the commoditization of urban public space (Le Goix, 2005). The gated lifestyle creates a permanent rift between communities as possibilities of interaction are minimized, leading towards isolation (Duany et al., 2000).

2.14.3.5. Inner-City Deterioration

The urban decay of the inner city is another cost of the sprawl as it compels families and businesses to move out of the city in case of economic viability and affordability (Nuissl & Rink, 2005). The compelling conditions and poverty-stricken neighborhoods dishearten those interested in moving into the inner city (Nuissl et al., 2005). The declining investment in the inner core city causes irreparable loss to the marginalized and ruins their prospects of upward mobility in the upper strata of society (Nuissl, Rink & Steuer, 2005). However, the societal impact may worsen the social and economic outcomes of moving into urban cities from rural areas.

2.15. Measuring Urban Sprawl

Urban sprawl is hypothesized in academic works as a multi-dimensional phenomenon that needs to be investigated on various sets of measures (Torrens & Alberti, 2000; Galster et al., 2001; Ewing et al., 2002). This study attempts to measure sprawl from a landscape perspective. The measures and indices used are derived from various research disciplines, such as urban research, urban planning, ecological research, and geometry. Meanwhile, literature presents various indices as a primary method of measuring urban sprawl in cities. It is prudent to choose appropriate scientific methods and approaches for measuring urban sprawl because of its broader applications (Maier, Franz & Schröck, 2006).

The Sierra Club, USA Today and Smart Growth America are among the influential indices to evaluate and measure urban sprawl. The Club (1998) considered population trends, aerial land growth, traffic congestion being caused by increasing automobiles, loss of open spaces and extinction of wildlife as important indicators of sprawl after ranking US Census-defined urbanized areas. US-FHA (2001) put forward the share of the population beyond SMSA (Standard Metropolitan Statistical Area) as an indicator for measuring sprawl. Smart Growth America (2002), in their research to study the impacts of sprawl on life quality, used four indices to measure urban sprawl: residential density, mixture of residence, employment and service sector.

The study by Frenkel and Ashkenazi (2008) performed an urban land-use survey in seventy-eight urban settlements in Israel and divided the measurements into five major groups: "growth rates, density, spatial-geometry, accessibility and aesthetic measures." Later, all measures were weighted into one integrated sprawl index through factor analysis, thus enabling a description of sprawl rates and their dynamics over a time period of approximately two decades. The results revealed urban sprawl as a multi-dimensional phenomenon. In their research study, Galster et al. (2001) used eight dimensions for measuring urban sprawl by using qualitative and quantitative techniques. These dimensions are:

- Density: The average number of residential units per square mile;
- Concentration: The degree to which development is located within a relatively few square miles of the urbanized area;
- Compactness: The degree to which development has been clustered;
- Centrality: The degree to which development is located closer to the central business district;

- Nuclearity: The extent to which an urbanized area is characterized by a single center of development;
- Proximity of land uses: The degree to which different land uses are close to one another;
- Continuity: The degree to which uniform development patterns could be observed at urban densities in a continuous and unbroken fashion;
- Mixed uses: The degree to which two different land categories exist within the same small area.

Barredo et al. (2003) described an urban-growth simulation model for the city of Lagos in Nigeria, in which an urban cellular automata (CA) prototype was used. The model for Lagos was calibrated and tested with the aid of measured time-series data on land use through a set of spatial metrics and k-coefficients. At the beginning of their study, the historical and current land-use datasets from 1984 to 2000 were used for simulation. During the sixteen-year period of 1984-2000, the measured built-up area in Lagos grew by 157.13 square km. It is noticeable that the land-use classes which showed the largest increase in this period were residential discontinuous urban fabric, with a growth of 125.5 square km, residential continuous medium dense urban fabric (24.74 square km), and industrial areas (15.18 square km). The simulation was also run from 2000 until 2020. The simulation results predict many challenges for the city of Lagos as it is expected to have an agglomeration of around 27 million people with an estimated area of 969 square km by 2020.

Remote sensing data and GIS have been used widely to analyze and study the patterns of urban expansions. Shahraki et al. (2011) measured the sprawling patterns of Yazd, an Iranian city, from 2000 until 2009. The data on impervious (built-up) areas was collected through satellite images. The study found that the expansion of urban land between 2000 and 2009 almost equals all urban land developed between 2000 and 2009. The land under urban usage was 13,802 ha, whereas population density decreased to 33.68 persons per hectare. The study indicated the sprawling patterns as disordered, disproportional, scattered and leapfrogged, defining all the features of urban sprawl.

Yeh and Li (1998, 2001) used geographical information system (GIS) analysis of remotely sensed data to measure the degree of urban sprawl in the urban areas of China. They featured sprawl as scattered development in isolated tracts. They calculated Shannon's entropy, a statistical measurement of dispersion to determine whether a city's development is dispersed or compact. Jat et al. (2008) measured the urban sprawl of Ajmer city, a medium-sized Indian city, through GIS and found that the city witnessed an increase of three times in population growth over a period of 25 years and the urban area expanded from 488 ha in 1997 to 1259 ha in 2002. Al-sharif et al. (2013) measured the urban sprawl of Tripoli, the capital of Libya, from 1984 to 2010 through the GIS and RS approach. The study demonstrates that Tripoli witnessed sprawling urban growth from 1984 to 2010 and showed an ascending mode in dispersion, resulting in a high consumption land rate per capita despite a decrement in population growth rate. The study conducted by Owoeye and Ibitoye (2016) thoroughly measured the sprawling trends of Akure from a remote imagery perspective from 1986 to 2014 and found incompatible conversions in land uses and undue encroachment into green areas in the adjoining communities.

The EEA (2006) report used a combination of six indicators to measure urban sprawl for the purpose of environmental monitoring, i.e.

- The increase of built-up areas (1950s–1990s);
- Population density of residential areas in the 1990s;
- New areas with low density (the mid-1950s onwards);
- Residential density (1990s);
- Changes in the growth rates of the population and of built-up areas (1950s–1990s);
- The available built-up areas per person (1990s).

Sprawl, between 1990 and 2000, was quantified as urban land development as a percentage of the total area (EEA, 2006). Many scholars have focused on measuring urban sprawl by establishing multi-dimensional indicators by GIS analysis or descriptive statistical analysis (Ewing et al., 2002; Frenkel & Ashkenazi, 2008; Galster et al., 2001; Barnes et al., 2010; Siedentop & Fina, 2008; Song & Knaap. 2004; Schneider & Woodcock, 2008; Tsai, 2005). The researchers have used remote sensing and GIS to monitor and measure urban sprawl (Yeh & Li, 2001; Sudhira et al., 2004; Huanget et al., 2007; Li et al., 2007; Jat et al., 2008; Iyer, Kulkarni & Raghavaswatmy, 2007; Wei Ji et al., 2006; Yu & Ng. 2007). Doan and Oduro (2012) employed spatial modelling (ArcGIS) and regression analysis on the population census and described a pattern of urban development in Accra (Ghana) as a combination of a spreading pancake, development node, village magnet and ribbon patterns.

The study is interested in measuring the urban sprawl of Karachi from 1975 to 2017 through the lens of GIS and RS and intends to investigate the correlating factors accelerating the sprawling process in the city. There is a general consensus that sprawl is primarily responsible for the air contamination, segregation, ghettoization, fragmentation and deterioration of urban areas. Researchers and broader academia are looking for quality information, measurement tools, and information on the pitfalls of urban sprawl (Ewing, Pendall & Chen, 2002). The study aims to know sprawling trends and contributory factors to understand this phenomenon comprehensively. The urban transformation in the form of sprawl has altered the physical boundaries of the cities. The earlier urbanization after the Industrial Revolution changed its structure and dynamics post-2nd World War, resulting in chaotic, congested, messy and spatial cities. Urban sprawl is the primary form of rapid urban expansion, posing a serious challenge to urban planners and policymakers as it has been the catalyst for shaping modern cities. The study by Ewing (1997) mentions that sprawl leads to fundamental changes in the city landscape by overburdening the public utilities, creating mobility issues, severely impacting the vegetative land and resulting in psychic costs.

The popularization of automobiles has played a major role in dispersed urban development. According to the findings of Southworth (2001), in 1920, one automobile was available for eleven people in the USA, and by 1930, the figure had changed to one automobile for every four and a half people. The proliferation of automobiles forced the governments to make huge investments in the form of highways and road networks. Urban sprawl is very popular among developers as it offers them enormous opportunities to work on the least expensive lands and Greenfield sites, thereby incurring lower costs as infrastructure is financed by the general public through rates and infrastructure costs (Carruthers & Ulfarsson, 2002). The findings by Carruthers and Ulfarsson (2003) showed that the political elite, due to the compulsions of their electorate, are unable to make any move against the sprawling environment, which might diminish their political fortunes.

2.16. Sustainable Forms against Urban Sprawl

The 20th century witnessed human migration towards cities because of industrialization and seeking better opportunities to transform lives, causing a massive wave of urbanization supported by free trade, liberalization of the economies and globalization (Jaspar, 2008). However, this unending expansion with scant resources has thrown serious challenges in the form of urban decay, infrastructure deterioration, inequalities, unrest, pollution and the crisis of governance (Mensah & Castro, 2004). The sprawling trends in the cities have come under severe criticism because of their negative impacts not only on the environment but also on socio-economic fronts, coupled with an increasing awareness of human impacts on the environment and the emergence of 'sustainability' as an important concept in the urban planning literature (Patel, 2014).

The extant literature has emphasized a universal mechanism to mitigate the negative effects of sprawl and encourage sustainable development based on humane values of equality, affordability and efficiency (Scoging, 1993). Aguirre (2002), in his study, used the term 'sustainability' to ensure the suitable consumption of water, energy and soil to protect the environment from human hazards. Sustainable development as a process can be an effective tool in urban centers to overcome the issues pertaining to sprawl and the environment as a whole (Schwab, 1996). In this regard, urban scholars and environmentalists have resurrected "sustainability" as a concept to discuss the shape of current cities and urban settlements, keeping an eye on environmental concerns (Jabareen, 2006). Modern urban settlements, towns and cities can progress through the lens of sustainable urban development by encouraging proper and effective utilization of natural resources (Watanabe et al., 2005). Sustainable development is a holistic approach to improving the quality of human lives meanwhile protecting the diverse species in our environment (Mebratu, 1998; Torjman, 2000; Dixon & Fallon, 1989; Beatley & Manning, 1997; Newman & Kenworthy, 1989). The main purpose of this chapter is to overview the concept of sustainability, its uses and models of sustainable urban development. The concept of sustainability will be evaluated to tackle the growing challenges posed by sprawling cities across the world.

2.17. Sustainability or Sustainable Development

Sustainability approaches have a leading role in improving human lives in multi-dimensions and curbing environmental challenges in societies throughout the world (Gaffron et al., 2007). The detailed discussion will revolve around sustainability, its forms, features, characteristics, and associated links with urban sprawl. The half of the 20th century had a series of discussions about "sustainable development" between 1972 and 1992, when various conferences were held on this subject (Hurley, 2009; Drexhage & Murphy, 2010). The World Commission on Environment and Development (WCED), established in 1983 and comprised of representatives from developed and developing countries, has carried out several pieces of research on sustainable development (Jaspar, 2008). The final report, under the title "Brundtland Report," was published in 1987 and invited universal attention to the concept of sustainability (Bell & Cheung, 2009).

The report defines sustainable development as "Development that meets the needs of current generations without compromising the ability of future generations to meet their own needs" (WCED, 1987). The study conducted by Mebratu (1998) summarized two key concepts from Brundtland's report:

- Priority should be given to the needs of the poorest segment of the population.
- Limitations must be put on the environment's ability to meet present and future needs.

The "Rio Conference," also known as the "Earth Summit," held in Rio de Janeiro in 1992, was aimed to pursue a comprehensive framework for the implementation of goals under "Sustainable development." The conference framed the following important documents: "Agenda 21, the Rio Declaration, and the United Nations Framework Convention on Climate Change" (Bell & Cheung, 2009). The "Agenda 21" accepted sustainability as a universal object and was signed by more than 170 countries across the globe, presenting practical actions to strategize sustainability at local, national and global levels (Blanc et al., 2012; Niwa, 2012). The "Agenda 21" emphasizes the integration of the environment for the fulfilment of basic needs, improving the quality of love, addressing disparities and dealing with hunger, poverty, and illiteracy, coupled with the protection of eco-systems on which we depend for our well-being and demands global partnership for the sustainable development (Quarrie, 1992).

2.17.1. Dimensions of Sustainable Development

The structure of sustainable development contains three important dimensions: economic, social, and environmental, which are characterized by social equity and equal development

(WCED, 1987). The dimensions are explained in figure 2.1 as follows:

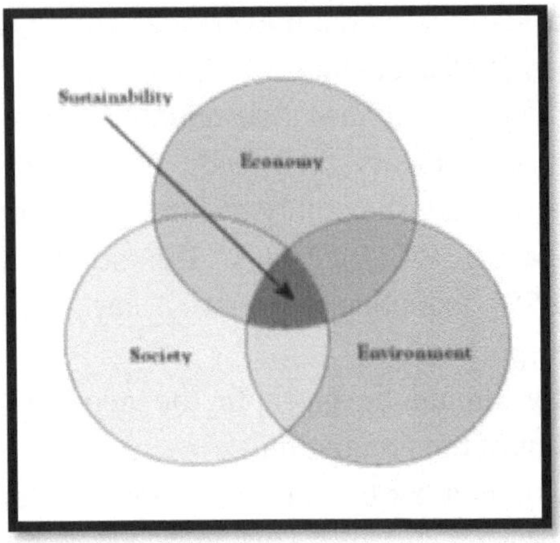

Figure 2.1: Three Pillars of Sustainability
Source: IUCN, (2004)

2.17.1.1. Social Dimension

Social cohesion in society can be maintained through equitable distribution of resources, bridging the gap between the rich and the poor, providing universal services to all residents, providing a level playing field to all citizens and pursuing a classless society based on the notions of sustainable development (ICT, 2003). The social well-being of society should mean the entitlement of quality living to everybody, with the best utilization of resources to safeguard the interests of future generations, and its failure leads to chaos and deviance (Lapalme, 2003).

2.17.1.2. Economic Dimension

Economic growth, being the foundation of human development, must cater to the existing needs and wants of the households and should never compromise on the better future of the generations by better management and utilization of natural capital such as animals, plants, fish, soil and avoiding excessive damage to the environment and water reservoirs (ICT, 2003). The sustainable economic growth requires change in demand and supply patterns of the economy by altering present consumption and generation patterns to obtain substantial benefits and should be the savior of the environment (Declaration, 1992).

2.17.1.3. Environmental Dimension

Environmental sustainability is the major concern of ecologists, who want to ensure the conservation of natural resources and shield against over-exploitation of the resources by maintaining equilibrium in the system (Register, 2002). The environmental balance can be achieved by attaining atmospheric equilibrium and protecting biodiversity and non-economic capital by recognizing the environmental boundaries (Rauhala, 2007).

Environmental sustainability would mean containing population growth, over-consumption, soil erosion, deforestation and framing policies to discourage overdependence on fossil fuels and non-renewable resources (ICT, 2003). The sources of energy generation throughout the world mainly rely on non-renewable resources such as oil, gas, and coal, creating emissions that are detrimental to planet Earth and human health, as well as depleting natural resources (Romiguer, 2011). "Agenda 21" and "Brundtland Report" generally focus on sustainability based on the protection of resources, conservation and efficient use of non-renewable resources at length (Declaration, 1992; WCED, 1987).

An increasing number of urban researchers and planners are adopting the idea of applying the theory of sustainability to urban and architectural forms (Kärrholm, 2008). Sustainable development is a powerful tool to improve the quality of urban lives and address the environmental issues threatening the cities, thus requiring approaches that permit a smaller environmental footprint (Heberle, 2008). The UN (2001) document desires universal acceptance of sustainable urban development and demands that nations must envision their local and national policies on the basis of this document for achieving sustainability. The nation-states are on course to accept and recognize the sustainable urban development model to overcome their depleting social and environmental conditions (Salman & Qureshi, 2009). The study undertaken by Camhis (2006) concludes that sustainable urbanization is key to global sustainable development, and there is a global push for environmentally friendly and livable cities free from ecological footprints.

Sustainable urban development guarantees the long-term strength of the urban system, and it needs to be integrated at all tiers of the government to minimize excessive utilization of natural resources and prevent the production of pollutants (Nijkamp & Pepping, 1998). Sustainable urban development focuses on different levels of "socio-economic, demographic, environmental and technological performance," contrary to conventional development, which has a direct effect on the basis of the urban structure and system (Kenworthy, 2006).

2.17.2. Sustainable Urban Forms

Statistics confirm that the world's urban population has reached 50% of the total population, and it demands policies based on sustainable urban development for universal sustainability (Aronson et al., 2017). Sustainability as a process is directly linked to the form, size, compactness, and land use of an urban settlement (Williams, Burton & Jenks, 2000).

The best methods of sustainable urban development are being implemented in developed countries compared to developing nations, where challenges of urban expansion are altogether different, as revealed by research (Williams, Burton & Jenks, 1996). The academics related to urban studies have consensus that urban centers must be livable, economically equitable, socially justifiable and ecologically viable to achieve long-term goals of peace, progress and prosperity (Beatley & Manning, 1997; Haughton, 1999; Newman & Kenworthy, 1989).

The extant literature pinpoints sprawl as an undesirable outcome of urban development and the main reason for various urban-related issues, such as economic, environmental and social problems (Haughton, 1999). The developed world, particularly the USA, is taking countermeasures that are alternatives to sprawl for the betterment of the cities, but it has a complex structure and operates differently from one country to another (Razin, 1998). The alternative strategies to deal with sprawl will be discussed at length in the following lines.

2.18. Neo-Traditional Development

Neo-traditional development is a movement in which historical built environments have encouraged designers, planners and architects to focus more on urban forms based on several physical qualities (Nasar, 2003). Generally, neo-traditional development is a form of sustainability that supports pedestrian orientation and walkable urban settlements and encourages greater residential densities than usual suburbs (Fulton, 1992). The neo-traditional city is strongly clustered with different street patterns, having a variety of buildings and congested streets promoting street life and connecting people through more open spaces (Nasar, 2003; Audirac & Shermyen, 1994; MacBurnie, 1992; Sutro, 1990).

2.18.1. New Urbanism

New urbanism is the best approach in the neo-traditional movement as it supports processes to stop suburban sprawl and inner-city decrease by building and reconstructing neighborhoods of cities (Jabareen, 2006). New urbanism as an approach was proposed in the mid-1980s to deal with sprawling metropolises (Besussi et al., 2010). New urbanism is designed and planned to foster a sense of community among residents, encourage a walking lifestyle and forge residential density outside the suburban localities (Leccese & McCormick, 2000).

The new urbanism features solutions for various income ranges and family structures, strengthening the relationships of residents within the neighbourhood and providing suitable conditions to increase people's presence by decreasing automobile attendance (Audirac & Shermyen, 1994). The

Congress for New Urbanism (CNU) advocates for free choice of people to ride a motorcycle, take transit, drive a vehicle or walk but does not encourage the environment with easy car access and easy parking (Hikichi, 2003). The study by Beatley (2000) evaluated new urbanism projects and found inconsistent and weaker relationships with the environment. He stressed the need for more environmentally friendly policies and execution.

2.18.2. Transit-Oriented Development

Transitional-oriented development (TOD) is a form of neo-traditional development which proposes to design and provide livable communities that are placed on "high-quality train systems" (Gunay, 2007). The development of residential areas close to rail stations for better commutation purposes is considered transit-oriented development (Boarnet & Crane, 1997). Belzer and Autler (2002), in their study, defined TOD as "a development that lowers dependence on automobiles by encouraging communities to live near metros or rail systems." Transportation Research Board of the National Academy (1996) defines TOD as a pattern of living interconnected with street networks and mixed-use development that is conducive to transit riding.

2.18.3. Urban Village

The concept of the urban village surfaced during the era of the 1980s in the USA, followed by the United Kingdom (Aldous, 1992) and further defined that it is a mixed-use area, densely populated, consisting of mixed social groups with easy accessibility to public transportation points. An urban village has been defined as "a line drawn around a city at a distance sufficient to accommodate expected urban growth" (Gunay, 2007). Kelbaugh (2008) recommended urban villages in cities and suburbs on the ground; they are economical, walkable, interconnected streets, transit-friendly, offer a lively environment and, above all, sustainable.

2.18.4. Urban Containment

This form of neo-traditional development is explained through urban growth boundary and smart growth in the following passages.

2.18.4.1. Urban Growth Boundary

Urban growth boundary (UGB) is a form of urban containment, which is a buffer line between urbanized and rural lands with the provision of public facilities, and preservation of farmlands and greenery outside the boundaries (European Environment Agency, 2006). Any development outside the boundary is strictly forbidden and termed the "urban limit line" (ULL) with distinguishing features such as a green line or blue to mark the difference between rural and urban areas (Hirt, 2007). The UGB was successfully implemented in Portland during the 1970s, which brought meaningful changes for the city, such as growing density inside the UGB, pedestrian-friendly environments, decreased use of automobiles and supporting other modes of public transportation (Jabareen, 2006; Johnson, 2001).

2.18.4.2. Smart Growth

The American Planning Association defines smart growth as planning, designing, developing, renovating, promoting location sense, preserving natural and cultural resources, and fairly delivering development advantages and disadvantages (Blair & Wellman, 2011). Smart growth is aimed at core issues like traffic congestion, housing diversity and ecological confusion (Gunay, 2007). In this context, Talen (2003) defined smart growth as a type of urban containment that features compactness, higher density, and walking-friendly characteristics, as opposed to automobile-driven growth. The study by Dempsey (2010) concludes that essential features of smart growth mentioned in the following:

- Mixed land uses
- Advantages of compact building design
- Housing opportunities and choices

- Pedestrian-friendly neighborhoods
- A shared sense of community
- Preservation of open spaces and green fields
- Strengthening direct development towards existing communities;
- Provision of multiple transportation choices;
- Cost analysis of development decisions
- Encouraging participatory decision-making for the benefit of communities

Smart growth as a type of containment operates in multi-model locations, focusing on mixed-background families and various housing options. The accessibility of walking, cycling, and public transit systems is supported by a system of smartly designed streets (Downs, 2005; Litman, 2012).

2.19. Compact City

The idea of a compact city was proposed by Dantzing and Saaty (1973), who aimed to improve the quality of urban life without compromising the interests of future generations. It can be argued that the compact city model consists of strategies, approaches and procedures to substitute compactness and density as solutions for ever-expanding modern cities (Laghai et al., 2010). Compact development recommends the density of the built areas, land planning, and viable transportation systems (Breheny, Gent & Lock, 1993; Leccese & McCormick, 2000). A compact city as an approach suits an ecologically sustainable urban environment due to its high compactness, a mixed-use city with well-defined borders and provides an opportunity to walk between the functions (Williams, Burton & Jenks, 1996). The research conducted by Williams, Burton and Jenks (2000) reveals the reasons in favor of the compact city model, such as:

- It has the capacity to provide sustainable systems of transport
- It encourages sustainable use of land
- It is linked with social diversity, social cohesion, and cultural expansion

- It is ecologically viable and cost-effective
- It increases population density, which supports local services and businesses

2.20. The Eco-City

The eco-city is a model of development that presents an essential policy framework to mitigate environmental risks related to urban sustainability (Shwayri, 2013). The model covers an extensive environmental agenda through a set of official tools and can be classified as "formless" due to its compactness (Jabareen, 2006). The main features of this model are briefed here:

- Compact
- Pedestrian-oriented
- Public transport-oriented
- Mixed-use neighborhoods

An eco-city presents attractions through nicely designed public spaces, green areas and cultural heritage in its surroundings (Mayerhofer & Skala, 2005). The eco-city model provides (Figure 2.2) impetus to urban life and immensely contributes to the well-being, welfare and safety of the residents by associating its residents with a greener environment (Jabareen, 2006; Mayerhofer & Skala, 2005).

The 20th century witnessed the massive expansion of cities due to the large influx of people and changing lifestyles, thereby creating issues for cities in developed and developing countries. Sustainability is accepted as a global concept to overcome the mess caused by urban sprawl. The adaptation of a sustainability model will not only resolve impending issues related to cities but will also pave the way for sustained urban growth.

The literature presents the antithesis of sprawl models such as neo-traditional development (new urbanism, transit-oriented development, urban village), urban containment (urban growth boundary, smart growth), compact city and eco-city models as a solution to deal with environmental degradation in metropolitan cities. Table 2.2, recommended by Dempsey (2010), summarizes the characteristics of sustainable urban form such as density, accessibility and transport infrastructure, housing/ building type, land use and layout forms versus urban sprawl.

Sustainable urban form against urban sprawl	Density	Land use	Layout	Accessibility & transportation infrastructure	Building / housing type
New Urbanism	High densities	Mixed land use	Grid street layout	Low car dependency & medium public transport	Small scale and diversity of building type
Transit Oriented Development	High density	Mixed use	Interconnected street network, often in a grid or modified-grid pattern	Medium car dependency & rich public transportation	Mixed housing type
Urban Growth Boundary	High density	Mixed use	Grid pattern	Medium car dependency	Mixed housing type
Urban Village	High density	Mixed use	Grid pattern or modified grid pattern	Medium public transportation	Mixed housing type
Smart Growth	High density	Mixed use	Smart street or complete street	Medium car dependent & low public transportation	Diverse housing type
Compact City	High density	Mixed use	Narrow streets in an organic form	No car dependency & rich public transportation	Compact building typologies
Eco-City	High density	Mixed use	Smart streets	Public transport	Eco building typologies

Table 2.2: Characteristic of Sustainable Urban Forms against Urban Sprawl
Source: Dempsey (2010)

Chapter | 3
An Overview of Karachi's Urban Growth

3.1. Urbanization and Settlement Challenges

Karachi, the financial capital of Pakistan, is one of the largest metropolises, with an estimated population of 16 million, according to the census statistics of 2017. Karachi, representing one-fifth of the country's urban population, is unique due to diverse forms of economic, social, and political interaction. The city, being the hub of trade, investment, innovation, employment, and economic growth, is facing a lot of problems like disjointed governance, complex economy, lack of basic resources like water, gas, and electricity, and integration of government (Hameed et al., 2019). The city's physical boundaries are overburdened with dilapidated infrastructure, poor urban service provision and ever-growing slums threatening the city's ecosystem with traffic congestion, elevated pollutants, polarization among communities and increasing violence, causing hurdles for the city's development in an era of modernity and innovation. The city has witnessed multiple phases of migration, resulting in the complex distribution of communities and the allocation of resources between them.

The city of Karachi has been witnessing massive challenges in the form of informal settlements, lack of basic facilities, inadequate sanitation and solid waste management facilities, outdated public transport system and physical expansion of the city (Alam, 2010). Megacities like Karachi have complex land use systems, which is often a multifaceted phenomenon mostly observed in developing countries (Qureshi, Kazmi & Breuste, 2010). Karachi, the business capital of Pakistan in the past, has been referred to as the "Glory of the East", "City of Lights",

"Liverpool of India and Pakistan" (Pithawalla, 1950) and the "Bride of the Cities" (Kazmi et al., 2008).

Karachi always had a flourishing status after the independence of Pakistan, as reported by Zaidi and Zafar (2018). The city, with a glorious past and as a main revenue contributor for the province and country, is turning out to be a complex phenomenon with an unending sprawl and a lack of foresight to mitigate the risks to be borne by citizens in the foreseeable future. Since Karachi is also known as the hub of opportunities, people from rural areas come to the city to seek the urban lifestyle or urban source of income, and Karachi's population is increasing continuously (Verkaaik, 2016). Karachi has grown nearly 25 times since 1947 and is growing at the rate of about 5.4% per annum (Afsar, 2001; KDA, 1991), making it one of the fastest-growing cities in the world (Azad, 2007). The city has witnessed exponential growth, and at present, over one-half of Karachi's population lives more than 10 km from the city centre. The city's major growth trajectory has been observed along major arterials because of commercial enterprise development and connectivity with the rest of the country.

The pattern of growth and urban structure of Karachi has attracted the attention of numerous researchers and scholars with specified objective-driven approaches. The city needs scientific, evidence-based studies and a multi-disciplinary approach to address the various challenges faced by the citizens of Karachi in this colossal ecosystem. The unprecedented and haphazard growth of the city deserves a pluralistic and holistic approach to understanding the urban dynamics of the city. It is worthwhile to expect timely policy interventions to offset the challenges of physical and spatial land use changes in the city of Karachi.

3.1.1. Urbanization Trends in Pakistan

Pakistan has one of the highest rates of urbanization in South Asia, with an annual urbanization rate of 3.1%, as shown in table 3.1 and a projected population of 335 million by 2050. The provinces of Sindh and Punjab have half of the population in the urban environment. More than half of the country's population is living in the eight urban agglomerations: Karachi, Lahore, Faisalabad, Rawalpindi, Multan, Hyderabad, Gujranwala, and Peshawar, as exhibited in table 3.1.

Year	Total %	Rural %	Urban %
1951	1.7	1.4	4.1
1961	2.4	1.8	4.9
1972	3.7	3.3	4.8
1981	3.1	2.6	4.4
1998	2.6	2.3	3.5
2012	1.6	1.2	3.1

Table 3.1: Total, Rural & Urban Population Growth Rates
Sources: Various GOP Census Reports; Hasan & Mohib (2003)

Pakistan's urban journey began with the expansion of primary (megacities like Karachi), but development in recent years has been the growth of smaller cities of between half and one million inhabitants (Hasan & Raza, 2009) and further estimated to be double in size between 2000 and 2025 (Burki, 2011). The recent Statistics (2017) categorize 38% of the population living in the cities, contributing an estimated 75% of the country's GDP to projections at 50% for 2030 (UNDP, 2012). The country is undergoing a youth bulge, which will certainly fuel the urban growth process as an increasing number of younger Pakistanis are migrating from rural areas to cities in search of employment opportunities. Most of the urban population is concentrated in eight urban agglomerations, as exhibited in figure 3.1.

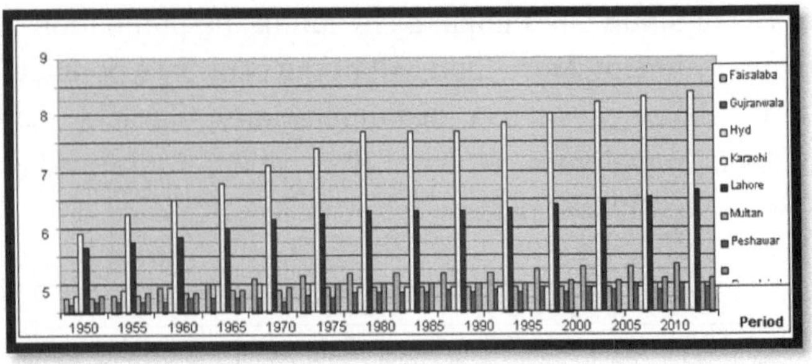

Figure 3.1: Percentage of Pakistan's Urban Population Residing in Eight Urban Agglomerations with 750,000 or More Inhabitants, 1950-2015

In order to relate the statistics in the case of Pakistan, these demographic transitions from rural to urban areas call for integrated urban planning to ensure universal delivery of basic municipal services, control of the spread of slums, minimization of pollution and the control of crime and political violence (Kugelman & Hathaway, 2011).

The Planning Commission of Pakistan contends that peri-urbanization trends have already pushed the country towards the 50% mark, and taking Karachi, for example, some urban planners posit that approximately half of the population reside within a radius of 10 km from the city centre (Qureshi et al., 2010) and they may not have been counted as urban in official censuses or research, but the lives of these residents are almost certainly urban in character. Urban population growth is related to excessive attention to population, overburdening cities with the problems of infrastructure deficiency, delivery of municipal services, rapid decline of institutions, and environmental degradation (Basit et al., 2018). The study conducted by Shirazi and Kazmi (2016) reports that urbanization is the basic and unspoken statement in the development theory of the country; it is the expression of modernization.

The 'urban question' in Pakistan is very contentious and debatable not only due to methodological conundrums about defining the 'urban' but also because such classification carries important outcomes for the national political economy. The urban researchers state that in the case of Pakistan, the actual urban picture is not clear in this scenario, when small towns are quickly turning into cities and rural areas are being developed to the standards of cities. This misrepresentation has important implications for the national political landscape in terms of job quotas, electoral constituency delimitations and formal municipal governance structures. Unfortunately, these political implications (shifting power balances and resources from rural to urban) may have something to do with this misrepresentation.

After independence, Pakistan witnessed a huge influx of migrants from India, thus quickly changing its demographics. Pakistan went through an urbanization phase from 1950-1970 on the back of green revolution technologies that displaced small producers and landless laborers. The massive wave of industrialization geared inter-provincial migration, forming new industrial urban nodes such as Karachi.

Pakistan has one of the highest birth rates among South Asian countries and is the sixth most populous country in the World, causing an alarming increase in the natural growth of the population and putting immense pressure on the haphazard growth of the cities (Khan, 2010). The country's five-fold increase in population from 1950-2017 can be analyzed as shown in table 4.2. The country's future population growth is uncertain, but according to Sathar et al. (2013), the fertility rate might drop to 2.3 in 2027, which is still projected to be higher than peer countries. Pakistan's 'youth bulge' with an estimated 60% of the nation's population below the age of 30 years denotes a demographic transition with an urban bias as the growing young population would migrate for education and skill development prospects as well as for seeking employment opportunities. These changing dynamics are equally supported by an increase in the number of urban literacy rates, as reflected in table 3.2, showing marked improvement from 1981 to 2012.

Total Population (millions)		Female Population	Male Population	Urban	Rural	Annual Population growth rate	Total Fertility Rate	Life Expectancy at Birth	
								Male	Female
2012	187.3	91.1	96.23	67.32	119.7	1.55	3.07	64.5	64.4
2006	156.3	75.14	81.09	53.85	102.4	1.8	3.28	63.9	63.8
1998	133.3	64.16	60.17	43.32	90	2.61	4.7	62.7	60.9
1981	84.25			23.8	61.2	3.1			
1972	65.3			16.59	48.71	3.67			
1961	42.88			9.64	33.24	2.43			
1951	33.74			6.01	27.72	1.79			

Table 3.2: Demographic Trends 1951 – 2012
Sources: SDPI (2008); GOP, Federal Bureau of Statistics; CIA World Factbook; UNDP (2008); Various GOP Census Reports

The Social (2015) data shows that the literacy rate is higher in urban areas (76 percent) than in rural areas (51 percent). However, the official government statistics are shown in table 3.3.

Cohort	1981			1998			Karachi (1998)	Rawalpindi (1998)	Islamabad (1998)
	Natio nal%	Rural %	Urban %	Nation al%	Rural %	Urban %	Urban%	Urban%	Urban%
Total	23.17	17.33	47.12	43.92	33.64	63.08	61.23	76.3	62.52
Literacy									
Male Female	35.05	26.24	55.32	54.81	46.38	70	65.5	81.87	75.09
	15.99	7.33	37.27	32.02	20.09	55.16	55.96	69.8	48.78
15 - 24									
Years:	35.76	24.52	58.28	53.71	43.56	71.65	73.65	82.00 *	75.68
Total									
Male Female	45.5	35.79	64.42	65.36	58.96	76.15	76.05	87.00 *	83.95
	24.7	11.99	51.05	41.69	28.16	66.7	70.19	76.00 *	66.49

Table 3.3: Literacy Rate 1981 to 1998 with Karachi & Rawalpindi/Islamabad Breakdowns
Sources: GOP, 1998 & 1981 Censuses, UNESCO 2004, 'Literacy Trends in Pakistan'

Migration on a large scale is another contributory factor behind the rapid urbanization of the country. The partition of Pakistan and India involved an influx of millions of refugees from both sides of the border. In 1947, nearly 4.7 million Sikhs and

Hindus left Pakistan for India, and in contrast, 6.5 million muhajirs (migrants) left India for Pakistan. This event increased Sindh's population by 6%, with the main cities of Hyderabad and Karachi being affected the most. Between 1941 and 1951, the cities of Karachi and Hyderabad witnessed massive growth of 150%, putting strain on the resources of these cities. The migrants preferred Karachi, Hyderabad (Sindh) and Lahore and Rawalpindi (Punjab), neglecting the northern region of the country due to matters of political economy and availability of suitable infrastructure in the provinces of Sindh and Punjab (Ansari, 2005).

The displacement of the Afghan population due to persistent wars has immensely disturbed the dynamics of the population, as figures suggest that 6 million Afghans settled in Pakistan from 1992-2001, making Pakistan the host to the largest refugee population in the world (Malik, 2013). It is reported that an estimated 600,000 Afghans eventually settled in the city of Karachi; the majority of these refugees are ethnically Pakhtun, and their migration to Karachi has quickly increased the ethnic Pakhtun population to around 25%, challenging the socio-political balance of power (Kronenfeld, 2008). The studies by Hasan and Raza (2009) and Memon (2005) posit that within Pakistan, both international and internal mobility remains unrestricted, as evident from the continuous influx of people from interior Sindh and other parts of the country due to the changing socio-economic landscape.

In its recent annual report Bank (2018), the State Bank of Pakistan estimates that the population in urban centers are poorer than rural areas and that inequality has been on the rise for the past decade. The report further states that the top 20% of urban households receive 60% of total income, and in contrast, the bottom 20% share only 5% of total income and expenditure. The migration to urban centers is an attractive option for landless rural poor who settle in 'unplanned settlements' where service provision is weak and there is greater exposure to vulnerability in terms of various health impacts and hazards

(Ghani, 2012). In Pakistan, the proportion of the urban population living in unplanned settlements or *katchi abadis* varies between 35 and 60 percent. The growth of these *abadis* in cities such as Karachi has particularly been massive. In Karachi, *katchi abadis* increased from 212 in 1958 to more than 500 presently (Arif & Hamid, 2009). In cities such as Lahore, there are more than 300 unplanned settlements and in Faisalabad, at least 40 percent of the population lives in such *abadis*. Residents living in unplanned urban areas find work in the informal economy and mostly depend on brokerages to provide services.

The changing urban dynamics in the country are creating serious challenges in service delivery, resource allocation, quality of life, rising inequalities, crime and violence, as well as struggles for political and social power. The recent trends are more sprawling based on state policies for population dispersal and conversion of agricultural to urban land. The sprawling trends are visible all over the twin cities of Islamabad-Rawalpindi to Faisalabad, Lahore and Karachi, in the form of outward expansion of metropolitan regions or the areas. The urban areas in the country have chronic housing shortages, forcing the in-migrants, unemployed, homeless or poor migrants to find affordable shelter on the city's expanding periphery. The state policies are also friendlier for launching housing schemes in peri-urban areas, often through the conversion of agricultural land, thus resulting in sprawl (Anwar et al., 2014). In the context of Karachi, since the 1980s, housing schemes such as Taiser Town and *Khuda Ki Basti* and unplanned settlements such as Orangi Town and Baldia in the western regions have expanded the metropolitan boundaries by conversion of land, causing a decline in density gradient (Akhtar & Dhanani, 2013). The vast improvement and laying of new physical infrastructure has further redefined the city's metropolitan limits (Ahmed, 2013).

3.2. Urban Growth in Karachi

The city of Karachi has a long history dating back to 1839, when it was conquered by the British, who needed a port for landing troops for their Afghan campaigns. The city was recognized as the trading post by the British, so in 1843, under the supervision of Charles Napier, they took over the city and province of Sindh, and it was captured as the District of British Indian Empire (Saleem, Farooq, & Masood, 2016). The conquest of the British triggered the rapid expansion of the city because they developed perennial irrigation schemes in Punjab and Sindh (Karachi's hinterland), increasing agricultural production, which was exported through Karachi. The railway was initiated in Karachi to connect the city with the rest of the upcountry to transport agricultural produce, and as a result, Karachi became the largest exporter of wheat and cotton in India in 1869. The city of Karachi was the headquarters of British India during the First World War to counter the Central Asian countries. Karachi was made the capital of Sindh after its separation from the Bombay Presidency, and as a result, the first industrial estate in Karachi was created due to the relocation of Government offices and trade organizations from Bombay to Karachi. Finally, in 1947, Pakistan was created, and Karachi became its first capital.

Under colonial rule, Karachi emerged not as an industrial center but as a commercial port, making it an attractive destination for traders drawn from the coastal districts of the subcontinent. The British Empire, due to their vested interests and suitability of the location, scaled up the development of Karachi in line with modern cosmopolitan cities of that time, making it a bridgehead of imperial culture and modernity, setting it apart from its rural hinterland. The city's vast infrastructure, swathing gardens, tram transit system, artisan buildings, and beautiful beaches made it a hub of all business and recreational activities.

The city witnessed massive demographic changes after the independence, as illustrated in table 3.4, which changed the cultural and ethnic identity of the city, as mentioned in table 3.5, increasing the city's population by 161 percent in just 10 years. This was the result of the migration of 600,000 refugees from India. During the early phase of the independence, migrants settled squatter settlements on the city's periphery and within the city itself, occupying open areas, turning the city into a high-density and compact mode with a cosmopolitan culture. The city's population continuously accumulated into large numbers, and once the country was taken over by the military, new townships under the names of Landhi-Korangi and New Karachi were built 20 km away from the city centre to settle the people living in the squatter settlements. The city's transport started to worsen from this point as people had to travel long distances to reach their workstations. The Green Revolution and large-scale industrialization triggered rural-urban migration, and people started to settle in the squatter settlements, thus increasing the population of the *katchi abadis.*

	1941	1951
Population	450000	1137000
Sindhi spoken as mother tongue (%)	61.2	8.6
Urdu spoken as mother tongue (%)	6.3	50
Hindu population (%)	51	2
Muslim Population (%)	42	96

Table 3.4: Demographic Changes
Source: Official Census Reports Various Years

Year	Population	Increase or Decrease %	No. Of Years In Survey	Increase or Decrease%	Average Annual Growth Rate
1941	435,887	135,108	10	44.90	3.70
1951	1,137,667	701,780	10	161.00	11.50
1961	2,044,044	906,377	10	79.70	6.05
1972	3,606,746	1,562,702	11	76.50	5.00
1981	5,437,984	1,831,238	9	50.8	4.96
1998	9,802,134	4,364,150	17	86.29	3.52
2017	16054988	6252854	19	63.79	3.35

Table 3.5: Karachi, Population Growth
Source: Official Census Reports various years

The city's "Master Plan 1974-1985" was designed to make the city more livable for its residents and according to the standards of the World's best cities, but it could not be implemented effectively because of continuous political conflict and military takeover except for road networks and the bulk water supply. The city's institutions began to weaken during the rule of Bhutto and Gen Zia because of a lack of transparency and accountability. The military regime of Zia oversaw a strict implementation of "Islamic Laws," eventually leading towards the closure of Karachi's active nightlife, racecourse, bars, billiard rooms and a number of cinemas. The city, which was once the cultural and recreational capital, came to an abrupt end, denting its progressive pursuits in the long run.

Karachi, as a "buoyant city", witnessed another era of turbulence rife under the auspices of a new political party drawing inspiration from "Mohajir Ethnicity" known as Mohajir (refugees from India) Quami (national) Movement in the late 80s and early 90s, making the city unfriendly for new investments and business expansion. The city's homicide rate skyrocketed during this phase, and high unemployment led to the expansion of *katchi abadis* and the densification of inner city slums.

The city went through transformational change after the takeover of military leader Pervez Musharraf as the local government was empowered, and the economic situation of the country improved after the alliance with the USA due to post 9/11 events, resulting in greater fiscal space and funds for the betterment of the citizens. The city prospered under the mayorship of "Naimatullah Khan and Mustafa Kamal" with scores of new infrastructure projects, flyovers, underpasses, roads, new water projects, and expressways in the midst of political calm and stability. The improving economic situation further aggravated the outward growth at the edge of the city and the settlement of in-migrants from northern Pakistan due to the war on terrorism, natural calamities and rural poverty at the urban fringe.

The continuous vertical and horizontal growth of the city had a negative impact on municipal service delivery, infrastructure development, and ecological footprints. The city was a harbinger of deadly violence once the democratic set-up was dispensed in 2008 and continued till 2014, eventually inviting large-scale military operations for the maintenance of law and order. However, the main point to ponder is that with the worsening law and order, Karachi still has its charm and spirit alive, making it different from others. That city never loses hope of being in a crucial situation, but Karachiites never stop being lively and maintain their evergreen existence (Rafiq et al., 2016).

In Karachi, numerous communities reside liberally and have diverse identities. Major communities that are residing are Urdu-speaking, Agha Khanis, Hindus, Christians, Bohris, Parsis and so on (McGrath, 2005). These communities have their own concentrated areas in the city, where they live and practise their culture (Zubair et al., 2015). These communities have their own rituals and festivals, which they celebrate in the city with freedom and represent the city (Jamil, 2018). The most common language spoken in Karachi is Urdu, but it is a fact that many different communities have different accents and different pronunciations of Urdu words (Zubair et al., 2015). People with clear Urdu speaking skills are known as persons with pure Karachi instincts (Zubair et al., 2015).

Karachi is a highly urbanized area of Pakistan with a 48.9 percent urban population and characterized by an accelerating rate of suburban growth. Karachi, with a population of 16 million (Statistics, 2017), is considered one of Asia's fastest-growing cities. Karachi's unrelenting expansion is fueled by natural growth and particularly by rural-urban, inter-provincial, and transnational migrations. Metropolitan Karachi is a more complex region today than it was in the 20th Century. Even though the centre-periphery continuum is very useful for understanding the spread of vulnerability and social segregation, the pattern of urbanization and land uses is beginning to change again as Karachi's peripheral regions are also attracting new, upscale real-estate development schemes. The following sections will explain in detail the transformational changes in the form of socio-economic, demographic and physical expansion of metropolitan boundaries.

3.2.1. Population Growth

Karachi is one of the fastest-growing cities in Asia. Karachi Development Authority has estimated that during the 1980s, it received between 300,000 and 400,000 migrants each year from within Pakistan as well as from the neighboring countries, which has had a tremendous impact on the population explosion of the city. Consequently, Karachi's share in Pakistan's population increased from 4 percent in 1961 to about 6 percent in 1981. Its share in the country's population increased to 7.8 percent in 2001 and 8 percent in 2017 according to the official figures. The city's population, as evidenced in table 4.6, indicate that Karachi has grown from a small agglomeration of 1.13 million to a large metropolis of over sixteen million populations in a time span of less than 70 years. The rapid growth of Karachi is not only natural but also due to the net inflow of migrants. The city's population, as exhibited in table 3.6, shows an exponential upward trend, clearly indicating the huge population influx in Karachi, which is further confirmed in table 3.7.

Year	Population	Increase or decrease %	No. of years in survey	Increase or decrease%	Average annual growth rate
1941	435,887	135,108	10	44.90	3.70
1951	1,137,667	701,780	10	161.00	11.50
1961	2,044,044	906,377	10	79.70	6.05
1972	3,606,746	1,562,702	11	76.50	5.00
1981	5,437,984	1,831,238	9	50.8	4.96
1998	9,802,134	4,364,150	17	86.29	3.52
2017	16054988	6252854	19	63.79	3.35

Table 3.6: Population Growth in Karachi
Source: Census Reports, Government of Pakistan Various Issues

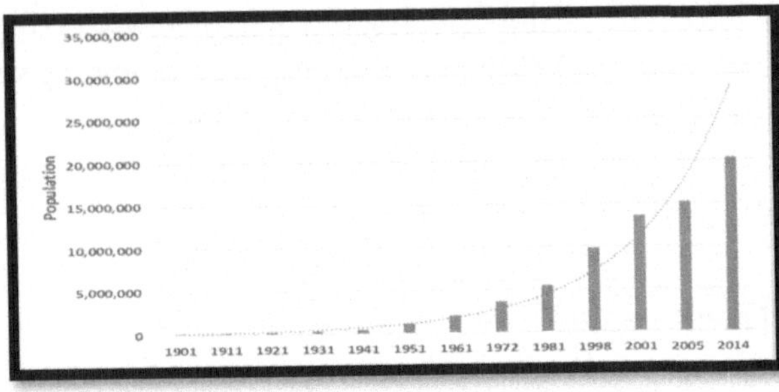

Table 3.7: Upward Population Trend
Source: Government of Pakistan, "Population Census Reports"

Successive phases of migration resulted in the complex distribution of communities and had far-reaching effects on the city's growth. The post-partition scenario witnessed a huge influx of migrants, mainly originating from India, seeking better life prospects. The number of migrants to Karachi from 1941–61 swelled to 1.3 million, of which about 300,000 originated from within the country. The city went through a massive demographic transition after the independence as it turned out to be a majority Muslim city after the migration, which shook both Pakistan and India. The city experienced growth of 58.4 percent during the decade 1941 to 1951 and exhibited growth of 80.5 percent during the decade of 1951 to 1961. The next two decades (1961–81) registered about 2 million migrants to Karachi, most of whom originated from within the country.

The city continued to attract immigrants as more people from the 1st Afghan War settled there for better economic opportunities and the safety of their lives. The poverty in the rural areas across Pakistan and the war on terrorism and natural calamities triggered the monumental growth of the city from the period (1981-2017), resulting in a 5% to 6% average growth in its population, touching 16 million. The study by Hasan and Raza (2009) reveals that 10.8 million Pakistanis (8 percent of the total population) are migrants. Some 64 percent of all migrants have migrated to urban areas and 25 percent of all migrants have gone to Karachi, Lahore and Rawalpindi, which are all large cities and 13 percent have migrated to Karachi alone due to pull and push factors. The study conducted by Ali et al.(2015) confirms that the urban-built of Karachi has changed by 53 square kilometers from (1989-2014), indicating a 2 square kilometers variation per annum while estimating a density of 50000 people per square km, the city can manage 0.1 million people per annum. However, this is not the case as more and more people are migrating, choking the whole ecosystem and increasing its vulnerability against external shocks.

A general explanation of the population growth of the city can be made as follows: the coastal location of the city of Karachi, its contacts with foreign countries and hinterland (facilitated by the improvement in means of transport by land, sea and air), increased trade and economic opportunities; these in combination attracted the migrants which caused the growth rate to rise substantially above the level of reproductive change.

3.2.2. Economic Dominance

Karachi is the economic powerhouse of the country and contributes immensely to most of its economic activities. The city, which is home to almost 5,000 industrial units, comprises textiles, pharma, engineering, cement, autos, glass, plastic, rubber, allied food, etc. These units are always looking for employee replacement, capacity enhancement, and automation. This generates the demand for skilled and unskilled labor, increasing the drive and incentivizing people to relocate from their native cities.

Karachi, the capital of Sindh, is the commercial and trading hub of the country, handling 95% of the country's foreign trade and contributing 30% to the manufacturing sector. It contributes 20% of GDP, adds 45% of the national value-added, retains 40% of the total national employment in large-scale manufacturing and contributes 25% of national revenues. The statistics of the Federal Board of Revenue reveal that 70% of the income tax and 62% of the sales tax is generated from the Sindh province, and of these, 95% is generated from Karachi. This implies that Karachi has a distinctive advantage in terms of wealth generation and business activities.

Karachi dominates Sindh's economy, as evident from the fact that a large-scale industrial sector employs 71.6 percent of the total employed labor force in Sindh, with a value of fixed assets that is 71.4 percent of the total and of the total number of large-scale units in Sindh, 72.7 percent are located in Karachi where 74.8 percent of the total large scale output produced in Sindh is produced in Karachi (Khuhro & Mooraj, 2010). The Gross Regional Product (GRP) of Sindh was Rs. 1019 billion[1] in FY 2003 contributing 28% in national GDP.

3.2.3. Transport Infrastructure

Travel is fundamental to almost all human activities. While the population has expanded extensively in recent years, the quality, coverage and reliability of transportation have not been able to develop accordingly. The Person Trips Study of Karachi City Imran and Low (2005) revealed that Karachi generates around 24.2 million person trips on a typical weekday, about 60 percent of which was generated by public transport. Subsequently, Travel Demand Forecasting Study for Karachi City conducted by JICA in 2008 (Koiznmi et al., 2013) showed that the overall modal share of public transport in the City's traffic is only 6%, however, about 54% of the persons traveling to various destinations use public transport as their means of transportation. Every workday, 24.2 million person-trips are taken in Karachi. Pedestrian trips represent about 20 percent of all trips. Public transports (buses) are thought to provide 50-60 percent of all trips, and private transport and para-transit account for the remainder. The city's vehicular ownership can be witnessed from figure 3.2.

---

1 Kaiser Bengali, Ph.D. Dissertation "Regional Account of Pakistan", 2004.

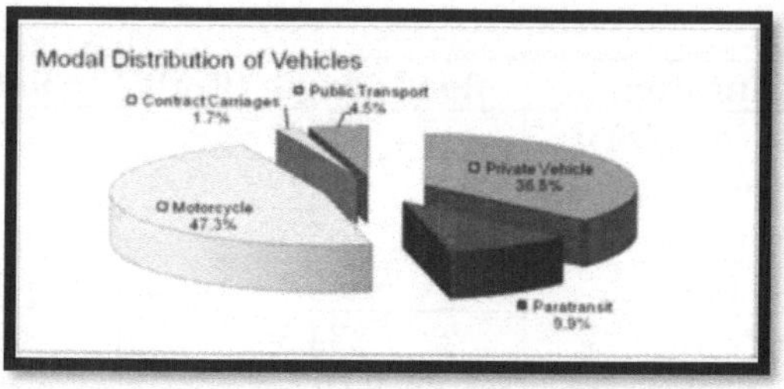

Figure 3.2: Modal Distribution of Vehicles
Source: Karachi Mass Transit cell (2012)

The shortage of bus route network coverage and generally poor access to transit provide no alternative for those who own private vehicles (Figure 3.3). Increased population, economic activity and vehicle ownership forecasted for the next several years (if not decades) are likely to contribute to a marked increase in traffic congestion.

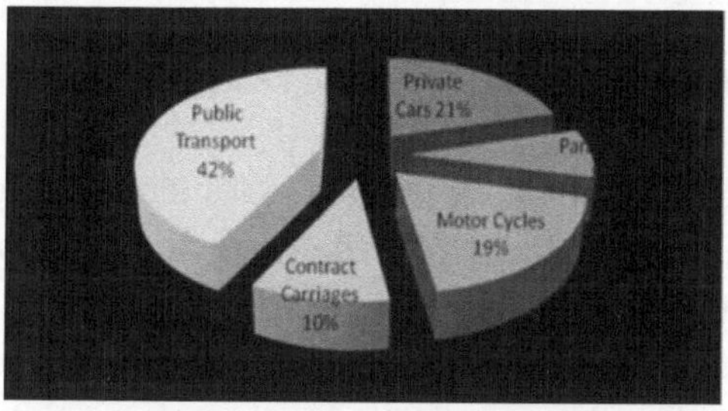

Figure 3.3: Modal Distribution of Passengers
Source: Karachi Mass Transit Cell (2012)

The transportation network of Karachi is dominated by roads with a total length of more than 9,900 km, as mentioned in table 3.8, and further supplemented by Lyari Expressway and Northern Bypass, accommodating more than 4.1 million vehicles, as confirmed by table 3.9. It has been observed in recent years that the city has been facing a massive increase in the number of vehicles due to easy lending policies by private banks and improvement in the socio-economic indicators. The upsurge in vehicular traffic has caused massive congestion, resulting in road accidents and waste of the valuable time of commuters.

Classification	Road Length (Km)	Ratio (%)
Arterial road Total	512.2	5.2
Expressway	77.2	0.8
Principal	265.9	2.7
Minor	169.1	1.7
Collector	234.3	2.4
Local	9,197.8	92.5
Total	9,944.3	100

Table 3.8: Road Infrastructure of Karachi
(Source: KDSP 2020, CDGK)

Total number of Vehicles REGISTERED / ON ROAD in Karachi								
Types of vehicles	**2013**	**2014**	**2015**	**2016**	**Growth 2014**	**Growth 2015**	**Growth 2016**	**Cumulative 2013-2016**
Minibus	16,152	16,834	16,542	16,623	4.2%	-1.7%	0.5%	2.9%
Buses	6,361	6,449	6,393	6,696	1.4%	-0.9%	4.7%	5.3%
Mini Truck	13,983	14,468	15,802	16,655	3.5%	9.2%	5.4%	19.1%
Truck	16,572	17,145	18,650	20,325	3.5%	8.8%	9.0%	22.6%
Van/Pickup	118,479	119,564	133,510	155,374	0.9%	11.7%	16.4%	31.1%
Taxi	47,107	47,016	46,923	46,923	-0.2%	-0.2%	0.0%	-0.4%
Rickshaw	130,340	153,996	199,165	229,826	18.1%	29.3%	15.4%	76.3%
Tanker	3,027	3,069	3,156	3,337	1.4%	2.8%	5.7%	10.2%
PVT Vehicles	1,079,443	1,126,486	1,181,648	1,275,317	4.4%	4.9%	7.9%	18.1%
Motorcycles	1,560,674	1,759,852	1,976,252	2,344,976	12.8%	12.3%	18.7%	50.3%
Others	9,400	10,413	12,849	14,660	10.8%	23.4%	14.1%	56.0%
Total	3,001,538	3,275,292	3,610,890	4,130,712	9.1%	10.2%	14.4%	37.6%
Source: Transport & Communication, KDA								

Table 3.9: Total Number of Vehicles in Karachi

Three national highways connect Karachi to the northeast (Super Highway to Hyderabad and Punjab), southeast (National Highway to Badin) and northwest (RCD Highway to Quetta). These all terminate at Karachi Port Trust. The essence of the intra-city road network is a series of arterials emanating north and northwest from Saddar, Karachi's traditional centre and the town closest to the port. These arterials create a radial pattern that defines much of Karachi's urban structure today.

'Signal Free Corridors' is a recent term introduced theoretically and practically in the urban transportation arena of Karachi. The major aim of signal-free corridors developed with huge capital investments is to facilitate fast-moving cars and other freight-carrying vehicles. The city of Karachi consists of 4 signal-free corridors, as exhibited in figure 3.4. Corridor I consists of 10.5 km connecting Sharah-e-Faisal with SITE, which started operating in 2007. Corridor II consists of a 19-Kilometer-long highway connecting Sharah-e-Faisal with Surjani, which began operating in 2009. Corridor III, consisting of a 28-Kilometer-long Signal Free Corridor connecting Karachi Toll Plaza to Saddar Dawa Khana, was inaugurated on August 13, 2009, and Corridor IV, a 28-Kilometer-long highway, connects Malir to PIDC through Shara-e-Faisal.

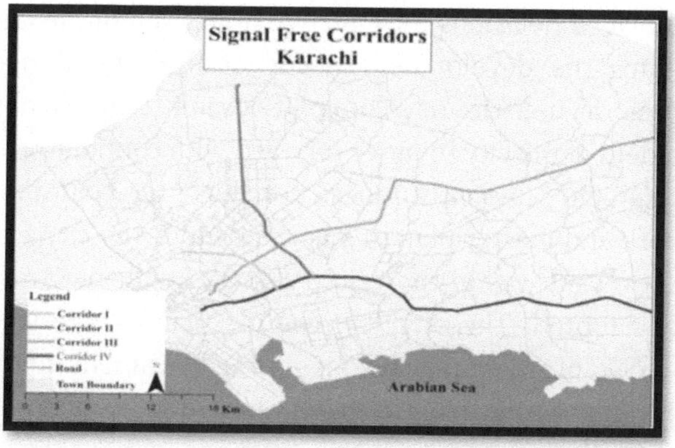

Figure 3.4: Signal Free Corridors in Karachi

The existing bus transport system in the city causes extreme hardships and mental torture for the people of Karachi, compounded by the wider urban transit problems of congestion, air and noise pollution, which cause not only significant economic and social costs to the city but also a decline in the health and quality of life of the residents. It is essential that the city's roads and highways network be restructured, reorganized and rehabilitated, ensuring smooth urban mobility of masses to provide relief to traffic congestions and boost commerce and trade activities. If this is not done at the appropriate time, these shortcomings would be immediately reflected by the sluggishness in the pace of development and also would be visible in the degeneration of the socio-economic structure.

3.2.4. Land Use Trends

The failing land market of Karachi adversely affects the efficiency of current development and restricts the future growth of the city at the same time. Any market-driven economic growth must have unrestricted availability and transferability of land and capital. It is the need of the hour to properly assess and evaluate failures of the urban land market and develop mechanisms to make informed decisions for effective utilization of the land that necessitates the development needs of the city. It needs to encompass a holistic development vision that involves all stakeholders of the city to move forward with confidence.

Karachi currently does not have a comprehensive framework and master plan to steer and guide the city's growth. The most recent was in the year 1986 till 2000[2] but was never formally adopted. The city has complex land ownership, and nearly 90% of the land belongs to government and allied agencies, consisting of 17 major institutions. The housing facilities for the citizens cannot be extended without the consent of owning agencies. There is no provision of land for incremental housing, which means:

- Employment centers are far away from employee housing
- Half of the city's population is living in *katchi abadis* and slums.

There is a dearth of institutional mechanisms to open up the land for serviced plots and fill up genuine demand. This failure has caused an informal private sector to illegally possess the public land, subdividing and selling plots to people at lower prices.

The CBD of Karachi, located in Saddar, Jamshed and Keamari towns, represents a huge concentration of retail trade establishments, wholesale markets, warehouses, business offices, banks, financial and commercial institutions, transport terminals like truck and bus stands, etc. More than 50 percent of

---

[2] Karachi Development Plan 2000; KDA, UNCHS, 1991

the city's jobs or employments are found in this section of the inner city. Since the CBD is the most preferred location for most businesses, there is heavy pressure for commercial space. As a result, congestion, overcrowding, and heavy traffic movements, punctuated by regular traffic jams and air pollution, are prevalent features. With the mounting pressures exerted by population growth over the last two decades, two basic trends in land use are observed. Recently, commercial growth has taken place along major arterials. While most residential neighborhoods have acquired one or two-storey structures, significant densification has taken place through the construction of upper floors and subdivisions of large plots.

3.2.5. Land, Planning and Municipal Control

In the city district, land planning and municipal control are fragmented and divided into twenty federal, provincial and local agencies with overlapping powers/functions and an utter lack of coordination. These agencies include: Six Cantonment Boards, Port Qasim Authority, Karachi Port Trust, Defence Housing Authority, Pakistan Steel, Pakistan Railways, Export Processing Zone, Sindh Industrial Trading Estate, Government of Sindh (Board of Revenue), City District Government Karachi, Lyari Development Authority, Malir Development Authority, cooperative housing societies and private owners as exhibited in figure 3.5.

The multiplicity of ownership, overlapping functions and fragmented municipal control have resulted in the following problems:

- Lack of holistic and unified vision for the city, hampering the formulation and implementation of development plans for the city in an integrated manner
- Unplanned and haphazard growth, leading to acute civic problems
- Environmental degradation and deterioration of living conditions

- Widespread *katchi abadis* and slums, promoting unsustainability
- Grossly deficient infrastructure/utilities
- Lack of unified town planning and building regulations
- Inter-organizational conflicts in the provision of basic infrastructure, municipal services and revenue collection
- Problems in disaster/crisis management

Most of these problems were also one of the major reasons outlined in the household survey questionnaire to compute the perceptions of the citizens scientifically.

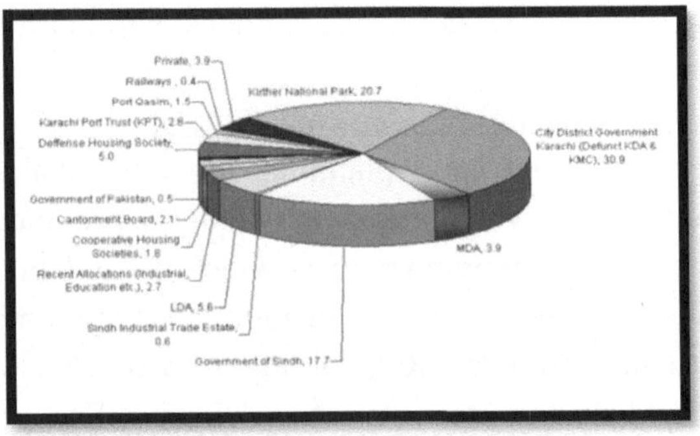

Figure 3.5: Land Control in Karachi
Source: Ud Din Ahmed (2016)

3.2.6. Housing Trends

The housing needs of the population are increasing as the size of Karachi is very large, and gradually, they are becoming dependent on the government for better opportunities. The phenomenal growth rate is due to the continuous inflow of people that has generated massive demand for affordable and low-cost housing. The rising demand does not meet adequate supply, resulting in severe strain on the urban ecosystem and pressure on physical infrastructure in the form of vertical construction. The formal sector has badly failed in the provision of housing facilities for the urban middle classes and lower strata of society. The costly land in the metropolitan area due to the supply constraints and speculation has effectively turned off the option for middle-income groups to settle in the middle of the city, near their workstations. The urban middle and lower classes of the city, roughly consisting of 40% of the city's population, have been compelled to live in squatter settlements or the *katchi abadis* in or around the metropolitan area.

The CDGK (2007) reports reaffirm that 100,000 new units will be required to be added per year to meet the requirements of 3.8 million households/units in the year 2020. Of this, about 50 percent of the increase in housing provision will be required for the poor and low-income households to be formed in the existing *katchi abadis*. The issue of regularization and non-provision of leases are some of the major bottlenecks hindering the investment and the much-needed improvement in the overall living conditions of the inhabitants living in the squatter settlements and slums.

Formal housing in Karachi has been a highly coveted but largely unavailable commodity for decades now. Even today, according to the study by Hasan et al. (2015), more than 60 percent of Karachi's population lives in *katchi abadis* or informal settlements, whereas the poorest of the people live in the slums or *jhuggis*, lacking all basic amenities. By numbers alone, this is, in fact, Karachi's vast majority. The city's housing dynamics exhibit vertical and horizontal expansion in all the corners of the city, devoid of any policy mechanism and direction, presenting a gloomy picture for overall aesthetics and morphology.

Gaining rights to land and housing, by extension, remains a highly contentious process which has remained inaccessible to most Karachiites for decades now and has pushed scores of people into vulnerable informal housing arrangements. The people residing in informal settlements will always be vulnerable to harsh climatic conditions, forceful evictions due to brutal planning regimes and continuous threats of dispossession. Housing is set to become an ever rarer commodity with each passing day, and more and more people will be pushed into buying lands or houses that are environmentally unsound.

3.3. Urban Morphology of Karachi

Urban morphology refers to presenting the main elements of urban form – streets, urban blocks, plots and buildings. The city of Karachi has grown from the old town to the port at the sea outwards, along with radial avenues that connect all city segments to the port. The inner city is manifestly the historic Karachi and has proud possession of an array of historic structures and heritage buildings, protected and preserved under the Sindh Cultural Heritage Act 1994. Along the Bundar Road stand the oldest Mandir, the Mereweather Tower, the KMC Building, Khaliq Dina Hall, and the old Sindh Assembly Building, whereas the Lea Market, Spencer Eye Hospital, and residential quarters of Napier Street and Pakistan Chowk mark the historic quarters of the city. It is prudent to have an effective conservation policy for the urban regeneration of the inner city. There are a few means of circumferential movements. As the city continues to expand, future economic growth is expected to have an impact on the morphology and physical pattern of the megacity. As Karachi's economy grows, the space requirements/needs of the growing economic activities will have to be taken care of through appropriate allocation of land or developed spaces in suitable locations, where these can grow in a harmonious relationship with the rest of the city. In particular, the demand for industrial space for manufacturing is increasing despite several adverse factors, such as power shortages or high business costs.

In Karachi, the pattern of population density and urban sprawl has been changing continuously since Partition. Karachi is valued for its enormous diversity in terms of ethnic and cultural cross-section in a unique urban scenario. The city, due to massive neglect and inaction, has lost its flair and its title, the "Queen of the East." Karachi is surrounded by an aesthetically poor environment as its coastline receives an estimated 200 mgd of untreated sewer and up to 1000 tons of dumped solid waste every day. It is further supplemented by an estimated 92 mgd of industrial waste discharged to the stormwater drainage system.

The critical factor to the poor and deteriorating environmental conditions is a lack of urban planning and unplanned development in environmentally sensitive areas.

The rapid, unregulated and uncontrolled urban growth of the city has changed land dynamics, resulting in inhumane, poorly serviced and heavily polluted informal settlements known as *katchi abadis*. The lack of a mass transit system has led to more congestion, overcrowding, degraded air quality, and an increase in the number of accidents. The following sections explore the different forms of physical transformation in the metropolitan city of Karachi.

3.3.1. Suburbanization

Karachi is a migrants' city. It has been the destination for, and home to, millions within and outside Pakistan – both economic migrants and refugees fleeing war and natural disasters and their aftermath – for decades. Consequently, migration has played an important role in shaping Karachi's urban development trends and its socio-economic and political character. Karachi's haphazard and humongous growth has been a major impediment to realizing its true potential for urbanization. The city's sprawling trends have been a major reason behind its inadequate provision of infrastructure and basic urban services, along with insufficient and poor quality housing and a failure to deal with pollution.

The increase in the natural population due to continuous migration from different regions and within the country has fueled the horizontal growth of the city. Of the estimated 3.35 million 'illegal' immigrants in Pakistan, 75 percent (or 2.5 million) are settled in more than 100 migrant-concentrated residential areas in Karachi. With an estimated population of 16 million according to the census of 2017, as suggested in table 3.10, Karachi is considered one of Asia's fastest-growing cities. Population growth has been presented as the main cause of urban sprawl in Karachi. CDGK (2007) predicted that 45% of the population increase during the 15 years from 2005 to 2020 would occur in the three towns located on the outskirts of Karachi city, namely Keamari, Gadap and Bin Qasim (District West & District Malir) while the other 55% would occur in the remaining other districts. The causes of population growth and invasion of the cities are related to economic growth due to development and technical progress. An increase in population has led to urban problems, such as traffic, crowding, air pollution, noise and crime. The vast and expensive land within the city compels people to move and settle at the urban fringe as these areas are cheap.

Name	Area (km^2)	Population Census 2017-03-15	Density
Karachi Central	61.5 km^2	2,972,639	48,336/km^2
Karachi East	165 km^2	2,909,921	17,625/km^2
Karachi South	85 km^2	1,791,751	21,079/km^2
Karachi West	630 km^2	3,914,757	6,212/km^2
Korangi	94.8 km^2	2,457,019	25917/km^2
Malir	2491 km^2	2,008,901	806/km^2
Karachi	3527km^2	16,054,988	4552/ km^2

Table 3.10: Karachi's District Population
Source: Statistics (2017)

Table 3.10 reveals that Karachi's overall density is 4552/km^2, and the city's central, eastern and southern zones are showing stable trends, whereas district Central is denser, followed by district Korangi. The average population density in the existing urbanized area is 23,800 persons per km^2, which is relatively higher than other big cities in the world. It is evident from table 3.10 that the western part and district of Malir are less dense, and these are areas with vast availability of land and show signs of suburbanization as people prefer to settle in these areas due to low cost and low density. Density is the correlation between inhabitant and built-up area (BA) per census district (j). This index is given by:

$$D = \frac{P}{\sum BA} \quad n \tag{1}$$

Where Pj is the population of the district, which is the collective spatial unit in which the census organized the population, and BA is the built-up area in km^2. Density is the ratio of the people living in an area and the size of that area. Density for each district was calculated and then spatial density map was created using the arcmap 10.4 software. In the spatial map, as shown in figure 3.6, it is visible that Malir and Karachi West are the districts with large area sizes, but the population is comparatively less in these districts.

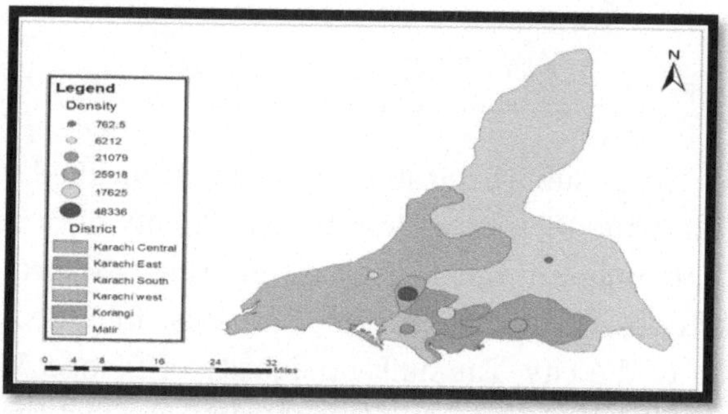

Figure 3.6: Spatial Density Map of Karachi District Wise
Source: Owner's calculation

The city of Karachi, due to its accessibility and connectivity on the outer fringe and within the city, as shown in figure 3.7, provides ample opportunity for people to relocate and improve their living standards. Road infrastructure is directly associated with the urban sprawl. The Karachi metropolitan region, as determined by the commuter zone, spreads over parts of the surrounding districts, Thatta and Jamshoro of Sindh to the east and Lasbella of Balochistan to the west. The coastline in the district is about 135 kilometers long, extending along the Gharo Creek westward beyond Cape Monze to the estuary of the Hub

River. Almost in the centre of the coast, sheltered by the island of Manora, lies the Port of Karachi, with entire Pakistan and Afghanistan forming its vast hinterland; the Port Muhammad Bin Qasim at Pipri on the Gharo Creek plays a complementary role.

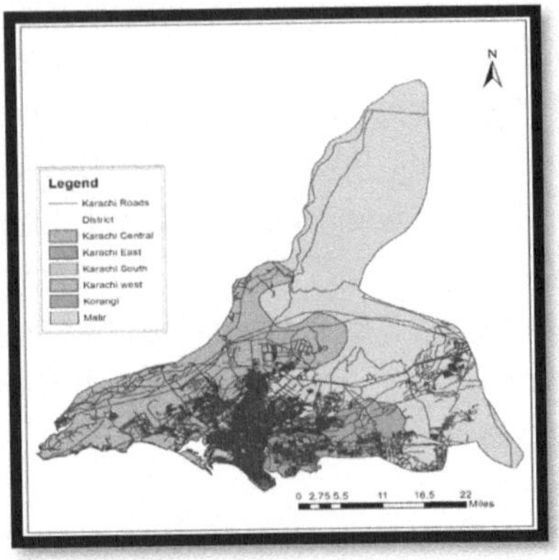

Figure 3.7: Spatial Map of Road Infrastructure in Karachi

The city's suburbanization is mainly inclined towards District West and District Malir as the availability of vacant lands is more prominent in these districts, and they are located near major arteries, providing further impetus for the physical expansion of the city. The built-up density of District West and Malir is evident from figure 3.8, confirming the fact that future sprawl is going to take place in these peripheries, which is further affirmed by big real estate projects of Bahria Town Karachi and Defence City projects already launched for many years.

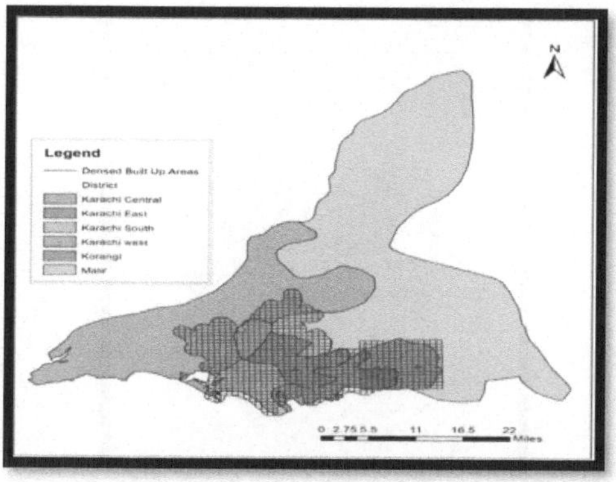

Figure 3.8: Spatial Map of Built Up Areas of Karachi

The official statistics of the 2017 population survey reveal that District West comprises 7.20% of the rural population, as shown in table 3.11, and District Malir comprises 42.60% of the rural population, as shown in table 3.12, presenting an ideal opportunity for developers to convert green spaces into planned and unplanned development.

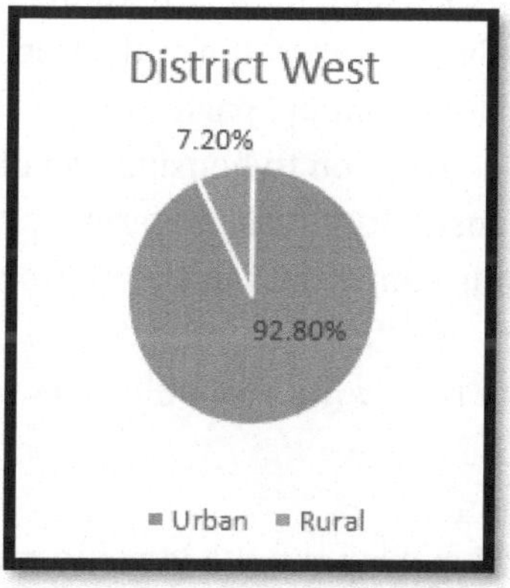

Table 3.11: Urban and Rural Population Pie Chart
Source: Statistics (2017)

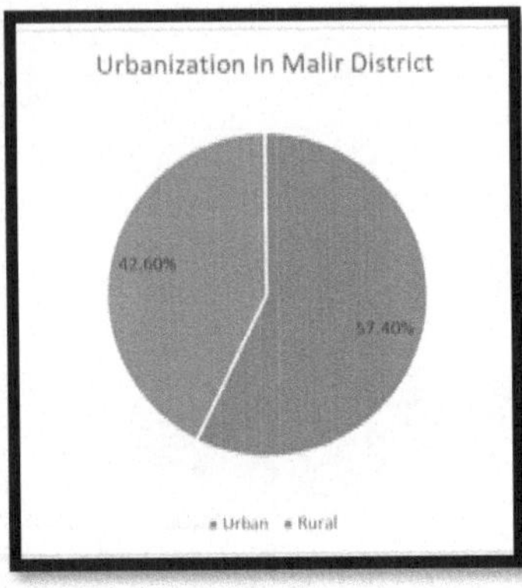

Table 3.12: Urban and Rural Population Pie Chart
Source: Statistics (2017)

In the Malir Valley, Kathore and Shah Mureed-Gadap zones, large cultivated tracts depend on irrigation from tube wells and shallow-dug wells. There is considerable potential for the development of cultivation and groundwater resources. Culturable land with good soils is generally constrained by a shortage of groundwater supplies. However, cultivation has witnessed some expansion in the Kathore and Shah Murad-Gadap zones, leading towards the reduction in the cultivated lands of the Malir River valley, particularly in its lower section, due to large-scale conversion to housing and other urban uses. It is the prime responsibility of the government to make prudent policies to contain urban sprawl in the metropolitan city as it is the economic hub of Pakistan and ensure its food security through agriculture reservoirs available in its vicinity.

3.3.2. Fragmentation

The social fabric of metropolitan has many groupings along the lines of a common culture, nationality, race, language, occupation, religion, income level, or other common interests. The high-income settlements of the city are becoming increasingly isolated from the rest of Karachi. They are developing sports facilities, shopping centers, entertainment activities, libraries and educational institutions in their own areas. Their residents now do not have to go out of their areas except to work. In addition, most houses have armed guards, and many are looked after by security companies that have computerized security arrangements. There is a new concept of gated communities signaling out the urban poor from affluent people of the city, leading towards long-term psychological problems and hindering their social mobility.

In middle-income settlements, there is a constant struggle with the local authorities to improve services. Citizens' associations lobby with politicians and government agencies to this end. They initiate court proceedings when they do not succeed in getting what they desire and often help in making the issues of their areas into election issues for the national and provincial assembly elections. Ethnic issues dominate the politics of these areas and give rise to a number of social welfare organizations. In the *katchi abadis*, which are not in the city core and which have been marked for regularization and improvement, community organizations are developing to protect open spaces and to create sports clubs, lending libraries and cultural organizations. In these settlements, services and housing gradually improve over time. A large segment of the population lives in slums and squatter settlements in very inhumane conditions, and their struggle with lives continues almost on a daily basis as they are completely secluded and ghettoized, and they do not have any meaningful say in the decision-making.

3.3.3. Encroachments

According to the findings of Jamil (2018), there are many encroachment mafias who acquire land illegally and pose various threats to the management of these landholding parties. The encroachments are carried out at the back of political patronage with vested interests. Land grabbers have, at times, the support of law enforcement agencies in conducting their illicit activities. The city of Karachi witnessed "China Cutting" term used for bisecting the amenity plots into piecemeal for the commercial purposes. The encroachment mafias have linkages with the black economy of the city, which runs into billions annually. The political patronage in Karachi is mostly comprised of a number of political parties which are present in this giant city (Basit et al., 2018). Most of the time, the illegal settlements are formed on the outer edge of the city, fuelling urban growth, and are regularized with the help of government functionaries to increase the vote bank but massively damage the city's urban environment.

3.3.4. Master Plan Fiasco

Cities facilitate human interaction. From a traditional perspective, master planning is shaping and foreseeing this interaction through spatial development plans, providing amenities, housing, transport systems, and community facilities, and determining land use. The range of dynamics and dimensions that govern this megapolis is more complex than any other city. However, this diversity is the strength of the city. With its 16 million population and an urban sprawl of 1600 sq km, the city of Karachi is the 7th largest urban agglomeration in the world.

The city has witnessed many urban planning documents since 1947, but interestingly, none of the documents was officially notified by the Sindh government; hence, they are not legally binding. The Greater Karachi Plan of 1951 aimed to expand the administrative functions of the Capital, Karachi, some 20 kilometres away in Gadap. The city of Karachi witnessed the massive arrival of migrants after 1947, changing the demography and ethnicity of the city in a very short span of time. The Greater Karachi Resettlement Plan was prepared in 1958, which aimed to house newcomers in satellite towns named Landhi-Korangi and North Karachi, linked with industrial and commercial hotspots but could not achieve the desired results as residential development outpaced industrial and commercial activities.

The city had another Master Plan document for 1973-85, but it could not be implemented fully except for road networks and the bulk water supply. The reasons for non-implementation were the military takeover, political conflict and lack of legal cover. Another Master Plan 1986-2000 was adopted to implement the rational strategies to check and contain the city's growth scientifically. Although the 1973-1985 and 1986-2000 plans were both different in approach, content and outputs, both offered a useful mechanism to guide development. The CDGK (now defunct) prepared the Karachi Strategic Development Plan (KSDP) 2020, adopted by the city council in the year 2007, but it lost its credence after the devolution plan was undone by the provincial government some years later. The strategic plan was aimed at providing basic municipal services to the citizens, prioritizing the infrastructure, checking the sprawling growth through scientific means, revitalizing the old city, preserving its historical heritage and affordable housing, integrating the management system and working with the private sector to reclaim the "City of Lights".

The built environment of a city is envisioned through its city plan and enforced by building control agencies to ensure the city is developing and functioning in a rational manner. In today's fast-paced world, old master plan documents are becoming obsolete and irrelevant. Planning literature has been identifying density, resiliency, multi-functional and walkable neighborhood, cellular city and smart city urbanism approaches as more responsive towards the contemporary challenges. Moreover, the literature has also discussed the changes in the role of the planner from the sole originator to a mediator, advocate, and collaborator in strategic planning, collaborative planning, co-production, and just city.

Urban planning does not need to come from the government only; it can be a product of social interventions and public involvement. The urban development teams need to extend beyond town planners. City management is all about people, not just infrastructure. So we need economists, sociologists, historians, anthropologists, public health professionals, psychologists and other professionals to work together to develop the city's vision instead of entrusting engineers to do it by themselves. The city of Karachi must be built through cooperation, not compulsion.

3.4. An Outlook of City's Major Challenges

3.4.1. Urban Transportation

Urban transportation is instrumental for economic development and a sustainable environment. The city lacks an efficient and modern public transport system at par with other urban centers across the globe. The studies indicate that the city's private transport is growing at an alarming rate of 9% annually, causing more congestion and personalization of vehicles. This growth is the main contributory factor to the heavy traffic and prevailing congestion on the city's roads. The CDGK and other competing authorities did partially offset the traffic woes by constructing signal-free corridors, overhead bridges and underpasses, but these proved futile as these were short-driven efforts and did not yield long-term benefits for those travelling on buses and two-wheelers. The personalization of vehicles in the cities compounds the miseries of the traffic system (Weisbrod et al., 2003), as evident from table 3.13.

The CDGK (2007) document stresses the revival of the Karachi Circular Railway, Bus Rapid Transit and Light Rail Transit to provide modern transportation to its citizens by 2020.

Cities	Private transport%	Public transport%	Motorized transport%
Lahore	24	16	60
Karachi	27	23	50
Delhi	18	40	42
Mumbai	18	60	22
Kolkata	5	78	17

Table 3.13: Urban Transport in South Asian Cities
Source: Transport & Communication, KDA (2016)

The transportation infrastructure of Karachi is very weak because it has been unable to provide the required support for the development of an adequate culture in Karachi (Umair & Naz, 2019). According to the research article by Soomro et al. (2018), the transport system in Karachi does not meet the demands of the public because only a few people can travel through public buses launched by the government. The exponential growth in private transport will create delays in reaching the destination, waste of precious time besides lowering economic productivity, polluting the environment, overcrowding the roads, and causing accidents, injuries and stress among the citizens.

3.4.2. Water & Sanitation

The provision of water to residents is another uphill task of urban institutions in Karachi. It is the basic responsibility of the Karachi Water and Sewerage Board (KWSB). The core function of this institution is to supply, transmit and distribute water. It is also responsible for wastewater collection, treatment, drainage and sewerage. The entity is separate from KMC, and its annual budget is approved by the government of Sindh. The demand for water outstrips the supply, inviting informal players to fill up the gaps with inflated costs.

These players operate illegal hydrants by involving concerned officials through kickbacks. The water supplied is mainly unhygienic and prone to water-contaminated diseases because of sub-soil water mixing. The water supply system of Karachi largely depends on the following infrastructure, as mentioned in figure 3.9. It can be said that Karachi is getting water from 7 different points in Sindh. As the figure illustrates, the last developed project in this water domain was K-III, which was developed in 2006. However, even after 14 years, there has been no water project carried out in Karachi, as progress on K-4 has yet to be determined.

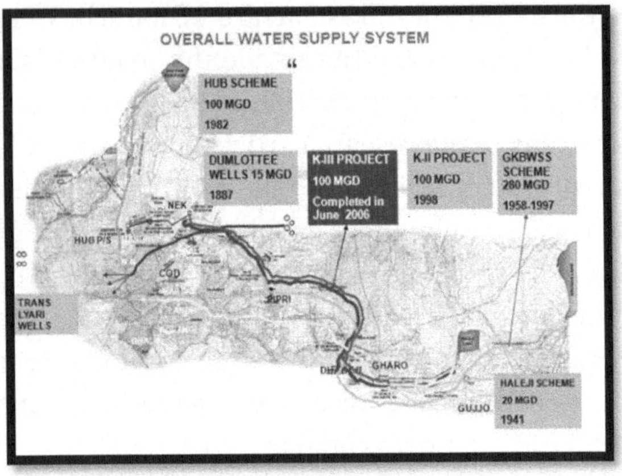

Figure 3.9: Karachi's Water Supply
Source: KW&SB (2019)

A staggering 40% of the water is estimated as non-revenue water in South Asian cities, according to the reports of the World Health Organization and UNICEF (2010). This indicates institutional incapacity as a large quantum of revenues is not realized along with the non-provision of essential utility to the consumers. This can be improved by putting emphasis on the usage of benchmarking tools to evaluate and analyze the performance of service providers, addressing service gaps and ensuring broader reforms. Table 3.14 reflects water and sanitation accessibility across the country.

	Urban (36% of population	**Rural (64% of population)**	**Total**
Water	96%	89%	92%
Sanitation	72%	34%	48%

Table 3.14: Access to water and Sanitation in Pakistan in 2010
Source: World Health Organization (2011)

The economic impact of inadequate and non-availability of proper sanitation is estimated at $5.7 billion, resulting in productivity losses, increase in mortality rates, environmental degradation and higher costs of bottled water. It has been observed that water infrastructure in Karachi could not develop at a rapid pace because it is only controlled by the Karachi Water and Sewerage Board (KW&SB). According to the findings of Whitelegg and Haq (2017), the performance of different companies declined because the water supply was inadequate, and the sewerage department did not receive the investments. The statistics of the demand and supply gap can be gauged from table 3.15.

Year	Population (Million)	Demand (MGD)	Supply (MGD)	Gap (MGD)
1998	9.8	567	410	157
2017	16.0	820	650	170

Table 3.15: Water Demand and Supply Gap
Source: KWSB (2017)

The statistics show a major decline in investments in the sewerage sector, which was already pretty low. This indicates that sewerage issues are present in almost all areas of the city. Based on the component-sharing model, there is evidence from the private sector and NGOs working to fulfil water and sanitation facilities in different communities. The examples of the Orangi pilot project (OPP) and the Lodhran pilot project are prominent in this regard, as these innovative projects were conceived and funded by the communities themselves.

3.4.3. Solid Waste Management

The growth in the city's population has significantly enhanced the production of solid waste, with estimates of around 18000-20000 tons of waste generation per day by 2020, according to the projections of CDGK (2007), creating severe repercussions for the overall drainage system in Karachi. The Karachi Metropolitan Corporation, responsible for disposing of the waste, now rests with the Sindh Solid Waste Management Authority. The city of Karachi, which is spatially built, has two landfill sites for solid waste disposal situated in Gond Pass and Deh Jam Chakro next to each other in the District West. The distance to these landfill sites is 40 km from the eastern edge of the city, making it very difficult to effectively dump the waste due to the time and costs associated with it; therefore, most of the solid waste is dumped into streets, open plots, public amenities turning the city into full of garbage, filth and litter.

The solid waste management in Karachi is neither efficient nor collected, transported and disposed of according to the set international standards. The urban experts pinpoint that nearly 30% to 40% of solid waste is dumped into landfill sites (Figure 3.10), leaving the remaining for scavengers, *kabbaris*, middlemen and sweepers involved in the waste disposal recycling business, which has quite turned out to be lucrative in recent times and according to the 2001 study by Karachi Urban Resource Center, nearly 40000 families directly or indirectly venturing into this business can easily touch 100000 figure according to the latest studies.

The city, being the commercial and industrial hub, comprises all types of solid waste. The recyclable material is acquired from two streams: clean stream and dirty stream. The clean stream objects involve bottles, newspapers, metal objects, cans sold to *kabbaris* and recyclers. The dirty stream objects are picked from *kachra kundis* or neighbourhood dumps by young boys, mainly of Afghan origin, appointed by contractors to extract recyclable materials and objects.

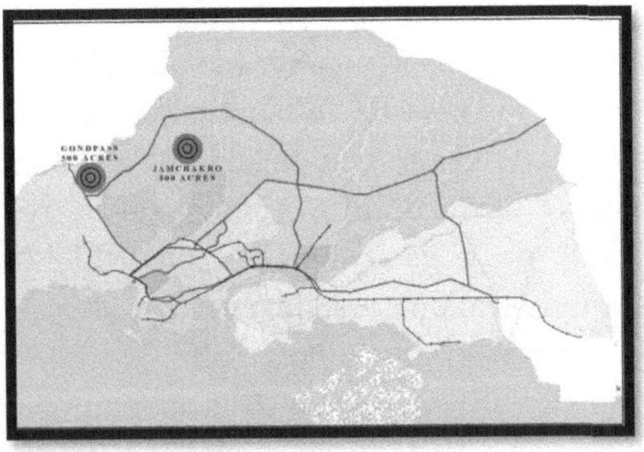

Figure 3.10 Landfill Site
Source: KMC (2007)

3.4.4. Urban Slums and Informal Settlements

Urban growth will raise housing demand, with an estimated backlog of six million housing units, mainly in urban areas (Haider & Haider, 2006). Karachi covers 3,300 square kilometers, of which 1,300 square kilometers fall into the urban mass. The city's land is regulated by 13 different entities, leaving little room for comprehensive urban housing, which is followed across the globe in the metropolitan regions.

The mushroom growth of *katchi abadis* in urban areas is not a good sign for equitable distribution of the resources, as shown in table 3.16. The overwhelming majority of the *katchi abadis* are settled in urban vicinities and are considered safe havens for criminals and gangs escaping from law enforcement agencies. The land of Karachi is distributed unevenly as 62% of the population lives in 8% of the residential area, thus ballooning the rate of densification in the city, whereas 38% of the population is settled in 92% of the area consisting of the urban middle, elite class, bureaucrats and politicians. Slums are present in many areas of Karachi (Zakir et al., 2016). According to the latest statistics, Orangi Town has been rated as the biggest slum in the world because many people live in this big region and pollute the environment (Zakir et al., 2016). According to the findings by Soomro et al. (2018), the slums in Karachi have increased in many regions and areas, and there is a need to resolve these issues as soon as possible.

	1974	1986	2000
Population	709000	1036000	1064400
No. of households	109077	164000	148000

Table 3.16: Population of Slum Areas
Source: Hasan A (1992), calculated by the author from KDAMPD/AERC (1989)

The voluminous increase in shanty towns and slums is widening the gap between urban rich and poor classes. Table 3.17 indicates the spread of slums across Karachi. The urban residences in the city are classified as slums, *goths* (villages), apartments, houses, schemes, and cantonment areas. Choices are made depending on income levels, net worth, and purchasing power.

District	No. of Slum Areas
Central	119
West	191
East	105
Malir	63
South	61
Total	539

Table 3.17: District Wise Slums Distribution
Source: Sindh Katchi Abadis Authority (1998)

Urban housing in the city has turned into different shapes depending on income groups, net worth, and purchasing power parity. The residences are classified as: Slums, Goths, *Katchi abadis*, Apartments, Houses, Schemes and Cantonment areas.

3.4.5. Law & Order

The rapid growth of the urban population has created a law and order situation in the form of target killings, kidnappings, extortions, murders, robberies and vandalism. The inward migration of criminal outfits is aimed at pursuing their malafide agendas in the commercial and economic hub of the country. The capital city police officer (CCPO) is mandated to look after the law and order situation of the city. The security situation in the city for over two decades looks gruesome and demands further improvement. The city's economic contribution of nearly 20% of the country's GDP makes a strong pull factor for inward migrants. The rogue elements and criminal outfits have moved in large numbers, making the city a hotbed for criminal activities. The UN studies of the 13 largest cities point out a homicide rate of 12.3 per 100000, the highest among the largest cities. This confirms slackness from law enforcement agencies attributed as politically patronized, wrecked and incapacitated.

Law and order agencies have miserably failed to stop street crimes, terrorist activities, gang wars, killings, and other related crimes perpetrated on the streets of the metropolis. Despite the bleak scenario, Inskeep (2011) appreciates the city's tolerance, vitality, thriving civil society, and culture of charity. He lauds the spirit and resilience of people to live in a harmonious society and denounces all forms of violence.

The terrorism in KPK, economic deprivation in rural Sindh and insurgency in Baluchistan immensely contributed to the changing demographics in Karachi. It is a well-established argument that the city is well-represented by all major ethnicities, which is why there is a rivalry to compete for scarce resources. The socio-economic divide creates a chaotic situation and can be addressed through economic empowerment. The criminal outfits thrive on the back of illicit trade and are supported by the corrupt elite. The credible studies pinpoint that the city's black economy is worth 8 million dollars per day, thereby raising the stakes as the whole ecosystem is backed and supported by powerful mafias.

3.5. Karachi & Governance Framework

3.5.1. Administrative Paradox

Karachi is suffering from the problems of an administrative black hole because it is a hapless city, with no one owning it (Niazi & Azad, 2018). The city faces an administrative paradox as it is run by a host of agencies at the federal, provincial and local levels with separate legal and administrative frameworks. This creates a fragmented system as multiple agencies operate separately with their set of regulatory laws and frameworks. This impacts severely as the city suffers from a lack of coordination and effective planning. The city's fragmented and weak governance is a major impediment to the city's urban governance, delivery of municipal services, weaker enforcement of laws and visible fallout on the private sector, which otherwise would have spurred massive economic growth given the natural dynamism and growth potential of the city. The limited success of urban management and planning is primarily due to insufficient institutional capacity, coordination, and control among land-owning agencies at the federal, provincial and local levels. This has been exacerbated by the complex political economy of the city.

Nearly 90 percent of the city's land is under public ownership or control, but owners are reluctant or unable to make this land available for development and affordable housing in a coordinated manner. The local government itself only controls about 30 percent of Karachi Division's land. The GoS strategy of centralizing the planning and building control functions at the provincial level has yet to improve coordination between Karachi's planning, service delivery and urban management. A focus on integrated planning and service-delivery models is needed. It is prudent and viable to go for the decentralized and empowered 3rd tier of the government as per practices in international cities like London, Paris, New York, Singapore, and Tokyo to make a difference in the lives of the people residing in the metropolis.

3.5.2. Lack of Strong Local Government System

Until August 2001, local government in Karachi was structured according to the Sindh Local Body Ordinance (SLBO) 1978. The local government consisted of the Karachi Metropolitan Corporation (KMC) and five District Municipal Corporations (DMCs), one for each district. Local government was subservient to the provincial Ministry of Local Government and Rural Development (LG&RD), whose Secretary could supersede the KMC and DMCs for reasons of corruption and mismanagement. In August 2001, the Government of Sindh enacted the Local (City) Government Ordinance 2001. As a result of this enactment, the five districts of Karachi ceased to exist, and the city was now one district headed by a *Nazim* (mayor) and a *Naib*

Nazim (deputy mayor). The district was divided into 18 towns, and each town was further divided into approximately ten union councils. Each town and union council had its own nazims and naib nazims. As a result of the enactment of the Ordinance, the KWSB, KMC, KDA, MDA and LDA were dissolved. The CDGK had sweeping powers as primary education, basic health, and transport came under city government, including all planning, implementation, operation and maintenance. Hence, this system of local government, which was called "devolution plan" utterly restructured the district and Tehsil-level government structure (Cheema et al., 2005).

The devolution plan of 2001 ushered in a new era of 3rd-tier elected local governments backed by strong administrative and financial structures. However, soon after the completion of the second tenure of local governments, the Federal and Provincial Governments (2008-2013) led by P halted the local government system, and elections for local Government were not held until 2015 under SLGA 2013. In 2013, the Sindh government passed the Sindh Local Government Act, providing a framework for the reinstatement of elected LGs for the first time in the province since 2010. Municipal governance in the Karachi metropolitan region has been split between the Karachi Metropolitan Corporation (KMC) and six District Municipal Corporations (DMCs), working in overlapping geographical jurisdiction whilst the mayor heads the KMC and elected chairmen head the other entities. Rural areas are governed by the District Council. However, this law provides a multitude of powers to the provincial government, giving it strong control over the functions of the LGs and reducing their autonomy.

Many municipal functions are run through GoS departments or GoS-controlled entities. This results in city governments lacking authority to deliver on municipal service mandates. Numerous entities are fully controlled by GoS: Karachi Water and Sewerage Board, Sindh Solid Waste Management Board, Sindh Building Control Authority, Karachi Development Authority, Lyari and Malir Development Authorities, Sindh Mass

Transit Authority, Sindh High-Density Development Board, and others. The GoS strategy of centralizing the planning and building control functions at the provincial level has yet to improve coordination between Karachi's planning, service delivery, and urban management. The limited mandate for city governments and increasing fragmentation in local governance prevent Karachi from reaping the benefits of urbanization.

3.5.3. Municipal Finances

After the post-independence, the evolution of the local government system in Pakistan is attributed to military rulers, who used the local government system as the only "representative tier of the government" on the pattern of their colonial masters and supported the local government system, whereas, repressed the provincial and federal political systems (Cheema et al., 2005). However, successive governments experimented too much with this tier, resulting in a dismal performance. The non-serious and self-pursuit attitude of local politicians, the absence of a comprehensive legal framework and rampant corrupt practices have all led to the failure of local governments, which could have strengthened the delivery of services at grassroots levels.

Urban Pakistan, particularly Karachi, has suffered badly due to the inept, inefficient and centralized local government system, thus creating serious repercussions on the financial viability of the metropolitan city. The city of Karachi is governed through the Sindh Local Government Act 2013, which states that there shall be a Metropolitan Corporation in Karachi and a Municipal Corporation in all six districts of the city. The provincial government has mostly centralized all the major operations of the Karachi Metropolitan Corporation, including financial powers.

The Sindh government has also taken the advertisement/hoardings department, education and health sector from KMC and handed over these functions to the six district municipal corporations. Moreover, it may be noted that the Karachi Metropolitan Corporation performs the construction and maintenance of 30 major roads in the city, but it has been deprived of its biggest source of income — the local taxes (advertisement hoardings). The second major source of revenue for the KMC Master Plan department was already given to the Sindh Building Control Authority. Consequently, under the new local government laws, Mayor Karachi would have no authority. The Sindh Government has also taken control of the Water & Sewerage Board, Building Control Authority and city cleaning system (through the Solid Waste Management Board). The Karachi Development Authority is also not with KMC and is now under the control of the Sindh Government.

The Metropolitan Corporation depends on the provincial government for fiscal matters that include vertical programs and special grants without extending its financial base for more autonomy. Non-developmental expenses of KMC, including salaries and wages, account for 60% of budgetary outlays. Strong local infrastructure paves the way for sustainable growth and employment in urban economies. This must be backed by the mobilization of financial resources at the local government level. The KMC and DMCs must have financial autonomy rather than being dependent on direct transfers.

KMC comprises 87,000 workforce, of which about 30-40% comprises ghost employees, and the remaining 30-40% staff is inefficient and disinterested due to many reasons, which include low salary, lack of supervision, absence of training and commitment, political affiliations which exert political pressures, and absence of regulatory system for their grooming and accountability. KMC should, likewise, try to improve its asset management and utilize excess revenue income to develop assets under its jurisdiction. For that purpose, the finance department of KMC needs to maintain a proper balance sheet yearly so that the impact of excess Revenue Income can be realized.

A sound financial system is imperative for regulating the affairs of local government. It is essential to develop a joint mechanism with the Sindh Provincial Financial Commission to bring more transparency through strict compliance with regulations and utilization of finances according to best modern practices. KMC can mobilize more resources through the computerization of records, revamping the whole structure and charging fairly for improved municipal services. This will reduce the financial burden on provincial and federal governments. This can be achieved through an integrated system that offers timely information for budgeting, management, monitoring and reporting purposes.

The city's problems cannot be solved without adequate resources. KMC revenue can increase if it gets the devolved departments again for better fiscal discipline and revenue generation. The metropolitan corporation can execute many projects on its own if provided with amounts in various heads, including the betterment tax and commercialization charges. The main issue is the concentration of resources and authority on one hand and the inability to devolve power to the local bodies' representatives on the other.

3.5.4. Urban Vision

The Karachi metropolitan area needs a futuristic and sustainable urban development vision to address traffic and transportation issues, water supply, sewage and drainage, solid waste management, sanitary infrastructure, and social welfare. The development projects ought to be economically feasible and environmentally sound. Urban development projects are, by and large, not oriented towards sustainability. Sustainable growth can be ensured through better hygienic conditions, elimination of pollution, affordable housing and poverty reduction. Efficient cost financing and recovery are the key elements in guiding the choice of sustainable development projects.

The city's vision must be inclusive, non-discriminatory, non-ethnic, and free from prejudices of color and creed. The city needs social cohesion by bringing people closer socially and culturally. The equitable distribution of resources, provision of better education and health facilities, and employment opportunities to all population segments will create an environment of mutual bondage free from political and ethnic polarization. The social integration of the urban poor is a must for the overall livability and sustainability of the city.

Policymakers have to envision a modern city based on a cultural ethos that follows the universal principle of urban regeneration and urban revitalization. Revisiting the policies must meet the demands and expectations of the citizens of Karachi and reflect their aspirations and expectations now and for the future. It is in the very nature of a changing environment that it will require a flexible response that takes into account events and their impact, and that can only be done if the solutions and the strategies are proposed, managed and implemented by Karachiites, highlighting the concerns of all communities through consensus.

3.6. Quality of Life (QoL)

A sense of belonging and clean neighborhoods should be the cornerstone of urban life as they provide aesthetics and impetus to the urban ecosystem. Basically, quality of life is the well-being of people and the quality of the environment in which they live. The quality of life can be measured objectively and subjectively. The haphazard urban growth has worsened the living conditions and the environment. The rapid pace of urbanization and population growth in the city of Karachi has badly compromised the quality of life. Urban Karachi has grown manifold since independence and is still growing. Urban planning, management and service delivery have not kept pace with population growth, so the city is headed towards a spatially unsustainable, inefficient and unlivable form. The city's green, open, communal, recreational and cultural spaces are continuously under threat from commercial activities and are extinguishing at a faster pace.

Karachi is at high risk of natural and human-made disasters and is one of the most disaster-vulnerable districts in Pakistan. The citizens do not have access to the proper and prompt emergency response system due to poor land-use planning and building control. The annual monsoon season wreaks havoc on citizens due to poorly maintained and clogged drainage systems. The World Bank study finds that Karachi needs an estimated US$9 billion to US$10 billion in financing over a 10-year period to meet the infrastructure needs in transportation, solid waste and water supplies to improve the living quality of its citizens. The McArthur and Robin's (2019) study featured Karachi in the bottom 10 of the annual Global Liveability Index of 140 cities around the world based on considering more than 30 qualitative and quantitative factors spanning five broad categories, weighted as follows: stability (25%), healthcare (20%), culture and environment (25%), education (10%) and infrastructure (20%). Table 3.18 presents the statistics:

Ranking	City	Country
1	Damascus	Syria
2	Lagos	Nigeria
3	Dhaka	Bangladesh
4	Tripoli	Libya
5	Karachi	Pakistan
6	Port Moresby	Papua New Guinea
7	Harare	Zimbabwe
8	Douala	Cameroon
9	Algiers	Algeria
10	Caracas	Venezuela

Table 3.18: The world's Least Livable Cities in 2019
Source: The Economist Intelligence Unit (2019)

Karachi underwent an intense heat wave in 2015, killing scores of people and raising questions about the resilience of the city to withstand climate shocks. The city needs enhanced green belts to mitigate the heat islands, reduce energy consumption and provide breathing spaces for an increasingly dense city. The city faces serious environmental challenges that affect productivity, economic growth and quality of life. The incidences of air, water and land pollution caused by raw sewage, industrial emissions, medical waste and vehicular pollution expose citizens to diseases linked to environmental pollution. The five major contributors in Karachi are industrial emissions (53%), soil/road dust (16%), and others, including vehicular emissions (18%), sea salt originating from the Arabian Sea, and secondary aerosols (Mansha et al., 2011). The study of the World Bank Group (2014) finds estimated annual losses of PRs 260 billion related to health caused by environmental disasters. Air pollution, particularly in large urban centers, damages the populations' health and quality of life and contributes to environmental degradation (Aziz, 2006; Aziz & Bajwa, 2004; Colbeck, Nasir & Ali, 2010; World Bank, 2006). The bad outdoor air quality is significantly exposing the citizens to cardiovascular and pulmonary diseases that may result in death or permanent disability. The Gallup survey of 2019 puts Karachi as the dirtiest city in Pakistan, further signaling the low quality of life in the metropolis.

3.7. Ecological Changes in Karachi

In a study by Shirazi and Kazmi (2016), many ecological changes have been observed in the context of climate changes in this city. Karachi, being the main economic hub, is influenced by a huge rise in the temperature of the globe. Several environmental studies (Kazmi et al., 2008; Qureshi et al., 2007; Mehdi et al., 2002; Hasan, 1999; Zaidi, 1996, 1990; Kazmi, 1995; Ahmed, 1994; Shaikh & Rizvi, 1990) reported Karachi as one of the most vulnerable cities prone to face the environmental challenges of this century. The increased motorization spurred by sprawling patterns, traffic congestion, high-rise buildings, and changes in population density have contributed to poor air quality. However, in Karachi, the increasing number of vehicles and private transport resulted in elevated levels of smoke pollution. Water quality remains a question of all time. Water treatment facilities are not enough for this gigantic population; about 60%

of water is filtered, and the rest is only disinfected through chlorination.

The harm caused by air pollution in Pakistan's urban areas is one of the highest in the South Asian Region and exceeds several high-profile causes of mortality and morbidity in Pakistan. In Karachi, Mansha et al. (2011) reported a characterization and source apportionment of ambient air particulate matter (PM2.5). The study found five major contributors: industrial emissions (53%), soil/road dust (16%), and others, including vehicular emissions (18%), sea salt originating from the Arabian Sea, and secondary aerosols. The studies by Ghauri, Lodhi, and Mansha (2007) and Khan (2010) mention emissions from large-scale facilities, such as cement, fertilizer, sugar, steel, and power plants, as a major source contributing towards poor air quality as they run on furnace oil that is high in sulfur content.

Karachi metropolitan, due to its accessibility, connectivity, higher road density, local transfer of knowledge, and access to international supplier and buyer networks, provide further impetus to industrial activities and reasons for relocation. These factors, in conjunction with motorization, would further harm the air quality and stir high levels of traffic noise. These factors are putting a vast number of people subject to psychological and cardiovascular disorders and inducing hearing loss in due course of time. The exceeding levels of pollution observed in the city are significantly higher than all the available international standards. The city recently witnessed alarming levels of rainfalls and heat strokes, causing costly lives and collateral damage due to environmental degradation.

Karachi, being the country's major urban hotspot, needs a greener environment through good governance and participation of citizens in decision-making. Hameed et al. (2019) argued that there are different departments that need to increase legal regulations to promote green energy in this city. The city's resources, if mobilized diligently, can change the landscape within a short span of time. There is an acute need for empirical research to evaluate environmental conditions and correlate them with human systems. A cleaner and greener Karachi would better serve the interests of all citizens.

The critical review of the chapter finds that Karachi is a big metropolis, and because of that, it has many challenges in the form of infrastructure provision and governance framework. The city has various overlapping government entities, leading towards chaos and failure in service delivery. The non-serious and self-pursuit attitude of local politicians, the absence of a comprehensive legal framework, inept attitude, and rampant corrupt practices have immensely contributed towards urban decay and bad aesthetics.

The evolution of land-use patterns over the last few decades suggests that Karachi is now at a tipping point and could be heading toward a spatially unsustainable, inefficient and unlivable city form. The city is undergoing rapid development, as observed on the north and northeast periphery. The leapfrog pattern of development beyond the city core is clearly visible in the post-2013 scenario when developments belonging to housing societies and satellite towns such as Bahria Town and DHA City started to appear on the map. As the city expands to accommodate a growing population, travel from housing locations on the periphery becomes costly and time-consuming, significantly impacting the urban poor living on the peripheries. Better land use, urban design, and urban transport integration are needed to serve residents and businesses and manage congestion.

The mass transit project must be envisaged with good local area planning and urban design to better serve the interests of the citizens. The competent authorities need to find innovative solutions to bridge funding gaps and complete mass transit and other infrastructure projects in the city. The Public and Private Partnership (PPP) can be instrumental in bringing much-needed investment. Given the population size and land area of Karachi, the city can look towards a more polycentric approach in tandem with downtown rejuvenation as a strategy to reorganize the city more efficiently and sustainably for the long term.

Chapter 4| Methodology

This study was conducted looking at urban sprawl modelling of Karachi based on spatial and temporal remote sensing data. The specific aim of this study is to achieve a broad understanding of the main patterns of urban sprawl in Karachi using statistical and spatial analysis and the districts that are the main contributors to urban sprawl. The research was done using a mixed method approach to evaluate and assess the causative factors, consequences, and public perceptions about the infrastructure facilities and come up with policy tools to contain the unending expansion of the city.

This is an explanatory research study which aims to explore the phenomenon of urban sprawl in Karachi. Against this background, we present a methodological framework for measuring and assessing land use patterns and dynamics based on a broad review of previous sprawl measurement studies. We employ Remote Sensing and GIS techniques to measure and identify the sprawling techniques and assess its land dynamics from 1975 to 2017. The study is further supplemented by a mixed methods approach to find the determinants and consequences of urban sprawl, monitor suburbanization trends, and find a direction for better policy implementation. The detailed discussion is as follows:

There are several methods and techniques to quantify and characterize the urban growth process and patterns. However, with the emergence and availability of high temporal and spatial resolution remote sense imagery, the accuracy of monitoring urban sprawl problems become more promising and important at the global level (Guindon & Zhang, 2009). It is strongly argued and believed that remote sensing imagery is a powerful tool to analyze, detect and map spatiotemporal land use change and urban growth processes at different spatial scales (Huang et al., 2007; Yang & Lo, 2002; Yu et al., 2011). Remote sensing could be instrumental in providing observations related to urban growth and environmental conditions that are not available from other sources in the context of developing countries (Miller & Small, 2003). This process might still lack the ability to fully depict urban sprawl processes (Herold et al., 2005). There are several remote sensing satellite systems that provide medium to high and very high resolution imagery, such as Landsat (TM & ETM+), ASTER, IKONOS, GeoEye, QuickBird, RapidEye, WorldView, etc.

This dissertation involves remote sensing classification techniques and spatiotemporal analysis of spatial metrics to objectively quantify and describe the structures and patterns of the urban landscape from geospatial data (Pham & Yamaguchi, 2011). Spatial metrics are essential tools for characterizing and understanding urban landscapes. The phrases 'spatial metrics' and 'landscape metrics' are used interchangeably in the field of urban planning. These metrics are defined as numerical indices that describe the structures and patterns of a landscape (Bhatta, 2010).

Remote sensing is gaining traction for analyzing and measuring LULC processes. Remote sensing offers unique advantages over early techniques. When land change research was undertaken in the field, data was collected using land surveys and field-based instruments. Remotely sensed images provide cost-effective, multi-spectral, and multi-temporal data to monitor landscape processes. Satellite imagery provides synoptic views of large areas at a given time, which is not possible using conventional survey methods.

The techniques of remote sensing and GIS provide a visualization of phenomena in different periods. Remote sensing is an advanced technique that does not require physical contact with the Earth's surface (Campbell et al., 2011). Remote sensing of urban location is vital for determining the shape and direction of future sprawl and the consequences related to urban sprawl. The integration of remote sensing with GIS is helpful in data processing and presentation of data analysis. GIS interprets spatial data with socio-economic data, making the analysis meaningful and effective. This dissertation also aims to examine the spatiotemporal pattern of sprawl in Karachi using remote sensing techniques and spatial metrics. This dissertation employs census data and satellite images to evaluate sprawl and its impact on land use changes in the study area from 1976 to 2016. The application of RS and GIS techniques has been utilized to look for urban sprawl and associated land changes in Karachi. Figure 4.1 explicitly mentions the geographical limits of the study.

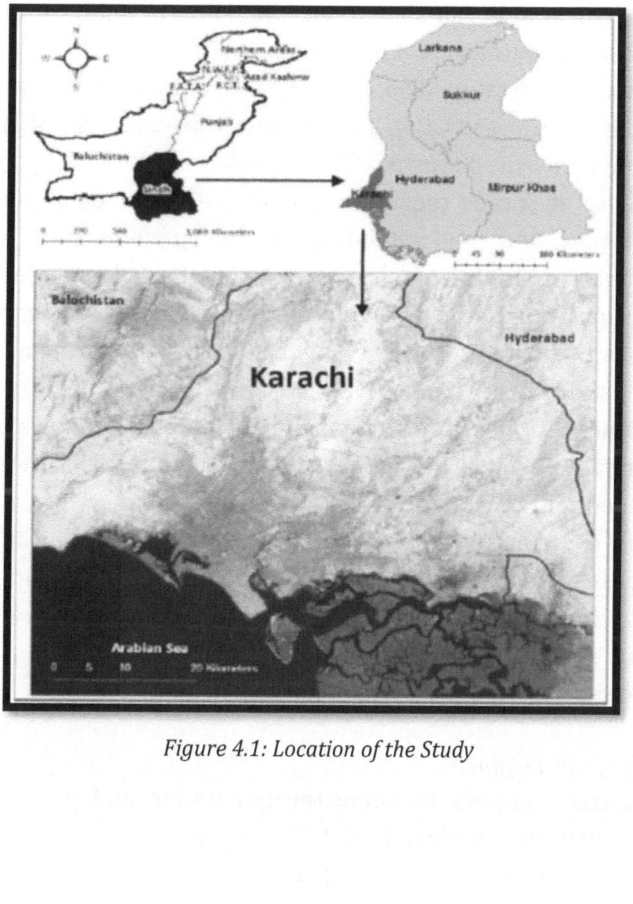

Figure 4.1: Location of the Study

4.1. Theoretical Framework

This dissertation aims to check and monitor the overall sprawling patterns in Karachi. The sprawl causes built-up areas to expand and encroach on agricultural land and open spaces. These changes in land dynamics give rise to complex socio-economic issues, adversely affect the urban environment and create policy implications (Allen & Lu, 2003). Urban sprawl can be monitored properly with the application of GIS and RS. These are useful applications as they lead towards the establishment of reliable, effective and well-integrated databases for better policy decisions (Saleh, 2007; Lata et al., 2005). RS provides the flexibility of multi-spectral, multi-temporal, multi-resolution data, which are valuable assets for urban analysis, urban modeling, and urban sprawl modeling.

This dissertation also employs a mixed methods approach to evaluate the causative factors and consequences of urban development in Karachi. The qualitative and quantitative methods, if used together, provide a rich database for description and understanding of the phenomenon under investigation. In the qualitative section, the phenomenon of urban sprawl in Karachi is explored through in-depth interviews. Afterwards, data is formed and categorized into themes for analysis. In the quantitative section, causative factors that contribute to urban development in Karachi are evaluated empirically through the monocentric city model. This model is extended and amended further to check the impact of variable factors contributing to the spatial growth of Karachi. Citizen's responses are recorded in the last phase of the quantitative section through household surveys for an overall assessment of the city's infrastructure that may have been negatively impacted due to the haphazard growth of Karachi in all directions.

4.2. Research Design

The mixed methods combine the qualitative and quantitative approaches to complement the findings in research studies, as explained in figure 4.2. Mixed methods encompass both theoretical assumptions and the methods of investigation. The use of qualitative and quantitative perspectives in combination leads towards a better understanding of the research problems (Clark & Creswell, 2010). Mixed methods design involves both quantitative and qualitative techniques to collect, interpret and analyze the data.

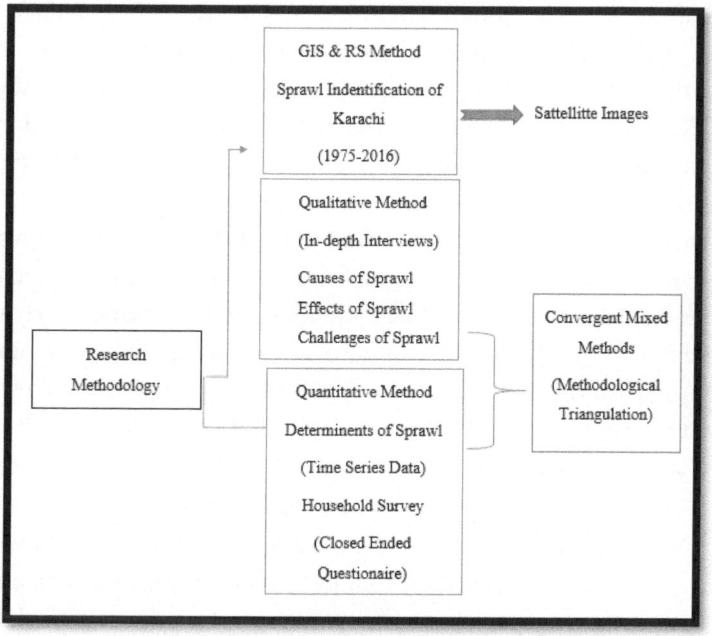

Figure 4.2: Diagrammatic Representation of Research Methodology

As a methodology, it involves philosophical assumptions that guide the direction of data collection and analysis and the mixture of qualitative and quantitative data in a single study or series of studies.

The mixed methods as a design can employ various sequences, which include the use of qualitative methods, followed by quantitative methods, or any other methodological choices adopted by the researcher to achieve the objectives of the studies (Creswell, 2009). Both qualitative and quantitative methods are essential to forge cooperation in the interdisciplinary research field of urban development. According to Borkan (2004), mixed methods provide a platform to synthesize the research traditions and equip the investigator with supplemental insights and perspectives that are beyond the scope of any single technique. Mixed methods offer extensive and comprehensive research opportunities, thereby resolving the issue of methodological dominance (Foss & Ellefsen, 2002).

This dissertation combines qualitative data through in-depth interviews conducted by experts in the urban field related to Karachi and collects quantitative evidence from secondary data along with a survey to determine causative factors and consequences that led to the haphazard expansion of Karachi towards the urban fringe. Understanding the causes and consequences of urban sprawl is a subject of immense importance in the context of developing countries, particularly in Pakistan. The study has adopted a concurrent mixed model approach to testify to the results and make a contribution to the field of urban studies. Methodologically, the dissertation aims:

- To employ concurrent mixed model design for the area of the study to seek the convergence of the results.
- To apply qualitative techniques to enhance the richness of the data and underpin philosophical assumptions and research paradigms with respect to urban sprawl in Karachi.
- To quantify the empirical results through time series data by adopting a monocentric city model in the Karachi Metropolitan and extend it further to correlate more causative factors related to urban sprawl.
- To conduct a public opinion survey of the citizens living in Karachi as urban sprawl analysis without knowing socio-economic conditions, pattern of development, land valuation and standard of living of urban residents cannot exhibit the significance of results for competent authorities and urban planners.

- To seek triangulation for a better understanding of the results under investigation.

The basic aim of using a mixed methods approach for this study was to validate the findings from two different perspectives and present comprehensive results related to the sprawling phenomenon in Karachi. Mixed methods research leads to the integration of quantitative and qualitative data to comprehend the phenomenon under investigation. Mixed methods research is further categorized into qualitative and quantitative methods as under:

4.3. Research Method

4.3.1. Qualitative Method

The qualitative part of the study will depend on the interpretations of the participants on the basis of their experiences and observations with respect to urban sprawl, in this case, the 'relationality' (Marton & Booth, 1997). The study aims to add and construct knowledge free from any bias and presuppositions to validate the interpretations made by participants. The study adopts a methodology whereby all data collected was included without preconceived ideas from the researcher on what range might be included. The study also includes necessary measures to ensure effective communication free from any bias and judgment. In qualitative research, questions and procedures are entailed in the research process, data are collected in the participant's settings, and data analysis is inductively developed from particular to general themes in a valid and reliable way. The study has extensively adhered to the principles of ethical dimensions to complement its rigour and reliability. The study uses phenomenology and narrative analysis as tools to achieve the objectives of the study, contribute towards the ever-evolving phenomenon of urban sprawl, explore in detail its causative factors, effects, and consequences and recommend policy measures to contain the process for the sustainability of Karachi.

This study method is characterized by inductive approaches to knowledge-building aimed at generating meaning (Leavy, 2014). Researchers use this method to explore, describe and explain processes or phenomena under observation. The qualitative method values the subjective experiences of the people and builds knowledge extracted from the sampling population. This dissertation applies the phenomenological approach of the qualitative method to robustly investigate the phenomenon of urban sprawl in Karachi and gain an understanding of causative factors, consequences and policy implications from participants through detailed, in-depth interviews. The semi-structured specialized interviews were conducted with a small population sample to give meaning and describe the richness of data in the form of categories.

The extent of the literature is divided on the sample sizes for conducting interviews in qualitative research. The study by Mason (2010) attributes the concept of saturation as a significant factor to consider when deciding on sample sizes in qualitative research. Saturation is the point at which the data collection process offers no information or insight about the subject under investigation. The saturation point can also be reached when gathering fresh data offers no theoretical insights nor reveals new properties related to theoretical categories (Chamaz, 2006).

The saturation depends on many factors, and not all of them are under the researcher's control. It may include the following: What is the timeline of the study? How much is the budget available for the study? Are there any conceptual and demographic stratifiers involved for an in-depth understanding of the topic being examined? How experienced and seasoned is the researcher to determine the point of saturation? (Strauss & Corbin, 2007) The experts of qualitative research are divided and avoid the topic of "how many" interviews could be conducted as a minimum to achieve research objectives. Morse (2000) concludes that it all depends on the nature of the topic, the quality of the dataset, the scope of the study, and the qualitative method used in the study. However, the extent of literature, manuscripts, research publications, book chapters, and books recommend 5 to 50 participants as adequate (Baker & Edwards, 2012). This dissertation conducted ten in-depth interviews from the sample to evaluate and explore the perspectives of participants about the phenomenon of urban sprawl in Karachi. The data was later analyzed with all ethical considerations to validate the findings and provide rigour to the study. The philosophical underpinnings, epistemological and ontological perspectives and research paradigms related to the qualitative method are mentioned in detail in the methodology chapter of this dissertation.

4.3.2. Quantitative Method

This method of the study uses a deductive approach while proving, disproving or lending credence to existing theories. The quantitative method measures variables and tests relationships between variables to reveal patterns, correlations or causal relationships and generalize results to wider populations. Quantitative research is widely used by social scientists to observe phenomena or occurrences affecting individuals. This method is shaped by empiricist and positivist philosophies. In quantitative methods, data is usually collected through readily available secondary data, questionnaires, polls, and surveys, or pre-existing statistical data is manipulated using computational techniques (Brannen, 2017). The data is then analyzed further to testify and find the relationship between explanatory variables and predictor variables.

This dissertation uses the standard 'Monocentric City Model' to draw a causal relationship between variables as a starting point, which was developed by Muth (1969) and Mills (1972) and was elaborated further by (Wheaton, 1974). The economic view of a monocentric city assumes that sprawling cities and location processes are regulated by a market process where land allocation is determined by opportunity costs (Tiebout, 1956; Brueckner & Fansler, 1983). The important variables of the monocentric city model are population, income, transportation cost and agriculture land rent price. The model stipulates that urban development at the fringe underlies an orderly, predictable market process and is not the result of an economic system that is out of control (Richardsson & Gordon, 1993).

This dissertation has extended and modified the monocentric city model to evaluate further variables with respect to Karachi, which are resulting in the expansion of the city. The extension and amendment in the monocentric city are consistent with the contributions of McGrath (2005), Wassmer (2008), Spivey (2008), and Paulsen (2012, 2013) as changing lifestyles, consumer preferences, socio-economic conditions, degradation of the inner city and other factors push people to shift at the urban fringe (Pirotte & Madre, 2011; Oueslati et al., 2013). This dissertation has used time series data from 1981 to 2017 to test the empirical model.

This dissertation also used the survey method as a primary form of data collection to evaluate the responses of citizens living in Karachi with respect to urban infrastructure, municipal services, utilities and other related factors, as the expansion of the city negatively affects the availability of the services and makes them costlier at times. The survey was conducted scientifically to validate the results, and data was collected through closed-ended questions. The data was further mined and interpreted to determine the suitability of the study. The method is scientifically discussed and elaborated in the quantitative part of the methodology section.

Massive suburbanization and motorization generally contribute to urban land use and transportation systems that are socially, economically and environmentally unsustainable (Qureshi & Lu, 2007). The historical context of gender, social capital, infrastructure and violence across urban Pakistan and, more specifically, in Karachi have been noted by researchers (Sawas et al., 2014). The city's development challenges have created socio-economic and environmental challenges at different scales that are likely to exacerbate the impacts of climate change-related weather events taking place within the city and elsewhere in the country (Hasan, Pervaiz, & Raza, 2017). The study by Shaikh (2019) pinpoints weaknesses of the metropolitan's budgetary and accounting systems, which failed to support local government in its decision-making.

The undertaken research study strives to investigate urban sprawl in a holistic manner. The study contributes significant knowledge by overhauling the historical evolution of sprawl and its growth patterns in developed and developing nations. The sprawling trends in the city of Karachi and its physical transformation have been thoroughly discussed through the lens of urban planning, geography, morphology and ecology. The city's historical and present growth has been measured and analyzed by Remote sensing data, and GIS is now widely being used for change detection analysis and applications because of cost-effectiveness and efficiency by utilizing satellite data available online in the form of present as well as historical images in different spatial resolutions.

A meaningful contribution has been made by projecting future growth to assist urban planners and competent authorities in taking corrective steps. The study quantifies the causative factors of urban sprawl by empirical tools in the form of ARDL regression to establish cause-and-effect relationships of different variables interchangeably, quite a missing link in previous scholarly work. The study transcribes and finds meaningful themes from interviews conducted by specialists in urban planning to ascertain important facts and impart innovative ways of looking at the city's problems caused by the sprawling phenomenon.

The citizen's perceptions have been incorporated to find out the missing link between urban dwellers and planners to vouch for a better living environment in the city. The study suggests creative solutions and policy mechanisms to contain and mitigate the sprawling trends and ensure the path of sustainable development. In brief, better links between historical studies and new urban planning and design are needed.

Globally, remote sensing imageries and techniques demonstrated considerable potential for urban growth and urban sprawl analysis. Land use and land cover classes (LULC) are a great help in understanding the connections between the environment and human activities, which can be efficiently obtained from satellite imageries through image classification (Bihamta et al., 2015). These are especially appropriate for countries like Pakistan, where ground monitoring data are scarce and inaccessible (Qureshi, Rajabifard, & Olfat, 2009).

The extent of urban areas can be automatically analyzed from satellite imagery using remote sensing algorithms, and change detection analysis can be executed through the use of transition matrices, which measure the changes between two LULC maps from different periods of time (Maktav & Erbek, 2005). They, in turn, help to assess the extent of urban sprawl through the differences between urban extent across multiple temporal periods (Suribabu, 2012). In addition, the spatial and physical characteristics of urban features, urban patterns, and their forms were evaluated using several landscape metrics (Alkan et al., 2013). These metrics can be derived from thematic maps created from remotely sensed data. Moreover, diversity values, such as Shannon's Diversity Index, which is widely used to describe and diagnose the degree of spatial dispersion and concentration of urban areas, were computed from remotely sensed images and effectively used to quantify the level of urban sprawl (Van, 2008).

4.4. Work Flow

The overall methodology for modeling the Urban Sprawl of Karachi with the application of GIS and Remote Sensing is composed of the following procedures:

- Landsat Images of Karachi in 1975, 1987, 1995, 2003 and 2016 were downloaded from the USGS website in GeoTIFF format, and census data from 1981, 1998 and

2017 was downloaded from PBS. Furthermore, LULC, roads and administrative boundaries in shape file format were collected from the Department of Survey Pakistan.

- An accurate assessment of classified images from different years was done by linking ERDAS Imagine with Google Earth Pro Version 7.3.
- LULC change analysis of 1975-1987, 1987-1995, 1995-2003 and 2003-2016 was done.
- The extent of Urban Sprawl was measured in each ring of the ring buffer by analyzing landscape metrics (Number of patches, Total Area, Largest Patch Index, Clumpiness Index and Fractal Index) in FRAGSTATS version 4.2.
- The level of Urban Sprawl was determined in each ring of the multi-ring buffer using Shannon's Diversity Index. It is used to measure the pattern of urban growth by measuring the degree of spatial concentration and dispersion of built-up areas.
- Markovian change model was generated using LULC of 1975 and 2016.
- The transition model between 1975 and 2016 was generated from the Markovian change model, using the change/no change matrix obtained in change detection analysis.
- Suitability analysis was done using distance from roads, distance from built-up areas, and distance from forest and slope suitability for development of built-up areas.
- The CA Markov model in QGIS software (Version 18.3) was used to model the LULC of 2025, using the transition area matrix of 2003 and 2016, suitability classes (raster group file), considering 2016 LULC as the base map.
- Validation of the model was done using Kappa variation.
- The Level of urban sprawl for 2025 was modeled using Shannon's Diversity Index in Fragstats 4.2.
- Finally, the direction of urban sprawl from 1975 to 2016 was analyzed.

4.5. Data Used

Urban sprawl analysis of Karachi was evaluated using Landsat Images, administrative boundary and land use land cover map of Karachi. As mixed methods, research offers great promise for practising researchers who are interested in describing and developing techniques for researchers in practical use. Mixed methods research, as the third research paradigm, can also help bridge the schism between quantitative and qualitative research (Onwuegbuzie & Leech, 2004). The methodological work of mixed methods as a research paradigm is mentioned in detail (Brewer & Hunter, 1989; Creswell, 2003; Newman et al., 1998; Reichardt & Rallis, 1994; Tashakkori & Teddlie, 2003). The study by Biesta and Burbules (2003) concludes that all research in social sciences provides warranted assertions about human beings and the environment in which they live and evolve. The study by De Jong and Kemp (2003) posits that the goal of understanding social sciences leads to the examination of different cultures, intentions, experiences and phenomena.

The research paradigms in recent times of complexity are becoming increasingly inter-disciplinary and dynamic; therefore, researchers need to complement one method with another by adopting and showing an understanding of multiple methods to promote collaboration, facilitate communication and present superior research. The study by Howe (1992) contests that research procedures and methods are mostly linked to certain paradigms; this linkage between research paradigms and research methods is neither sacrosanct nor necessary. It elaborates that quantitative researchers should freely use qualitative methods, and researchers opting for qualitative methods can use quantitative methods as and when needed. We contend that epistemological and paradigmatic ecumenicalism is within reach in the research paradigm of mixed methods research.

The study conducted by Tashakkori and Teddlie (2003) observed that some individuals engaged in the qualitative versus quantitative research paradigm debate appear to confuse the logic of justification with research methods. It is pertinent to know that the logic of justification (an important aspect of epistemology) does not dictate the choice of data collection methods and data analytics pursued by researchers. There is rarely entailment from epistemology to methodology (Johnson et al., 2004). Creswell, in his extended work related to mixed methods, terms it as an approach to inquiry that combines qualitative and quantitative forms of research. It involves philosophical assumptions, using qualitative and quantitative approaches and mixing these approaches in research studies.

The qualitative and quantitative methods can be merged into a large database and then can reinforce each other side by side. The main objective of employing qualitative and quantitative methods in this study is to discuss the urban transformation process within the context of Karachi. The main criterion behind employing mixed methods research is that urban settings are subject to constant transformation and expansion and have a complex social setting. The identity of communities, multiple local networks and unstable mixed incomes create complex and inconsistent social urban settings. Therefore, a flexible research model that is sensitive to the existing conditions based on a mixed methods approach is required to evaluate and assess the different dimensions of the urban settings in Karachi.

In empirical research of urban studies, research methodologies are often based on two poles: the research itself and the research itself. The implementation of qualitative and quantitative methods is based on the design and aims of the research. In urban studies, research methods are often separated between quantitative and qualitative methods in both the fields of planning and sociology. Demographic surveys and geographical data are often used in quantitative data gathering. Qualitative methods in urban studies mostly employ narrative analysis, focus groups, in-depth interviews and community involvement.

Through justification of the chosen methodology as matched to the research questions, credibility and design of the research design can be strengthened and defended (Sikes, 2004). Researcher positionality is the key aspect of choosing a methodology. This study mainly chooses concurrent or convergent parallel design to address the suitability of the research objectives.

4.6. Research Philosophy

The post-positivist theorists of qualitative and quantitative methodology have reached a consensus on several contentious points of earlier philosophical disagreements (Phillips et al., 2000; Cook & Reichardt, 1979; Reichardt & Rallis, 1994). The consensus is reached on the following issues: (a) the relativity of the "light of reason", (b) theory-laden perception, (c) the under-determination of theory by evidence, (d) the idea of auxiliary assumption, (e) the problem of induction, (f) the social nature of the research enterprise, (g) the value-ladenness of inquiry.

This study does not incorporate the cases to solve the epistemological, metaphysical, axiological and methodological differences between the purist positions. The specific aim of conducting this study through mixed methods research is to find a method and philosophy to fit the insights provided by qualitative and quantitative research into a workable solution. This study advocates pragmatism as a philosophical underpinning supported by classical pragmatists (Charles Sanders Peirce, William James, and John Dewey). The studies conducted by Maxcy (2003) and Watson (2010) support the pragmatic and pluralist approach as it seeks to improve communication among researchers as they attempt to advance knowledge. The methods must be combined and mixed in such a way that they find the best answers within the research framework. This study approaches to mix qualitative and quantitative methods in a single study to make it robust and superior. The mixed methods research rejects dogmatism and is an inclusive, expansive and creative form of research. Its logic of inquiry includes the use of induction (discovery of patterns), deduction (testing of theories and hypotheses) and abduction (uncovering and relying on the best of a set of explanations for understanding one's results) (Johnson & Onwuegbuzie, 2004).

The mixed methods research process model comprises eight distinct steps:

- Determine the research question;
- Determine whether a mixed design is appropriate;
- Select the mixed-method or mixed-model research design;
- Collect the data;
- Analyze the data;
- Interpret the data;
- Legitimate the data; and
- Draw conclusions (if warranted) and write the final report

The mixed method research, as concluded by Greene et al. (1989), is conducted for the following important rationales:

- Triangulation,
- Complementarity,
- Initiation,
- Development and
- Expansion

4.7. Triangulation

This study uses a concurrent method multilevel triangulation design to achieve the objectives of the study. The convergence model represents the traditional model of a mixed models triangulation design (Creswell, 1999). Concurrent design is a methodology for data collecting that employs different forms of data acquisition, enabling us to compare the analysis and test the data in different forms. In this model, the researcher has the freedom to collect and analyze qualitative and quantitative data separately on the same area of interest, and then different results are converged during the interpretation. The aim and rationale of the researcher is to validate, confirm, or corroborate the results side by side. The purpose of this convergence is to draw valid and well-substantiated conclusions about the urban sprawling phenomenon in Karachi. The use of qualitative and quantitative methods and generalizing the conclusions has methodological relevance (Tashakkori & Teddlie, 2010; Creswell & Clark, 2017).

A triangulation technique was adopted using a mixed method approach (Figure 4.3) to answer the research objectives while adopting a qualitative method. This was done to help analyze and further validate the results under the same phenomenon. Moreover, to enhance credibility, the following diagram shows how the application of the model combined the best results.

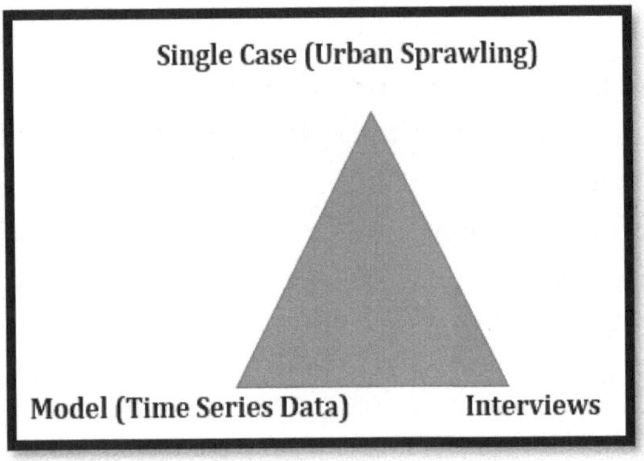

Figure 4.3: Triangualtion

The qualitative research design is generally based on the social constructivism perspective. Interpretivism and social constructivism have been associated with the post-modern era in qualitative research (Andrews, 2003). The qualitative research approach was deployed to collect multiple sources of evidence. The qualitative study allows for exploring the behavior of humans in their natural settings, such as the social, cultural, and political atmosphere in which they exist. This exploration could be carried out using various methods, such as the phenomenological model, grounded theory, historical methods, case studies, narrative models and ethnography. The researchers should use appropriate methods to answer questions about a phenomenon (Berry & Kincheloe, 2004).

How urban sprawl is perceived has an effect on the researcher. The researcher considers urban sprawl as a complex and dynamic process involving numerous factors, such as experiential, personal, and subjective, and that it needs in-depth inquiry from the people involved in this process. A qualitative approach was needed to encourage participants to describe the phenomenon of urban sprawl, and an interpretative approach was required to analyze those descriptions. The study also aimed to explore the phenomena and meaning and form a personal understanding. The involvement of individuals in posing problems and seeking solutions, as envisaged by Szydlik et al. (2003), is significant for learners to reason, apply, test and critically reflect (Cockcroft, 1982).

A phenomenographic approach was chosen as one which can 'describe an aspect of the world as it appears to the individual' (Marton, 1986). The social constructivist considers interactions of individuals within society as a source of knowledge creation and adopts an interpretive framework, as evident in the extensive literature review for phenomenological research studies (Andrews, 2003). This interpretive framework is useful in phenomenological research studies. A phenomenographic approach concentrates on the relation between the experience and the phenomenon (Marton & Booth, 1997) and is appropriate for the research whereby the relationship between the object [urban sprawl] and the subject [the people engaged] is not considered separate (Marton, 2000) since the focus is on the relational aspect between urban sprawl and people who are engaged to seek answers about the phenomenon of urban sprawl.

The detailed review of the literature presents urban sprawl as a complex phenomenon, and as such, phenomenography provided a vehicle for exploration that was considered 'particularly appropriate for engaging with complex, controversial or deeply held issues or viewpoints' (Cherry, 2001). The exploration of urban sprawl through qualitative tools was one of the important aspects of this dissertation. The phenomenographic methodology enabled the determination of the range of variation of 'qualitatively different ways of experiencing' (Linder & Marshall, 2003), providing the means to 'move up conceptually' through analysis beyond individual experience and contexts. In phenomenography studies, the different ways of understanding a phenomenon or aspect of the world are seen as the main outcome of the research (Dall'Alba, 2000). This dissertation further extended the phenomenological method to contextualize the causative factors, consequences, and policy measures taken by participants to evaluate and assess the phenomenon of urban sprawl in Karachi.

4.8. Method of Data Collection

4.8.1. In-Depth Interviews

The overall methodological strategy is: 'One should apply methods that are best suited to answering questions about a phenomenon' (Kincheloe & Berry, 2004). In a qualitative study, a number of research strategies are implemented, including face-to-face interview analysis. Interviews are the most common method of obtaining phenomenography data, as applied in this dissertation, to seek a detailed description of the urban sprawl phenomenon in Karachi via participants' accounts of experiences. A pilot study was carried out with a group of people similar to the intended interview sample (Bowden & Green, 2005). Small-scale analysis was used to ascertain any modification of questions which were minimal, and then pilot interviews were discarded and not used as part of the study as advocated by Bowden & Green (2005).

4.9. Sample Size

The sample size was consistent with phenomenographic study, forming a cross-section of ages, degree specialisms, culture, ethnicity and occupation, thereby enhancing the likelihood of variation in perceptions being determined. In view of this, the study by Miles and Huberman (1994) suggested that 9-20 participants can be sufficient to create a viable data set. Thus, through snowball sampling, 25 professionally and academically qualified persons were selected for interviews to collect data regarding causative factors and the effects and consequences of urban sprawl on the city structure of Karachi. Sample sizes were based on the criteria and available resources. The dissertation designed the semi-structured interviews that allowed the research participants to fully describe their own experiences. In-depth interviews were continued until the position was reached, where the experience and perceptions had been described. Phenomenographic 'bracketing' was maintained throughout the research, whereby emphasis was placed on trying to see urban phenomena through the eyes of the participants, so a conscious decision was made to focus on their descriptions and not impose the researcher's views within the interviews. In a qualitative framework, the researcher has to carefully craft the views and interpret the findings based on the background and experiences of the participants (Creswell, 2013). Therefore, an interpretive framework was adopted to gain access to the views and nuances that may have influenced the research participants.

4.9.1. The Interview & Interviewees' Background

The participants' real-life experiences involved in the planning and designs of the city of Karachi were taken into consideration to determine the determinants of urban sprawling. The data was collected through face-to-face interviews with planners, experts, architects, and the civil society of Karachi. Further, the professors and experts in the academic institutions played a great role as respondents in the interviews. Appointments were arranged by making calls and visiting the officials' offices. The participants were ensured their profiles would be kept confidential. Therefore, their names have not been declared (Annexure A). The interviews were conducted in Urdu and English, and then the recorded audio data was translated into English. The data was classified and arranged according to the research questions and objectives. Then, the data was passed through the coding process to categorize the variables in the study. In addition, the coded data was analyzed and interpreted to obtain the study objectives. The interview questions were prepared, keeping in view the factors and determinants of urban sprawling. Interview questions are attached in Annexure B.

Generally, the participants cooperated with the researcher in a good-mannered way. The least-educated participant was a graduate degree holder (BSc), while the highest was a doctoral degree holder (PhD). The majority of the respondents belonged to the age range between 40 and 60 years. The interview sessions commenced in March and April of 2018. The interview process was carried out at a time and place that was convenient for the participants. The maximum interview period was between 1 and 1.5 hours. The list of the participants is attached in Annexure A.

Population data was collected using different censuses conducted by the government of Pakistan. The population projection of 2025 was considered for the objectives of urban sprawling in comparison to current practices. Also, the population data was available in tabular form for both males and females.

4.10. Road Network

The road network system was collected from the survey department of the government of Pakistan. Furthermore, the data consists of highways, primary roads, secondary roads, tertiary roads, and local roads of Karachi and adjoining districts to evaluate connectivity.

4.11. Software Employed

The modeling of urban sprawl of Karachi was applied using GIS and Remote Sensing methods. ERDAS Imagine 2015 software was used for image processing and ArcGIS 10.5 was used for spatial analysis and map preparation; likewise, Fragstat Version 4.2 was used for urban sprawl measurement in Karachi and QGIS software (Version 18.3) was used for Urban Sprawl modeling and modeling for 2025. Moreover, the data was then placed in tabular form in Excel and MS Word for further analysis.

4.12. Instrument of Data Collection

The tempo-spatial method of GIS and RS was used to identify and assess Karachi's sprawling phenomenon. The study extensively used Landsat images, road network data, and administrative boundaries to model urban sprawl, as stated in Chapter 4. Furthermore, landscape metrics, an urban landscape analysis tool and a CA-Markov model were used to model urban sprawl in Karachi for the year 2025.

4.13. Data and Pre-Processing

The Landsat Operational Land Imager (OLI), Enhanced Thematic Mapper (ETM+) and Thematic Mapper (TM) with a 30m spatial resolution were used that covered the temporal scenes from 1987/8, 1995, 2003 and 2016, and Landsat Multispectral Scanner (MSS) with a 60 m spatial resolution was used to cover the scenes from 1975. The images were freely downloaded from the United States Geological Survey (USGS) portal in Geo TIFF, which is already geo-referenced. The data was initially geo-corrected, rectified and cropped to the study area. The image pre-processing was performed using the ArcGIS software package, as shown in table 4.1.

Date	Sensor	Path/Row
23 November 2016	OLI	152/43
29 October 2016	OLI	153/43
22 October 2015	OLI	152/42
1 Mar 2003	ETM+	152/43
24 Mar 2003	ETM+	153/43
20 May 2003	ETM+	152/42
6 May 1995	TM	152/43

26 March 1995	TM	153/43
6 May 1995	TM	152/42
8 November 1987	TM	152/43
1 November 1988	TM	153/43
24 November 1987	TM	152/42
26 March 1975	MSS	164/43
8 March 1975	MSS	164/42

Table 4.1: Satellite Images Date
Source: USGS Earth Explorer (2017)

4.14. Land Use Land Cover (LULC) Mapping & Accuracy Assessment

The Unsupervised Classification technique was adopted to detect the LULC pattern of Karachi. The spatially cohesive features of the classified images were filtered using the post-classification processing ESRI for further results. The accuracy of the image classification was determined using the kappa coefficient (KC). The classified images were compared with Near Infrared (NIR), False Color Landsat Images (topographically and atmospherically corrected) and ground truth data obtained from Google Earth. Afterwards, a confusion matrix and KC were calculated using Open Office Calc.

4.15. Quantification of Extent and Level of Urban Sprawl (US)

4.15.1. Extent of Urban Sprawl

Six landscape metrics were used to quantify and characterize the extent of urban sprawl between 1975 and 2025 in Karachi. Five of them (Total Area, Number of Patches, Largest Patch Index, Clumpiness Index and Fractal Index Distribution) were applied just to the built-up class and another one (Contagion) at the landscape level. The division was further done using LULC classes that were built-up areas and non-built-up areas. The landscape metrics were calculated in the freely available FRAGSTATS software package (Version 4.2).

4.15.2. Level of Urban Sprawl

Shannon's Diversity Index (SHDI) was calculated to assess the level of urban sprawl between 1975 and 2016. First, classification was done through built-up and non-built-up, and then, the SHDI was determined using FRAGSTATS software; the SHDI value range must be equal to or greater than 0, without limit. SHDI is equal to 0 when the landscape consists of only 1 patch (i.e., no diversity). SHDI increases as the proportional area distribution among built-up and non-built-up becomes more equitable. The changes in SHDI values for the built-up patches during four decades, i.e., 1991–2016, show the change in the urban sprawl level (i.e., dispersion of urban areas) for Karachi.

4.15.3. Prediction of Urban Extent for 2025

The prediction of urban extent for 2025 was performed using the MOLUSCE plugin available in QGIS software (Version 18.3). The land change model was adjusted to predict the extent of Karachi for 2025 using a four-step procedure:

- Quantification of urban variation between 2003 and 2016;
- Transformation modeling between 2003 and 2016; and
- Urban extent forecast for 2025.

LULC change analysis was run using the LULC maps for 2003 and 2016 as primary inputs. The land changes between 2003 and 2016 were quantified, and the losses and the gains among the LULC classes were calculated. Then, a change map between 1991 and 2003 using a multilayer perceptron neural network algorithm was measured. These implicated constraints and factors were used in the prediction of urban extent. Also, the change map was made for the period of 2016–2025 using the computed changes between 2003 and 2016. Moreover, a change probability grid for the period of 2016–2025 was obtained. The built-up extent of Karachi was predicted for 2025 by applying the UEPM.

4.16. Ethical Considerations

The ethical guidelines and considerations of the qualitative research were implemented throughout the interviewing process. The ethical issues in qualitative research are increasingly recognized as an integral part of the research (Cannella & Lincoln, 2011; Christians, 2011). Anonymity was assured (Cohen, Manion & Morrison, 2002) to all the participants, and at the same time, the nature and purpose of the research and the use of data were explained. Signed consent for participation was received, and after obtaining consent from the respondents, interviews were audio recorded to be used for transcription to maintain the flow of dialogue and clarity of responses and ensure the interviews did not take too much time. Interview transcripts were provided to those who requested these, and at the same time, a second consent form was given to be signed by all participants to make them feel comfortable and ensure that their willingness to cooperate was never abused (Bowden et al., 2005).

The interviews were conducted at a suitable date, time and place convenient for participants, and the process was kept confidential (Akerlind et al., 2005). The participants gave reasonable answers to the questions and were given the option to decline the answer to any question to maintain the trust between the interviewee and the interviewer. The interview process was coded so that no other person, apart from the researcher, could know the identity of the participants, and all the records were deleted after transcription and once passed to the researcher. Transcriptions were completed immediately after the interviews to check for errors, omissions and tainted data (Akerlind et al., 2005). Afterwards, transcripts were provided to the interviewees for overall checking as per the research requirement. Transcripts were read and re-read to understand what the participants were describing.

4.17. Procedure of Data Analysis

Interviews were analyzed by applying a phenomenographic approach into categories of description that were content-oriented (urban sprawl), relational (how participants relate their knowledge and expertise about urban transformation in Karachi), experiential (based on participants' views on the transformation of Karachi historically), and qualitative (based on participants' descriptions of their experiences and perceptions). The qualitative mapping process was adopted to properly understand the concepts and terminologies used by the interviewees (Barnacle, 2005).

The transcripts of the interviews were continuously revisited to check context and meaning as the excerpts began to be categorized in terms of qualitative similarities and differences. The empirical evidence of the data, along with logical decisions made by the researcher based on background and knowledge, paved the way for the formation of relational links between categories. The researcher consciously made all efforts to remain as objective as possible and true to the data (Marton, 2000), which is central to phenomenographic rigour (Barnacle, 2005). Bowden et al. (2005) focus on the 'relation between the subject and the phenomenon' throughout the analytical process in qualitative studies and avoidance of imposing the researcher's own ideas (Ashworth & Lucas, 2000).

4.18. Conceptual Framework

A thematic analysis approach was used for the analysis of data. It is one of the most common approaches used in qualitative research (Guest et al., 2012). Researchers all over the world used this method of analysis for their qualitative studies because it is a relatively simple method that "minimally organizes the data and describes it in a rich detail" (Boyatzis, 1998). This method is based on the propositions of Braun and Clarke, who define it as a method used for "identifying, analyzing and reporting patterns (themes) within data" (Braun & Clarke, 2006). This method of analysis was chosen for this study because evidence suggests that it "can produce an insightful analysis that answers particular research questions" (Braun & Clarke, 2006).

All the steps of thematic analysis were employed during the analysis of the data. In the first step, once interviews were transcribed, they were read again and again to gain familiarity with the data. The contents of the data and initial codes were generated to capture the important features within the data. These codes were the recurring patterns (themes) across the data that were developed during this process of familiarization. In the third step, after all the data were coded and all the relevant extracts were highlighted, codes were correlated and examined to identify broader patterns of meaning (themes). After developing the potential codes within the data, all the relevant information was organized under these codes (Figure 4.4). In the next two steps, these themes, through the iterative process, were refined, organized and categorized meaningfully into sub-themes to develop a thematic framework. Similar themes and ideas were clustered in groups and organized in the thematic framework.

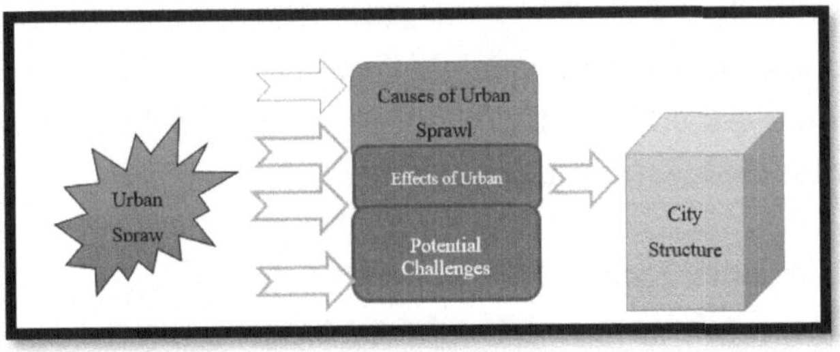

Figure 4.4: Conceptual Framework of the Qualitative Method

4.19. Reliability & Validity

In order to ensure reliability and validity in research, the test-retest measures have been used to check the responses over time. There are a lot of factors that are involved and taken into account to check the complexity of urban sprawling in Karachi. The purpose of asking questions to the respondents in the survey was to know the construct or idea of 'urban sprawling'.

Moreover, to draw conclusions, the theories were made during the study to ensure the reliability of the data being collected. The approximate authenticity of data was, hence, cross-checked and rechecked while answering all research objectives.

Urban sprawl is labeled as unending development, increasing congestion, reduction in green spaces, exorbitant property prices, infrastructure woes and class segregation (World Bank, 2007). Also, uncontrolled urban sprawl increases different environmental risks: food, biodiversity loss, and energy crisis (Cabral et al., 2016). The study by Gordon and Richardson (1997) concludes that sprawl results from free market decisions made by households and firms; it maximizes the overall welfare of society. The related studies have generally focused on the possible causes, pitfalls, and factors that subsequently led to the sprawl and have discussed the consequences and challenges set forth by urban sprawl.

Sometimes, Urban Sprawl (US) and unbalanced progress are the consequences of the switch from non-built-up to urban areas (Squires, 2002). Urban sprawl is often associated with low residential density, leapfrog, scattered suburban linear patterns, and dependence on private transport (Besussi & Chin, 2003; Batty, 2005). The accelerated population growth across the globe is generating global immigration from poor rural areas to cities, looking for a higher standard of living (Tacoli et al., 2015). The world's population is expected to rise by 72% in 2030, with a 175% upsurge in the bigger metropolitan areas consisting of more than 100,000 inhabitants (Lambin et al., 2001). This immigrant profile chooses cheaper suburbs in the city surroundings (Visalatchi & Padmanaban, 2012). Therefore, the urban area tends to enlarge, making it imperative for employment generation (Monishiya & Padmanaban, 2012).

Researchers working on urban sprawl usually define it depending on the context or the function of the term in (economic) models applied, while its operationalization critically hinges on the availability of appropriate data (Ewing, 1997; Sutton & Wheatley, 2003; Li et al., 2007; Paulsen, 2013). As it is often the case when analyzing social phenomena, valid and reliable operationalizations are essential for improving the (quantitative) knowledge base and thus, for objectifying the discourse about urban sprawl (Burchfield et al., 2006). To capture quantitative and qualitative aspects of urban sprawl, multidimensional measurements are suggested (Torrens & Alberti, 2000; Galster, 2001; Cutsinger et al., 2005; Torrens, 2008) but also challenged (Wassmer, 2008; Paulsen, 2013). In our study, we use three sprawl metrics (area of development, built-up, and population density) to capture the multidimensional nature of urban sprawl as well as possible.

A theoretical model that is able to provide basic explanations of urban expansion is the Monocentric City Model (Lewis-Kraus, 2006), which has long been the standard economic approach to studying the development of urban areas (Anas et al., 1998; Burchfield et al., 2006). The analysis of the current study is based on the Monocentric model. The model predicts that population, household income, transportation cost and the price of agricultural land are essential drivers of urban growth. Several empirical studies reported that some common elements exist in the urban development process independent of time and space, which are captured by the Monocentric City Model. However, other socio-demographic and economic variables are also contributory factors that have a significant influence on urban sprawl, which are not captured by the Monocentric City Model. In this context, the current study extended the Monocentric City Model by including various socio-demographic and economic variables.

It is essential to quantitatively measure the urban sprawl for fast-growing cities like Karachi (Dewan & Corner, 2014). However, with a few exceptions, this kind of study is rare in some countries, as in the case of Pakistan (Megahed et al., 2015). This study aims to determine the impact of local fiscalization, economic conditions, and social indicators on urban sprawl. In the specified model, urban sprawl (Measured by build-up area, population density, and Sprawl) is taken as the dependent variable, whereas population, household income, transport cost, local fiscalization variables, economic indicators, social indicators, utility and transport indicators are taken as explanatory variables. The time series data of the sample includes data from 1981 to 2017 extracted from secondary sources, as mentioned in table 4.2.

Model/Indictor	Variables	Data Description & Measurement	Source
Urban Sprawl Dimensions	Built-up	Change in LULC over the years, Unit of measurement (Square kilometer)	Official Maps and Satellite Images
	Population Density	Karachi's Population Density, Unit of Measurement (Persons Per Sq Km)	Calculated by author from Official Data of population Census (1981, 1998, 2017)
	Sprawl	Karachi's Change in Built up Areas, Unit of Measurement (Square Kilometer)	Official Maps and Satellite Images (1981-2017)
Monocentric City Model	Population	Karachi's Population Census, Unit of Measurement (Total Head Count)	Population Census (1981, 1998, 2017)
	GDP	Sindh's Yearly GDP taken as Proxy for Income, Unit of Measurement (Rs. Millions)	Government of Sindh Development Indicators (1981-2017)
	Transport Cost	Pakistan's Average yearly fuel price taken as proxy, Unit of Measurement (Rupees per litre)	Pakistan Burea of Statisctics (1981-2017)
Local Fiscalization Indicators	Karachi Metropolitcan Corporation Revenues	Karachi Metropolitan Corporation's Annual Budget figures, Unit of Measurement (Million Rupees)	KMC Financial Statements (1981-2017)
Economic Indicators	Interest Rates	Pakistan's yearly Interest rates, Unit of Measurement (%)	State Bank of Pakistan (1987-2017)
	Average Monthly Nominal Wages	Pakistan's National average taken as proxy for wages , Unit of Measuremnt (Rupees)	Pakistan Burea of Statisctics (1981-2017)
	Employment Oppurtunities	Taken as an average of employment in wholesale, employment in manufacturing, employment in transport, employment in construction, sindh's urban variable used as proxy, Unit of Measurement (%)	Labour Force Survey (1981-2017)
Social Indicators	Population per Doctor	Karachi's Population served by Doctors, Unit of Measurement (Total Population/number of Doctors)	Government of Sindh Development Indicators (1981-2017)
	School Enrolment	The children enrolled in schools for primary education (out of total enrollment in Karachi), Unit of Measurement (%)	Government of Sindh Development Indicators (1981-2017)
Utility& Transport Indicators	Electricity Consumption	The number of electricity units used in Karachi, Unit of Measuremnt (KW)	Government of Sindh Development Indicators (1981-2017)
	Private Vehicles	The number of cars used in Karachi, Unit of Measurement (Per Capita 1000)	Government of Sindh Development Indicators (1981-2017)

Table 4.2: Data Description and Sources

Table 4.3 presents the details of the explanatory variables and their expected signs against each dimension of urban sprawl.

The sprawl metrics we used imply that high urban sprawl corresponds to high values of the share of the settlement area (much land uptake of settlement area) and high dispersion of land. However, a high level of sprawl corresponds to low values of utilization density (less efficient use of space).

Model/Indicators	Variables	Sprawl	Built-up	Pop density
Monocentric City Model	Population	+	+	+
	Income	+	+	-
	Transportation Cost	+	+	+
	Price of Agriculture Land	NA	NA	NA
Local Fiscalization Indicators	KMC Revenues	+	+	-
	Vacant Plots Tax	-	+	+
Economic Indicators	Interest Rates	-	-	+
	Average monthly nominal wages	+	+	-
	Employment Opportunities	+	+	+
Social Indicators	Pop per doctor	+	+	-
	School Enrolment	+	+	-
Utility And Transport Indicators	Electricity Consumption	+	+	-
	Private Vehicles	+	+	-

Table 4.3: Expected Direction of the Effects of the Variables Employed in the Models for Each Dimension of Urban Sprawl

4.20. Analytical Technique

The extant literature used several estimation techniques, including the ordinary least squares method, ECM model, Johansen Cointegration technique, ARDL model and two stages least squares methods to estimate the Monocentric City Model. Recently, economic literature suggested that using the cointegration techniques for analyzing the time-series data is the best option as the cointegration techniques produce valid results in the presence of non-stationary data. In addition, the cointegration techniques also avoid the endogeneity problems (Hussain & Mazhar, 2018). Keeping in view the above problems, the current study applied the Auto Regressive Distributed Lag (ARDL) model (Pesaran et al., 1999) to obtain the required results. The reason for applying the Regressive Distributed Lag

(ARDL) model instead of other cointegration techniques, namely Johansen (1991) and Engel and Granger (1987) techniques, is that the ARDL model is a reliable and appropriate estimation technique in the case of the small sample size. Apart from this, the ARDL model is applicable in all cases, whether the underlying series are I (0), I (1), or mixed order (Oskooee & Oyolola, 2007). The second advantage of the ARDL model is that it can allow a significant number of lags of each variable. Apart from this, the ARDL approach allows the research to obtain both short-run and long-run results simultaneously. Based on the above explanations, we have developed the ARDL model to obtain the results. The procedure is to estimate the ARDL model by taking only one dimension of urban sprawl at a time, which requires the estimation of 3 different equations. The specifications of the unrestricted ECM-ARDL models are as follows:

$$\begin{aligned} \Delta BU_t = {} & \gamma_0 + \sum_{i=1}^{a} \alpha_1(\Delta BU_{t-i}) + \sum_{i=0}^{b} \alpha_2(\Delta POP_{t-i}) + \\ & \sum_{i=0}^{c} \alpha_3(\Delta HI_{t-i}) + \sum_{i=0}^{d} \alpha_4(TC_{t-i}) + \sum_{i=0}^{f} \alpha_5(LF_{t-i}) + \\ & \sum_{i=0}^{e} \alpha_6(EI_{t-i}) \sum_{i=0}^{g} \alpha_7(SI_{t-i}) + \sum_{i=0}^{h} \alpha_8(UI_{t-i}) + \sum_{i=0}^{i} \alpha_9(TI_{t-i}) + \\ & \beta_1(POP_{t-1}) + \beta_2(HI_{t-1}) + \beta_3(TC_{t-1}) + \beta_4(LF_{t-1}) + \\ & \beta_5(EI_{t-1}) + \beta_6(SI_{t-1}) + \beta_7(UI_{t-1}) + \beta_8(TI_{t-1}) + \\ & \beta_9(\Delta BU_{t-1}) + \mu_t \end{aligned} \tag{1}$$

Equation 2 of the econometric model 2 is as follows:

$$\begin{aligned} \Delta PD_t = {} & \gamma_0 + \sum_{i=1}^{a} \alpha_1(\Delta PD_{t-i}) + \sum_{i=0}^{b} \alpha_2(\Delta POP_{t-i}) + \\ & \sum_{i=0}^{c} \alpha_3(\Delta HI_{t-i}) + \sum_{i=0}^{d} \alpha_4(TC_{t-i}) + \sum_{i=0}^{f} \alpha_5(LF_{t-i}) + \\ & {}_0\,\alpha_6(EI_{t-i}) \sum_{i=0}^{g} \alpha_7(SI_{t-i}) + \sum_{i=0}^{h} \alpha_8(UI_{t-i}) + \sum_{i=0}^{i} \alpha_9(TI_{t-i}) + \\ & \beta_1(POP_{t-1}) + \beta_2(HI_{t-1}) + \beta_3(TC_{t-1}) + \beta_4(LF_{t-1}) + \\ & \beta_5(EI_{t-1}) + \beta_6(SI_{t-1}) + \beta_7(UI_{t-1}) + \beta_8(TI_{t-1}) + \\ & \beta_9(\Delta PD_{t-1}) + \mu_t \end{aligned} \tag{2}$$

Equation 3 of the econometric model 3 is as follows:

$$\Delta SP_t = \gamma_0 + \sum_{i=1}^{a} \alpha_1(\Delta SP_{t-i}) + \sum_{i=0}^{b} \alpha_2(\Delta POP_{t-i}) + \sum_{i=0}^{c} \alpha_3(\Delta HI_{t-i}) + \sum_{i=0}^{d} \alpha_4(TC_{t-i}) + \sum_{i=0}^{f} \alpha_5(LF_{t-i}) + \sum_{i=0}^{e} \alpha_6(EI_{t-i}) \sum_{i=0}^{g} \alpha_7(SI_{t-i}) + \sum_{i=0}^{h} \alpha_8(UI_{t-i}) + \sum_{i=0}^{i} \alpha_9(TI_{t-i}) + \beta_1(POP_{t-1}) + \beta_2(HI_{t-1}) + \beta_3(TC_{t-1}) + \beta_4(LF_{t-1}) + \beta_5(EI_{t-1}) + \beta_6(SI_{t-1}) + \beta_7(UI_{t-1}) + \beta_8(TI_{t-1}) + \beta_9(\Delta SP_{t-1}) + \mu_t \quad (3)$$

In the above equations, Δ represents the first difference, and i is the number of lags. Furthermore, BU represents build-up areas, PD is Population Density, SP denotes Sprawl, and POP is the Population in Karachi. While HI represents the household income, TC is the transport cost. LF represents the effect of local fiscalization, EI represents economic indicators, SI shows the effect of Social indicators, UI represents utility indicators and TI represents transports indicators. An error term denotes μ_t, whereas, γ_0 is the constant value. To identify the cointegrating relationship, the dissertations used a bound testing approach. So, β_1, β_2, β_3, β_4, β_5, β_6, β_7, β_8, β_9 are the long-run coefficients and α_1, α_2 α_3, α_4, α_5 α_6, α_7, α_8 α_9 are the short-run coefficients. To select the appropriate lag length, we utilize Akaike's Information Criterion (AIC) and other diagnostic tests. The (a, b, c……., l) are the numbers of lags used for each variable. After selecting the optimal lag length, in the first step, we tested the ARDL specification for the presence of cointegration among the concerned variables using the bound testing approaches. The null and alternative hypotheses for testing the cointegrating relationship based on the Wald test are:

$$H_0 = \beta_1 = \beta_2 = \beta_3 = \beta_4 = \beta_5 = \beta_6 = \beta_7 = \beta_8 = \beta_9 = 0$$

(No Cointegrating relationship)

$$H_a = \beta_1 \neq \beta_2 \neq \beta_3 \neq \beta_4 \neq \beta_5 \neq \beta_6 \neq \beta_7 \neq \beta_8 \neq \beta_9 \neq 0$$

(Cointegrating relationship)

In the case of evidence in favor of a cointegrating relationship, the second step is to estimate the conditional long-run ARDL models (4,5 and 6), which can be obtained from the Unrestricted ECM-ARDL model (1, 2, 3) as follows:

$$BU_t = \gamma_0 + \sum_{i=1}^{a} \beta_1(BU_{t-i}) + \sum_{i=0}^{b} \beta_2(POP_{t-i}) + \sum_{i=0}^{c} \beta_3(HI_{t-i}) + \sum_{i=0}^{d} \beta_4(TC_{t-i}) + + \sum_{i=0}^{f} \beta_5(LF_{t-i}) + \sum_{i=0}^{e} \beta_6(EI_{t-i}) \sum_{i=0}^{g} \beta_7(SI_{t-i}) + \sum_{i=0}^{h} \beta_8(UI_{t-i}) + \sum_{i=0}^{i} \beta_9(TI_{t-i}) + \mu_t \quad (4)$$

$$PD_t = \gamma_0 + \sum_{i=1}^{a} \beta_1(PD_{t-i}) + \sum_{i=0}^{b} \beta_2(POP_{t-i}) + \sum_{i=0}^{c} \beta_3(HI_{t-i}) + \sum_{i=0}^{d} \beta_4(TC_{t-i}) + + \sum_{i=0}^{f} \beta_5(LF_{t-i}) + \sum_{i=0}^{e} \beta_6(EI_{t-i}) \sum_{i=0}^{g} \beta_7(SI_{t-i}) + \sum_{i=0}^{h} \beta_8(UI_{t-i}) + \sum_{i=0}^{i} \beta_9(TI_{t-i}) + \mu_t \quad (5)$$

$$SP_t = \gamma_0 + \sum_{i=1}^{a} \beta_1(SP_{t-i}) + \sum_{i=0}^{b} \beta_2(POP_{t-i}) + \sum_{i=0}^{c} \beta_3(HI_{t-i}) + \sum_{i=0}^{d} \beta_4(TC_{t-i}) + + \sum_{i=0}^{f} \beta_5(LF_{t-i}) + \sum_{i=0}^{e} \beta_6(EI_{t-i}) \sum_{i=0}^{g} \beta_7(SI_{t-i}) + \sum_{i=0}^{h} \beta_8(UI_{t-i}) + \sum_{i=0}^{i} \beta_9(TI_{t-i}) + \mu_t \quad (6)$$

Where, all the variables and symbols are as previously defined. Finally, the coefficients of short-run dynamics are obtained by estimating the ECM. The ECM models (7, 8 and 9) are derived from the conditional ARDL-ECM model by a simple linear transformation. The short-run coefficients by estimating error correction models (7, 8, and 9) associated with the long-run estimates are obtained as follows:

$$\Delta BU_t = \gamma_0 + \sum_{i=1}^{a} \alpha_1(\Delta BU_{t-i}) + \sum_{i=0}^{b} \alpha_2(\Delta POP_{t-i}) + \sum_{i=0}^{c} \alpha_3(\Delta HI_{t-i}) + \sum_{i=0}^{d} \alpha_4(\Delta TC_{t-i}) + + \sum_{i=0}^{f} \alpha_5(\Delta LF_{t-i}) + \sum_{i=0}^{e} \alpha_6(\Delta EI_{t-i}) \sum_{i=0}^{g} \alpha_7(\Delta SI_{t-i}) + \sum_{i=0}^{h} \alpha_8(\Delta UI_{t-i}) + \sum_{i=0}^{i} \alpha_9(\Delta TI_{t-i}) + \mu_t \quad (7)$$

$$\begin{gathered}\Delta \mathrm{PD}_t = \gamma_0 + \sum_{i=1}^{a} \alpha_1(\Delta \mathrm{PD}_{t-i}) + \sum_{i=0}^{b} \alpha_2(\Delta \mathrm{POP}_{t-i}) + \\ \sum_{i=0}^{c} \alpha_3(\Delta \mathrm{HI}_{t-i}) + \sum_{i=0}^{d} \alpha_4(\Delta \mathrm{TC}_{t-i}) + + \sum_{i=0}^{f} \alpha_5(\Delta \mathrm{LF}_{t-i}) + \\ \sum_{i=0}^{e} \alpha_6(\Delta EI_{t-i}) \sum_{i=0}^{g} \alpha_7(\Delta SI_{t-i}) + \\ \sum_{i=0}^{h} \alpha_8(\Delta UI_{t-i}) + \sum_{i=0}^{i} \alpha_9(\Delta TI_{t-i}) + \mu_t\end{gathered} \tag{8}$$

$$\begin{gathered}\Delta \mathrm{SP}_t = \gamma_0 + \sum_{i=1}^{a} \alpha_1(\Delta \mathrm{SP}_{t-i}) + \sum_{i=0}^{b} \alpha_2(\Delta \mathrm{POP}_{t-i}) + \\ \sum_{i=0}^{c} \alpha_3(\Delta \mathrm{HI}_{t-i}) + \sum_{i=0}^{d} \alpha_4(\Delta \mathrm{TC}_{t-i}) + + \sum_{i=0}^{f} \alpha_5(\Delta \mathrm{LF}_{t-i}) + \\ \sum_{i=0}^{e} \alpha_6(\Delta EI_{t-i}) \sum_{i=0}^{g} \alpha_7(\Delta SI_{t-i}) + \\ \sum_{i=0}^{h} \alpha_8(\Delta UI_{t-i}) + \sum_{i=0}^{i} \alpha_9(\Delta TI_{t-i}) + \mu_t\end{gathered} \tag{9}$$

Where α_1 to α_{12} are the coefficients of the short-run dynamics and λ is the speed of adjustment. ECT_{t-1} is the lagged residual series from the long-run "level model."

4.21. Quantitative Data Selection

People's participation in development and municipal issues is crucial for efficient planning and policy formulation. The citizen's participation in public issues and their valuable feedback can be essential tools for improving the quality of public service delivery. This section covers the information provided by citizens through participation in the survey and can be used by service providers, policy-makers, planners and civil society to improve service standards. The study by Sarantakos (2005) concludes that research is an essential part of almost all professions. Research Methodology is one of the requirements of the science. The methods applied in the investigation of sociological phenomena are those that validate the study as scientific, reliable, and precise (Adams, 2010). In a common theory, research means the search for knowledge (Tossel et al., 2010).

The study by Serrador and Pinto (2015) finds that social scientists follow scientific research methods and prefer quantitative methodology. They accept data as scientific evidence only if it is collected by direct observation and through strict rules. In contrast, some other scholars adopt the non-positivist approach. They see knowledge as subjective and holistic. In their view, the scientific methods are social constraints. The quantitative, qualitative and participatory research methods have different disciplinary origins. Their research tools and techniques are also varied.

Zhang and Wildemuth (2009) argue that through semi-structured interviews, researchers observe the daily routine of the respondents, whereas Mason (2002) argues that the semi-structured interview technique has its own characters, variations, ways and practices. The quantitative approach is used as direct and primary interviews, while the qualitative approach is usually used for case studies in which the researcher needs in-depth knowledge of respondents. In the research in hand, the quantitative research method is also adopted.

According to Henslin (2005), the quantitative type of research emphasizes precise measurement and the use of statistics and numbers. The area from where the researcher has collected the research data is called the universe of the study. The selected universe for this study is Karachi as a whole. Therefore, due to a large population, the limitation of financial resources and time duration and COVID-19 lockdown restrictions and prevention, it was restricted to selected clusters. A brief review of the sampling framework and methodology for selecting households is presented to adopt the scientific approach for this study. The list of districts and cantonment areas presented in table 4.4 is extracted from official census blocks related to Karachi. The list of selected census blocks according to the 1998 population census is exhibited in table 4.5.

1.	LOCAITIES OF CENSUS CRICLE OF D.M.C EAST – 111
2.	LOCAITIES OF CENSUS CRICLE OF FAISAL (DRIG ROAD) CANTT – 112
3.	LOCAITIES OF CENSUS CRICLE OF MALIR CANTT – 113
4	LOCAITIES OF CENSUS CRICLE OF KORANGI CREEK CANTT– 114
5.	LOCAITIES OF CENSUS CRICLE OF D.M.C WEST– 116
6.	LOCAITIES OF CENSUS CRICLE OF D.M.C SOUTH – 117
7.	LOCAITIES OF CENSUS CRICLE OF KARACHI CATT – 118
8.	LOCAITIES OF CENSUS CRICLE OF MANORA CATT – 119
9-	LOCAITIES OF CENSUS CRICLE OF CLIFTON CATT – 120
10.	LOCAITIES OF CENSUS CRICLE OF D.M.C CENTRAL – 121
11-	LOCAITIES OF CENSUS CRICLE OF D.M.C MALIR – 179

Table 4.4: List of Districts & Cantonment Areas
Source: Pakistan Bureau of Statistics (2018)

Name of District	Name of Localities/ Cluster	Circle Code	Population
D.M.C - East	PECH society block- 02 (part) Tayyaba Mosque	111-02-06	4311
D.M.C - West	Data nagar (part) Orangi town Sector 1-B	116-02-02	6132
D.M.C - South	New Kalri area between Hingorabad road and Nala	117-02-03	4838
D.M.C - Central	Sector 5-D (Part) adjacent Surjani Chowrangi New Karachi.	121-02-01	13221
D.M.C - Malir	Gulshan-e-Qadri (part), Popular Villas	179-02-04	8077
D.M.C- Korangi	Sector 36-B, Landhi (part)	111-27-01	7797

Table 4.5: Areas of Population Sample
Source: Pakistan Bureau of Statistics (2018)

4.22. The Sample

The universe for this study is the city of Karachi, having a huge population. About 150 households across Karachi participated in this survey. All the respondents are residents living in six[3] districts of Karachi. The selected sample for the survey is well represented in terms of socio-economic characteristics. The enumerated sample had to go through multiple stages to make it unbiased and scientific to the extreme level. This city is administratively divided into districts. Therefore, to make it scientific, three-stage stratified random sampling selection criteria are employed.

In the first stage, Karachi was distributed in 6 districts (Keamari 7th[3]. The district wasn't notified till then). The localities were randomly selected at the second stage from District Municipal corporations. An appropriate number of circles [primary sampling units (PSUs)] listed under each tier in the District Population Census Report, 1998, were chosen randomly with the help of statistical software. The PSUs were selected using a probability-proportional-to-size (PPS) sampling

---

[3] Keamari wasn't notified as a 7th District

technique. The population of the enumeration block, according to the 1998 census, was treated as a measure of size for the selection of sample PSUs. In the third stage, twenty-five households were selected from each circle per district through a systematic sampling procedure with a random start. After one successful interview, twelve to fourteen households were skipped to select the next household for the interview. The framework of the survey is presented in figure 4.5.

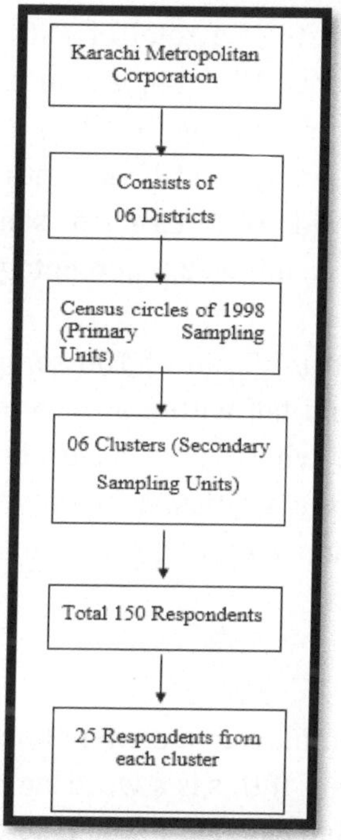

Figure 4.5: Conceptual Framework of Survey

The survey respondents were selected using a random probability method. The preferred method was to obtain information from the spouse or the head of the household. However, in case the family head was unavailable, any person above 18 years of age in that household was chosen as the respondent. The age profile of the respondents is summarized in figure 4.6.

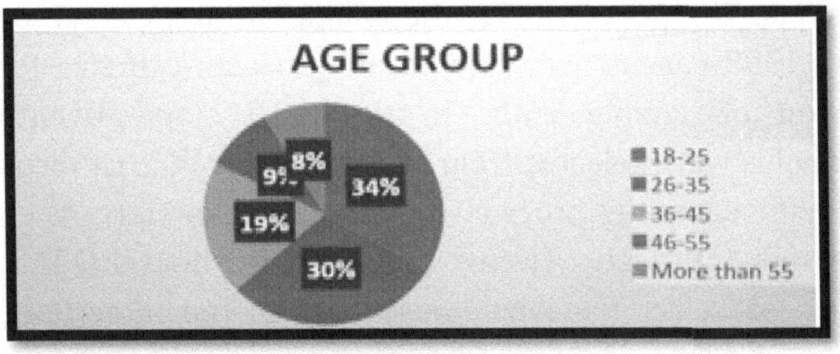

Figure 4.6: Age of the Respondents

The survey consists of a total of 150 respondents having face-to-face interviews. All sample surveys are subject to possible sampling error meaning that the results may differ from those which would be obtained if the entire population under study were interviewed. The margin of sampling error for the entire survey is plus or minus 2.5 percentage points at the 95% level of confidence.

This means that in 95 out of 100 samples of this size, the results obtained would fall within a range of plus or minus 2.5 percentage points of what would have been obtained if every individual adult in the particular town of Karachi had been interviewed. Other non-sampling errors may also contribute to total survey error.

4.22.1. Coding

The type of coding employed in content analysis depends on the type of unit of analysis. If this is a word symbol or character that is an easily identifiable element of the text, coding would consist of assigning codes to the collected elements; this is an easy task, but the interpretation of these words and their frequency is relatively difficult (Taheerdoost, 2016). A questionnaire was used for data collection (Annexure C). It consisted of two sections. Section 'A' consisted of personal data, and Section 'B' consisted of socio-economic data.

4.22.2. Pre-Testing

Pre-testing is the method of deducting the mistakes, unnecessary information, and difficult questions that are included in the data collection instruments before it is actually administered to the respondents (Nachimias & Nachimias, 1992). The pre-testing stage is a test of the research key. Without doing this, the researcher could not have been sure that the questions were appropriate or vague (Andrews, 2003). It also enabled the researcher to discover new aspects of the proposed problem and possibilities to study in the planning stage (Sowell, 1992). Therefore, the researcher used pre-test techniques that helped him identify ways to solve unforeseen problems using questionnaires. These problems included phrasing and sequencing of questions. For this, pre-testing was done by collecting information from 20 respondents. It helped to refine some of the questions. Corrections were made to the irrelevant questions before starting this study. At this stage, some questions were added with the help of the learned research supervisor. An easy and understandable questionnaire was developed in written form in English and Urdu.

4.22.3. Data Collection

In the study, the researcher used the interview schedule method along with other methods. It is a personal, face-to-face situation in which information is verbally extracted from the respondents through discussion. Which follows the interview guide? It is not easy to get information from male and female respondents who are reluctant to reveal confidential information for so many reasons. In the present study, the following method was used: In order to create and establish harmonious relationships with the respondents for the collection of such personal data.

As it was a personal type of data, the researcher had to create direct contact with the respondents. The questions asked were mostly close-ended.

This method made it easier for the researcher to explain meanings and overcome misunderstandings, which are usually developed among the respondents in the study. The researcher employed interview techniques, which helped the researchers (enumerators) complete structured questionnaires that contained several types of information related to the respondents' personal lives of men and women.

4.22.4. Questionnaire & Interviewing

The questionnaire used in this study was designed by a researcher with the help of a statistician. A draft of the questionnaire was subjected to a pre-test, resulting in modifications to the questionnaire both in terms of question wording and length. The researcher conducted fieldwork with his team in every 12th to 14th household, starting from left to right in all six selected clusters from census blocks representing all districts. If any household refused to answer or was found locked, the next household was selected to minimize the percentage of refusal.

This survey was conducted from November 2019 to May 2020 by a team of professionals under the strict supervision of the researcher. A team of enumerators was fully trained before conducting this survey. A team of four enumerators was hired, with two male and two female field workers under one field supervisor. The briefing session familiarized the interviewers with the sample specifications and the instrument for this study. The interviews averaged 20 minutes in length. The researcher monitored the interviewing process and data collection at all stages to ensure quality.

4.22.5. Procedure of Data Analysis

After data collection, the next step for the researcher was to analyze the data. The procedure depended on the type of questions and hypotheses developed and the characteristics of the collected data (De Leeuw, 2008). The step of analysis and interpretation of data is the most decisive phase of the research. After the data was collected, the researcher made full efforts and paid complete attention to the analysis and interpretation of a number of closely related operations. It can never be ascertained whether that is true or not about the universe from which data has been drawn. However, by statistical method, one can prove whether something is true about a universe or not. Selecting a suitable method helped the researcher trust the data quality (Llewellyn, Sullivan & Minichiello, 2004). After completing the data collection, the researcher used simple frequency distribution techniques to verify the existence of a relationship between two variables. The simple percentage and chi-square method was used to evaluate the results. The demographic characteristics of the sample, obtained via the selection methods described above, were matched to Census population estimates for the cluster. The collected data was weighted statistically to bring age and race into proper proportions for the population. The following table summarizes the responses of the survey participants.

Age Group		**Condition of Public Transport**	
18-25 Years	34%	Worse	45.8%
26-35 Years	30%	Bad	25%
36-45 Years	19%	Out dated	19.4%
46-55 Years	9%	Good	9.8%
More than 55	8%	Private M.Bike Owner	
Gender		Own	62.5%
Male	80%	Not own	37.5%
Female	20%	Stuck in Traffic Jam	
Size of Family		Yes	93%
1-3 members	15%	No	7%
4-7members	48%	Mode of transport prefer in future	
8-10members	27%	Rapid Bus Service	73.8%
More than 10 members	10%	Mass Transit	17.8%
Education		Tram	8.4%
Age Group		**Condition of Public Transport**	
Literate	93%	Water Tap Supply at Home	
Illiterate	7%	Yes	71.6%
Employment		No	28.4%

Status			
Employed	NA	Quality of Water	
Unemployed	NA	Dissatisfied	45.1%
Resident of Karachi		Satisfied	31.7%
By Birth	26%	Neutral	23.2%
Shifted	74%	User of Tanker Water	
Satisfaction of Municipal Services		No	66.7%
Satisfied	21.9%	Yes	33.3%
Un-Satisfied	78.1%	Performance of Solid Waste Management Departments	
Public Transport		Do not fulfill responsibility	27.2%
Used	77%	Fulfill responsibility	72.8%
Not Used	23%	Ownership of House	
Experience to effect by Street Crime		Yes	62.5%
Yes	66.9%	No	37.5%
No	33.1%	Family type	
Experience to live in Karachi		Joint Family system	62.5%
nice and livable	43.4%	Separate/individual system	37.5%
messy and more disorganized	24.8%	Major Household Expenses Head	
shabby and dirty	11%	Utilities	43.7%
worse	20.8%	Others (Food, education, transport)	56.3%

Table 4.6: Response Summary of the Survey Participants
Source: Data Taken from Present Study, Mentioned at Interpretation of Results

Chapter 5| Data Analysis

This chapter discusses the process and results of LULC classification using Landsat images, LULC change, urban sprawl extent using landscape analysis in FRAGSTATS 4.2, types of urban sprawl using an urban landscape analysis tool, and future prospects of urban sprawl in Karachi using a CA Markov model in detail.

5.1. Land Use Land Cover Classification

The satellite image classification technique was used for LULC map generation. Image Classification was used to create LULC maps in the temporal dimension (Dadras *et al.*, 2014). LULC patterns for five different years (1975, 1987, 1995, 2003 and 2016) were generated. Furthermore, an unsupervised classification technique was used to classify the Landsat Image. Also, several training areas for each LULC type with different characteristics were drawn before merging them into a single signature class. The supervised classification was performed, checking separately the signature of each class. The maximum likelihood technique was used for supervised classification. In the process of classification, landscape type and cover were detected. LULC were classified; categories of LULC were:

- Water Bodies
- Built-up
- Agriculture
- Bare Land and
- Vegetation

Table 5.1 lists four different LULCs and definitions of each category.

S.N	Classes	Definitions
1	Water Bodies	Water courses, water bodies, estuaries, and salt marshes
2	Built-up	Areas consisting buildings, roads.
3	Agriculture	Area consisting forest area, Shrub and bushes
4	Bare Land	Area consisting bare Land and no vegetation area.
5	Vegetation	Urban vegetation or urban parks or both

Table 5.7: Land Use Land Cover Classified Classes

5.1.1. Patterns of Urban Sprawling in Karachi between 1975 and 2016

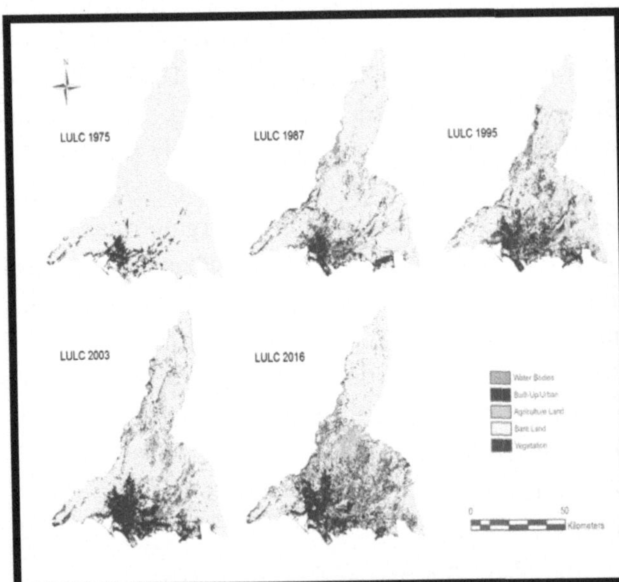

Figure 5.1: Karachi's Sprawl (1975-2016)

According to figure 5.1, most of the areas witnessed remarkable land cover changes between 1975 and 2016. Also, the growth of urban, i.e., built-up, areas was more than three-fold, i.e., an increase of about 42,019.38 hectares, as shown in table 5.2. This transformation influenced several classes, especially the bare land, which exhibited a big decrease, i.e., 35.55% and indicated that the growth of urban areas was accommodated mostly by diminishing bare land.

Metrics	Year					Changes in Urban Structure			
	1975	1987	1995	2003	2016	Δ% = 1975 - 1987	Δ% = 1987 - 1995	Δ% = 1995 - 2003	Δ% = 2003 - 2016
CA	18766.44	35625.51	51527.43	58872.51	60785.82	89.84%	44.64%	14.25%	3.25%
NP	58	640	1021	574	535	1003.45%	59.53%	-43.78%	-6.79%
LPI	3.25	5.37	6.04	11.3	10.65	65.06%	12.43%	87.26%	-5.78%
Clumpy	0.93	0.91	0.92	0.94	0.94	-1.30%	0.91%	2.16%	-0.56%
FRAC_AM	1.2	1.26	1.23	1.26	1.25	5.23%	-2.52%	2.57%	-1.02%
CONTAG	87.58	76.18	58.97	65.53	57.81	-13.02%	-22.59%	11.13%	-11.78%

Table 5.8: Change in Urban Sprawl Level in Karachi
Source: Author's Own Tabulations

The achieved KC for the LULC maps of 1975, 1987, 1995, 2003, and 2016 were 0.79, 0.81, 0.79, 0.77 and 0.74, respectively. These values indicate an acceptable accuracy level for land use and land cover classification. The landscape metrics announce that the urban class area (CA) has increased by 89.84%, 44.64%, 14.25% and 3.25% between 1975 and 1987, 1987 and 1995, 1995 and 2003, and 2003 and 2016, respectively. The NP for urban built-up areas has shown an associated increase of 1003.45%, 59.53%, -43.78% and -6.79% between the same periods, respectively. These values indicate a high level of land discontinuity during the first decade but decrease from 1987. The LPI increased by 65.06% between 1975 and 1987. This high value due to the large urban patches indicates a compact urban growth for the center, but fragmented and dispersed urban growth in the fringe areas, i.e., urban sprawl. LPI continued to increase from 1987 to 2003 (12.43% and 87.26%), confirming the continuation of the Urban sprawl process for Karachi until 2003. The CLUMPY is around 0.9 during all the study period, showing a high and constant aggregated urban patch. Likewise, FRAC_AM was very stable, around 1.23. The decrease in the CONTAG value between 1975-1995 and 2003-2016 indicates a high fragmentation of the landscape. However, this value increased slightly between 1995 and 2003 (11.13%), showing that the fragmented urban area has become denser than it was in the 1987–1995 period.

5.1.2. Change in Urban Sprawl Level in Karachi

The Shannon's Diversity Index (SHDI) value for Karachi was 0.2920 in 1975, which is rather moderately aggregated urban settlements, i.e., negligible urban sprawl level. However, in 1987, the index reached the value of 0.6332, indicating the initiation of dispersion, i.e., urban sprawl in Karachi (Fan et al., 2017). In 1995, the diversity index was 1.0829, which indicates a very high level of urban sprawl in the periphery of Karachi. In 2003, the index decreased to 0.9283, but in 2016, it shot up to 1.1255. This high level of urban sprawl in 2016 may directly be associated with the haphazard encroachment of the urban fringe. These results related to the urban sprawl, especially located in the suburbs, are caused by fast population growth and a lack of available land in the Karachi city center (Życzkowski, 2003).

Rapid urban sprawl overloads some urban infrastructure services (e.g., waste management, sewage water disposal, etc.), creating soil and water pollution in the area (Padmanaban & Kumar, 2012). This creates severe soil and air pollution and causes several health hazards, including respiratory disorders and cancers, for the city residents (Raman & Narayanan, 2008).

5.1.3. Urban Sprawl (US) Extent and Level Prediction for 2025

The $K_{location}$ and $K_{quantity}$ obtained from the validation between the classified and modeled LULC for 2016 were:

- $K_{location}$61.92%
- $K_{quantity}$58.32%

These values represent an acceptable level of accuracy for the calibrated UEPM (Rehman et al., 2005; Tewolde & Cabral, 2011). The predicted LULC for 2025 is presented in figure 5.2. It exposes an increase in the projected urban area of 10,238.94 ha (16.84%) from 2016. The vegetation class has decreased to 35,546.85 ha (-21.94%), as reported in table 5.3. Tabulations of different land categories are presented in figure 5.3, whereas bare land computed in different years shows a declining trend in figure 5.4.

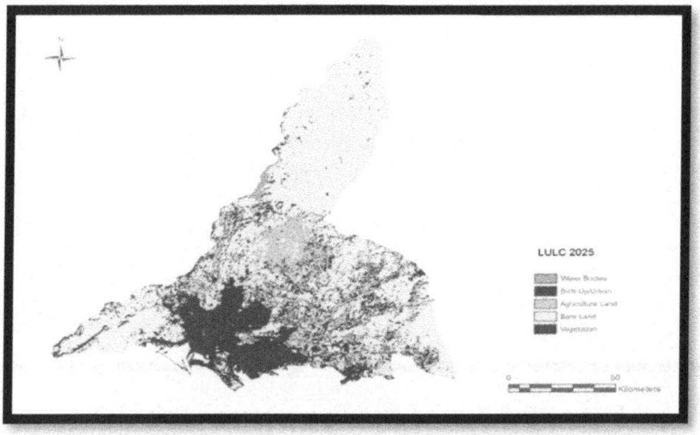

Figure 5.2: Karachi's Predictive LULC 2025

Land-Use Class	1975	1987	1995	2003	2016	2025	Forecasted LULC in 2025	
							ha	%
Water Bodies	0	4022.37	6296.14	3217.34	2214.49	2075.71	-138.78	-6.27%
Built-up/Urban	18761.22	35613.58	51504.71	58876.14	60789.3	71016.93	10227.63	16.82%
Agriculture	2171.64	2943.81	37623.38	23913.22	35174.91	35200.91	26.06	0.07%
Bare Land	336433.24	298421.63	232829.52	254024.02	216913.76	216798.52	-115.24	-0.05%
Vegetation	3268.97	19633.67	32381.3	20604.34	45542.61	35542.93	-9999.67	-21.96%
Total	360635.06	360635.06	360635.06	360635.06	360635.06	360635.06	-	-

Table 5.9: LULC 1975–2025
Source: Author's Own Tabulations

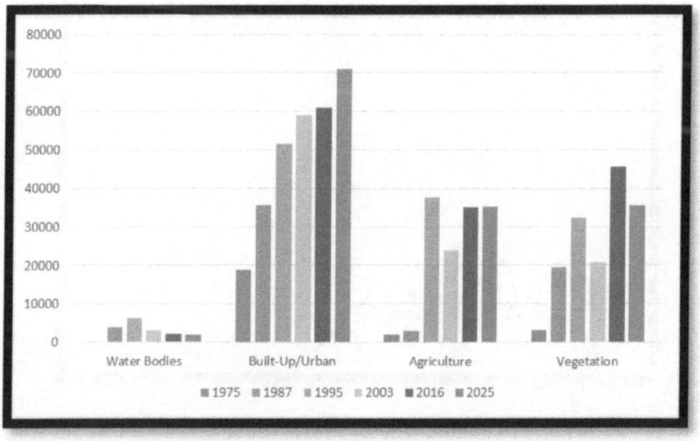

Figure 5.3: Comparative Chart of Different Land Use Class Represented in Different Years

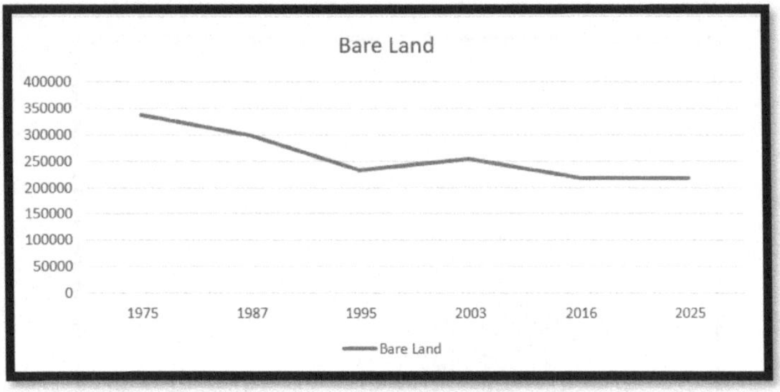

Figure 5.4: Bare Land Comparison Year Wise

The urban areas comprised 16.76% of the total landscape in 2016, which is predicted to increase to 19.58% in 2025. The SHDI of the predicted urban area in 2025 is expected to be 1.1111, which is below the resulting SHDI from 2016, indicating a trend change in the level of urban sprawl. Moreover, the extent of urban sprawl for the coming 8 years is expected to increase, as evident from figure 5.5, not at an alarming rate, but enough to cause an important degradation of urban ecosystem services.

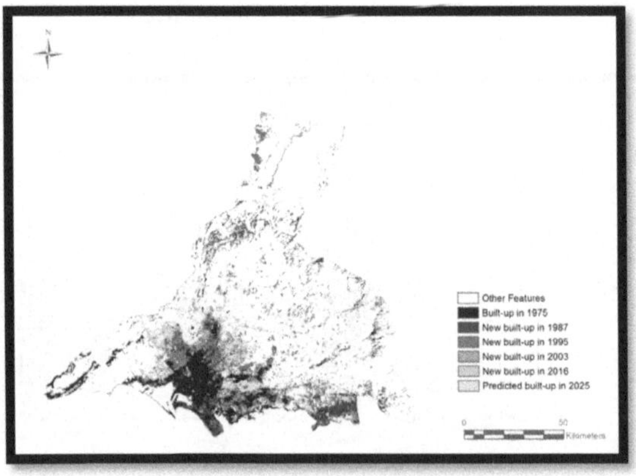

Figure 5.5: Mapping of Built-up (1975- 2025)

5.1.4. Direction of Urban Sprawl

The results from the LULC classification indicate that the growth of the built-up area is radially outward from the zero point. From

1975 to 1995, there was a vast expansion of new built-up areas, mostly at the northwest, northeast and north sides, converted into built-up areas. During the period from 1995 to 2016, there was evidence of stable trends indicating an infill development in already developed parts of the city. The results clearly indicate the concentration of built-up in all directions from the zero point. Built-up areas continuously developed in major road periphery and expanded outwards within the reach of major roads. Within a 10 to 15 km radius, vegetation and bare land were considerably transformed into urban areas. There was a major fragmentation of cultivation and bare land. Mostly, the leap frog form of development was observed from a 10 km radius and onwards.

The suburbanization in Karachi seems to have occurred in a horizontal dimension. The factors behind the development of built-up areas in urban fringes, suburbs and rural areas are low slopes, low land prices and the construction of new roads across the city. The development of road infrastructure across the city stands as an influential factor for multi-directional LULC transformation in Karachi. The city underwent a major infrastructure transformation during the phase of 2001-2007 as areas inside the ring roads were transferred to built-up. The costlier land within, due to higher demand, provided compelling ground to shift radially outwards. However, better connectivity and enhanced motorization provided impetus to rapid peri-urbanization.

5.2. Issues in Urban Sprawling

The content analysis was done carefully to examine and recognize the categories of data that describe the incidents. However, on the basis of inductive interpretation, the main categories of classification were inferred from theoretical models. Thus, the objective of content analysis in this study was a grouping strategy to obtain insights concerning the frequency and patterns of factors that influence the scenario under study. Hence, the interviews were guided by a checklist of questions. It also combines some areas of semi-structured interviews with probing questions. The interviewer began each interview by introducing and explaining the objective of the interview to the participants.

The essence was to describe to the participants how the data gathered from the survey would be used and to get permission from them to use a digital audio recorder. In this study, the interview technique was chosen to obtain a response to research questions 1–4. The aim was to ensure an understanding of how urbanization and urban sprawl issues influence city structure in Karachi. Nonetheless, as much as the data was collected via digital audio recorder, it was possible to examine them in their transcribed form.

The strategy involves a four-step process of grouping large groups of data into rational categories. The information in the form of transcribed interviews was coded. The coding process abides by the guidelines suggested by Campbell (2014). This technique separates the group data, which is based on responses to similar questions. This is because the open-ended questions posed to the interview participants were mostly the same for all respondents. The responses were similar enough to draw comparisons based on the generated responses. On top of this, through the process of frequently comparing the data and categories during and after the data collection process, important themes emerged from the data. The emerging themes are discussed in Section 4 of this study. Other sections of this study are sequentially arranged. The topics were built to establish a better understanding of urban sprawl issues on city structure in Karachi from the perspective of senior academics and planners in the field of architecture and urban and regional planning. At the end of all sections, the findings are presented and discussed, which shows the detailed themes of the interviews.

The content and thematic analysis strategy was adopted to analyze the data derived from the semi-structured interviews. Based on the document analysis, 3 inter-dependent subcategories (Table 5.4) within the context of urban sprawl and its causes and effects on city structure were uncovered and interrogated.

Sr #	Themes
4.3	Causes of urban sprawl
4.3.1	Migration
4.3.2	Industrialization
4.3.3	Lack of governance
4.3.4	Political instability
4.3.5	Lack of control over land agencies/developers
4.4	Effects of urban sprawl
4.4.1	Transportation
4.4.2	Pollution
4.4.3	Water scarcity
4.4.4	Rise of slums/unlawfulness
4.5	Challenges of urban sprawl
4.5.1	Unlawfulness
4.5.2	Damage to ecosystem

Table 5.10: Themes Extracted from Interviews

5.3. Causes of Urban Sprawl

These are different factors that the interviewers responded to when discussing the causes of sprawl in Karachi. This theme is divided into various sub-themes, which are explained in detail below:

5.3.1. Migration

According to the respondents, one of the reasons for sprawl in Karachi is the rapid migration of people from one area to another. There are many social, environmental, economic, and political factors that can cause people to migrate to other cities, but migration due to political events has been found to be the most significant in history. According to the views shared by the participants, a huge number of people migrated from India to Karachi after the partition, causing a sudden increase in the population of the city, doubling the population compared to the natural growth.

Karachi has increased its territory in many dimensions, and the expanded area is greater than the actual area of Karachi, which had a population of 450,000 at the time of partition; now, the population has increased to more than 20 million or around 20 million. This reflects how much the population has increased. IDI-09-M

Similar situations occurred with the migration of Afghanis. According to the participants, this was one of the most significant events in Pakistan's history, causing a population influx all over the country, thus contributing to the city's expansion.

The first phase was in the 80s when the Afghan Mahajirs arrived in the city, and the uncontrolled population influx occurred in Karachi, where the specific populations in Sohrab Goth (Village) and other areas became the hub of the Afghan community. So, there have been different phases in which the population has increased. IDI-09-M

Other environmental or political factors, such as natural disasters or terrorism, are also the reasons for the migration of people from one city to another. One of the participants summarizes these events of migration in the following quote:

Most of the time, the sprawl in Karachi has happened due to immigration to the city. There are some historical events which have contributed to the sprawl of Karachi. For example, in 1947, 1950, then in 1970, when East Pakistan and West Pakistan disjointed and then this insurgency in Pakistan due to this war and terror, people from Northern areas migrated to Karachi. Due to this recent flood in areas of Sindh and other cities of Pakistan, people migrated to Karachi. So when such an influx of population happens, it is almost impossible for municipal, local or provisional govt. to go to the planned development of the city. You can only plan to a certain extent. These events were so big that they had their own momentum and basically contributed to the sprawl of the city. IDI-04-M

5.3.2. Industrialization

As Karachi is the industrial capital of the country, it has a lot of job and growth opportunities. Therefore, people prefer migrating here compared to other cities in the country. According to the interviewees, almost 70 percent of the industries located in Karachi offer best employment opportunities.

> *Karachi is still the banking company of the country, the industrial capital of the country, and the commercial and insurance capital as well. This is the reason people from all over the country and from Afghanistan are coming here. Here, no one can stay unemployed as the city has a lot of employment opportunities. IDI-02-M*

It has also been noticed from the views of the participants that the reason for the expansion of this city is mainly economic, as it has been observed that the majority of people from rural areas move to Karachi for a better livelihood. As the city also has a port, people from other provinces are brought to this place to work here, and then they get settled in the cheapest areas where they can afford rent, mainly the outskirts of the city.

> *City expansion: There are several reasons why Karachi has gone through this population increase in different stages. One was when the British decided to establish Karachi as a port city. Port city, in this context, Karachi city port city, will provide Food navigation and transportation services (...). British-India also lent to Afghanistan. And during that time, huge population displaced from Gujarat and other areas of India from where the Kachi community, Bohra community, the Agha Khani community migrated to Karachi. IDI-09-M*

Karachi being the biggest city and cheaper than the other cities, people usually prefer moving here and settling in the suburbs of the city to get better education and other facilities for their families, which not only causes the increase in population but also the expansion of the city. Despite having many effects on the city, this expansion, for some participants, has a good side as well because these people usually provide cheap labor, which is helpful for the industrialists.

> *To be very honest, people think it is wrong that people from other places like KPK, Swat or Interior Sindh are coming here for jobs, but I consider it to be the strength of Karachi as it is impossible to run an industry unless you have the cheap labor available. This constant influx provides cheap labor that keeps the city functional. In Lahore, for example, if someone works, he cannot afford the accommodation as the rents are around 8k to 10k, whereas in Karachi, the whole family can rent a place in the slums for just 2 thousand rupees. IDI-02-M*

5.3.3. Lack of Governance

According to the participants, lack of governance and inability to take proper measures to control the population are the main reasons for sprawl in the city. They said:

> *When your municipal govt. and other govt. fail to accommodate this increasing population in the urban areas, then the result is the sprawl. Because as you get far from the main city center, the prices follow a certain decline. So it becomes cheaper to live outside the city in terms of residency setup; you can own a plot. There is less regulation when you are sprawling out of the city, and you can form so many things when you are sprawling outside the city limits. Because the municipality doesn't have a check on you, you don't pay tax, etc. IDI-04-M*

They further added that both federal and provincial governments are unable to develop mechanisms or policies to control the migration of people to this city. Because of their failure, the population of Karachi continues to increase, affecting the city's structure.

> *The federal government has no interest in the city. They are earning money from the city, but they are not*

interested in developing the city. Secondly, the provincial government; they do not have the capacity, they lack the capacity. Thirdly, the political stakeholders have no interest in developing the city; they do not own it. IDI-05-M

Furthermore, they also indicate that city planners and private organizations are working for their own profits; they take more interest in private societies and have no concern about how it impacts the other parts of the city.

The private sector normally never thinks of the long-term, but they just think of their own profit. For them, their confined area should be maintained, but they are least bothered about the impact of commercial activity on the entire city. IDI-09-M

5.3.4. Political Instability

During the analysis of the study, it was observed that political instability is also found to be a significant factor in the government's inability to control the population influx and the sprawl of the city. According to the views shared by the participants, due to different events in the history of the country, e.g., the Indo-Pak war, terrorism, military operations and Afghan migration, controlling the migration of people to the city seemed inevitable. The government failed to develop a policy and mechanism to control the increase in population, which resulted in the expansion of the city. One of the participants shared his views regarding this situation in a quote below:

The second major period was Ayub Khan's period, which took the capital from here to Islamabad. What he did was a mishit with the people and the province of Sindh. When he was building the Tarbela dam in Hazara, the displaced people shifted to Karachi. They were ang people; they must be given land near their own language group, but he shifted them to Karachi. The Hazara colony and all the others were developed during Ayub's period. And then came the Bengalis and the Barmis. Then, Zia caused

> *animosity among the people. He was afraid of Sindh due to the illegal murder of Zulfiqar Ali Bhutto, so due to this fear, he shifted the pukhtoon people or people from Afghanistan towards Karachi, and that was not the right thing to do as they must be settled in KPK because they have the same culture; instead, they were sent to Karachi. After the arrival of the Afghanis, the whole culture of the city was changed, the whole transportation system was changed, and all the statistics were changed, so the bad, unnatural migration settled. IDI-05-M*

5.3.5. Lack of Control Over Land Mafia

Most of the interviewees shared that the government's inability to control the land mafia and the excess of housing societies has resulted in the expansion of the city. According to their views, the government is not taking any action against those who are cutting off trees and removing natural vegetation just to create space for the construction of housing societies.

> *Certain areas of Karachi used to be harvesting areas for the city where they used to grow vegetables and other things, but unfortunately, this (...14:26...) has kept those areas in depth but a lot of private housing societies have been established; because of that, Karachi has become totally dependent for supply of all the thing from outside. IDI-09-M*
>
> *As you see, there has been a lot of unplanned construction on the coastal side. If you see from Itehad town and Baldia town, and then move forward to Sarjani to Korangi, these areas have been expanding to sea side. Societies near the sea have been increasing, and all of them are planned; there are no restrictions, and anyone can do anything. IDI-07-M*

Moreover, 90% of the respondents were of the view that the government is unable to stop these big shots from doing this unplanned construction because everybody has a personal gain in this scenario. Because of that, people are deteriorating the city's structure just because of their personal gains.

> *It depends on the need, and if entrepreneurs feel the need for something, they find their way out and make profits out of it. The current sprawl is the result of the nexus between the developers and the government. They have a strong connection and help each other out in their time of need. It is the outcome of the relationship of politicians, bureaucrats and developers, but the major player in all this is the government, which facilitates them by making laws and boards like the high development board or Sindh Special Development Board through which they facilitate them. IDI-08-M*

Moreover, there are so many vacant plots all over the city which are owned by the elite class; they don't sell or rent out them but keep them for better profit, which not only creates difficulties for the people to find places to live but somehow also contributes to the sprawl.

> *The main reason is speculation that middle-income and high-middle-income or high-income people buy land and keep it for better investment return. So, they keep it ideal, and as a result, the city has a lot of plots within the city limits that are not developed, and eventually, people have to find houses in the outskirts. This is how the sprawl is happening. IDI-01-M*

Similarly, they also complained that residential societies attract a particular class that can afford houses in posh areas, whereas the rest of the population is deprived of such housing schemes.

> *If you look at the house projects in the city, you will find that there are enough plots for development in the city. But you will see that most of the plot development is for the high-income or the higher middle class in Bahria and DHA. And then there are apartment projects that are being proposed in the city, but these are for the middle-income group, which accounts for only 25%, and the*

high-income group accounts for only 6-7%, while 75% of people are unable to get any formal housing provision in the city. IDI-01-M

The interviewees suggest that the government must initiate sprawl-controlling measures, as a quantum leap in population annually can pose a serious threat to the urban ecosystem of Karachi.

5.4. Effects of Urban Sprawl

This theme explains how urban sprawl is affecting the city. This theme is divided into various sub-themes based on the views of the participants. All these themes that emerged during the analysis process are explained in detail below:

5.4.1. Transportation

The findings of the study show that the sprawl in Karachi has greatly affected the transportation system, as the available public transport does not meet the needs of the population. According to the views shared by the participants:

"In Karachi, the latest research shows that every single passenger competes with 45 passengers for one bus seat. In similar conditions, in Mumbai, the figure is 10 or 11 people compete for one bus seat, and in Karachi, 45 passengers for one bus seat. So with this ever-expanding city, this is the present condition."

As Karachi is one of the biggest cities in terms of geographic area, it takes hours to reach from one end to another, and because of the expansion of the city, the distance has elongated, which causes more trouble for the people to reach their workplace by spending hours in the traffic.

The city has grown in distance, due to which the time of travel has increased. IDI-01-M

Because of the heavy traffic and the elongated distance, people who have jobs far from their residential areas have to face a lot of problems, and poor people have to travel on buses' roofs to reach their destination as the available transport is insufficient for the "16 million people."

> *In Karachi Defence, Gulshan and North Nazaimabad are 25km apart unless and until you have proper transport between the two areas; they are effectively two cities. IDI-06-M*

> *In Karachi, people are traveling on the roof of the buses and the buses are in very bad condition and now the rikshaws are introduced (10:10-18) and that has disturbed the whole infrastructure of the city. IDI-05-M*

Other than public transport, the number of private vehicles is also great. According to the findings of the study, "25 lacks motorcycles and 16 lacks vehicles are registered in Karachi," which not only causes heavy traffic but also creates parking issues in the city.

> *In the case of Karachi, you don't have proper bus terminals. The buses that travel to other parts of the country are parked in the city, and when they are parked in the city, they are impacting it. Karachi has one of the worst transport systems; there is no control. IDI-09-M*

5.4.2. Pollution

As the industrial capital, Karachi has been marked as one of the most polluted cities in the world because of air and water pollution. According to the views shared by the majority of the participants, the city lacks a proper waste management system and industrial management. The continuous release of toxic materials in coastal areas is not only the greatest threat to marine ecology, but it can also have a hazardous impact on people's health.

> *Karachi is a coastal city, so many people live in one place; it's all contributing to the creation of pollution. Sewerage and industrial waste that go into the coastal areas impact marine ecology, consisting of fish and aquatic animals. It also has an impact on the population of one*

place that needs more resources from the ecosystem. IDI-10-M

The lack of a proper drainage system is one of the biggest challenges for the people of Karachi, and the government's inability to deal with it is causing water pollution and health issues in the population.

The biggest issue, in my view, is the sanitation and drainage system because they are polluting your sea and your natural drainage system and causing many diseases. So sanitation and water supply are the big priorities. You cannot think of sanitation unless you think about water, and industrial waste is polluting the water, so these are the issues. IDI-08-M

Similarly, with the lack of trees or vegetation and the excess of heavy traffic and industrial smoke, air pollution has become a major challenge for the people of Karachi, creating severe health issues for them.

Air pollution impacts human health particularly, and you have all sorts of pollutants in the air. Smog in Punjab nowadays is a sort of air pollution, and the same thing can happen if you don't have the means to control it. If the air is polluted with these pollutants, then they can create this smoggy effect, which has a direct impact on human health. IDI-10-M

5.4.3. Water Scarcity and Wastage

With the transport issues, the people of Karachi also have to face water scarcity in several parts of the city. As the population has been increasing over the years, it is impossible for the city to meet the needs of the people as the current supply of water is inadequate for the people.

If you look at the statistics, only Karachi needs 800 million gallons per day of water supply; the current supply is only 400, and that is restricted to the proper urban area, which is 1200sr km and that too half of the urban area. Our need is 800, and in five years, our need will be 1000. Similarly, Karachi generates 600 million gallons of (10:38), and all of it goes into the sea without any increment (10:38-46). IDI-04-M

The interviewees were of the view that the water supply system of Karachi is not developed, which is why a lot of water gets wasted every year because of leakages.

Our 34% of water is wasted through leakages. The age of pipelines in the whole world is 20-25 years, and no one replaces them. What they do is a machine goes in and creates a line; you don't have to break the road for it for electricity and sanitation purposes. IDI-02-M

It has also been observed that other than the Hub dam, there are no dams available for storing water, and the Hub dam also has a limited capacity to store water. Thus, water is, most of the time, wasted during monsoon season.

Secondly, water is not scarce; fortunately, we had enough rain in the last season, and the Hub dam was filled to its limits; otherwise, people living in the eastern and the north-eastern parts would be facing scarcity of water. IDI-01-M

5.4.4. Rise of Slums

Most of the interviewees suggested that the greatest challenge the city of Karachi is facing is the increase of *Kachi abadi* in the suburbs of the city. People who are poor and cannot afford to live in the main city where rents are higher move to the periphery of the city and start living there illegally, creating issues for other people.

The slums are the first invaders in an area; people just find an area and then come there and start living there and make houses, so when people come, they exert pressure on the local resources; it may be sea, it may be water, it may be fish. People need basic economic opportunities and basic facilities to survive. So these slums will have more impact on local resources, mainly water, air, and land ecological resources; crime is also related to that, so there are social evils because people are poor and they don't find any job and social conflict arise with the local population. People from other places come and settle in these slums, so there are multiple issues. IDI-10-M

With the increase of slums, it has also been noticed that the events of unlawfulness have also increased as people living in the slums are not only living there illegally, but they are also stealing electricity, gas and water, and the administration is unable to get a hold of them.

The population of kachi abadis is not registered properly. And they are using all the facilities like electricity, by kunda system, water by cutting the main supply and gas theft. These are the issues which are illegal. IDI-05-M

According to the interviewees, these are serious effects that can harm any country's economy if left uncontrolled and unaddressed. In Karachi, the effects will be far-reaching.

5.5. Challenges in Urban Sprawling

This theme encapsulates the views of the participants regarding the challenges that urban sprawl may cause in the future. This theme is divided into various sub-themes, which are explained in detail below:

5.5.1. Unlawfulness

According to the participants, the increase in population might lead to clashes between different ethnic groups in the coming years. Such events have already been observed where Pakhtoons and Siraikis do not get along well, so according to their views, the migration of Pakhtoons or Siraikis to the city might lead to challenging situations in the future.

When I discussed the major issues with Qaiser Bengali, he was very afraid that the next fight in Karachi would be for the Pukhtons and Saraiki belt. Because the Saraiki belt has the same professions as construction and transportation, they have come in the last ten years in bulk. The new lash will be of these communities. And secondly, he was afraid that after ten years, it would not be Sindhi city, Urdu-speaking city, but Pukhtons city. So that situation has to be controlled, and all the ethnic groups should live here peacefully when the government and the stakeholders should realize that the majority of the population lives in the mega city. They have to live together with better life and better facilities. IDI-05-M

They also added that the crime rates will also increase if the government does not take any steps to control the current situation. The way things are going right now is not right. After all, 4 years plus the Karachi operation, street crime has not dropped by 1%. It has actually increased. So you can take administrative measures; you can try to control crime and everything; lakin jab tak small issues address nahi hote, we are going through a steep negative curve. IDI-02-M

Most of the interviewees were also of the view that if the current situation persists and the city continues to expand, it might have a drastic effect on the city's economy, which will not be good for the country's overall growth.

This is the city which gives you 6% of the revenue. This is the city which has 95% financial institution headquarters. This is the city that has functional ports for the whole year. So if this city suffers, basically, Pakistan suffers. IDI-04-M

Furthermore, the interviewees said that the government should take control of the current situation, play a mediator's role between ethnic group clashes, and develop a long-term solution and policy.

The state should have a clear policy on several terms, one of which is political. That is your permanent policy for this: if you are making some headlock, one political group, one ethnic group to achieve short-term goals, then, ultimately, it may give you relief for a short time, but, unfortunately, in the long-term, it will have negative impacts. In Karachi, for the last several decades, some political parties have been making arrangements for short-term, then religious groups and vice versa and keep on revolving those arrangements, and it affects you. IDI-09-M

5.5.2. Damage to Ecosystem

The lack of proper waste management systems and the increase in housing schemes pose the greatest threat to the ecosystem as there is no control over the cutting of trees and the abolishment of green spaces for the development of housing societies. If the situation remains the same in the coming years, it can have severe consequences.

> *So with increasing climate change impact, you will have more of these extreme events in future, and if you don't protect your ecology, the urban forestry with trees and green spaces, the city will definitely face the consequences of the heat wave. And urban flooding is another issue that may be impacted by climate change. You are concentrating your growth, and over-infrastructural development will lead to over-flooding in the urban areas. Poor people would be more affected by this. IDI-10-M*
>
> *They said that the destruction of green belts for industrial purposes could cause serious damage to the ecosystem and the marine ecology as "with increasing climate change impact, you would have more these extreme events in the future and if you don't protect your ecology, the urban forestry with trees and green spaces, the city would definitely face the consequences of the heat wave. And urban flooding is another issue that may be impacted by climate change. You are concentrating your growth, and over-infrastructural development will lead to over-flooding in urban areas. Poor people would be more affected by this. IDI-10-M*

Similarly, the increase in housing schemes not only results in encroachment on coastal areas but also creates social inequality in the region. Housing projects are limited to the high-income class, which can afford to buy houses in these societies.

So, a particular group is not only unlawfully constructing these societies but also creating a class difference in society because the poor are going to suffer the impacts of climate change, which is caused by these people destroying the natural ecosystem.

> *We have already experienced the impacts of the heat wave everywhere, and so many people died. U know, if there is any disaster like an earthquake, God forbid, we don't have a response mechanism to react. We live in a poor country; our institutions are very weak; if fire occurs, we are not even able to extinguish fire, so how can we face these disasters? Dengue was not here, but it has come now. It is spread everywhere. Basically, dengue was not here in Pakistan. This is an indication of how we are playing with our environment and ecology, so there will be more disasters; you can name any disaster that has not occurred that will occur in future if you continue to play with the environment or do not care for it. IDI-10-M*

The findings of the qualitative method are presented in figure 5.6:

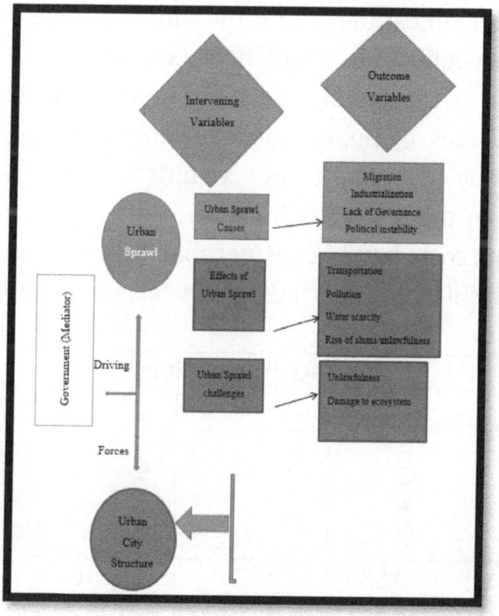

Figure 5.6: Finalized framework of the Study Findings

5.6. Monocentric Model

Table 5.5 presents the results of the monocentric model. We have taken built-up areas as the dependent variable, whereas population, household income (measured by GDP) and transport cost (measured by fuel prices) are used as explanatory variables in the model. For the existence of the long-term co-integrating relationship of built-up areas with the population, household income and transport cost, we have applied the bound testing approach. The sample size is 37 observations, while after adjustments, 33 observations from 1981 to 2017 were included to estimate the results. A maximum of four lags were used based on automatic selection, and an appropriate model was selected based on the Akaike Information Criterion (AIC). The results in table 5.5 showed that the F-statistic value [9.513] of the bound testing is greater than the upper bound value of Pesaran *et al.* (2001) at a reasonable significance level. It signifies that there is a long-term relationship among the concerned variables. In addition, the results of the short-term showed that all three variables, including population, household income and transport cost, have a significant effect on the built-up areas in the short-term as the coefficients of all three variables are statistically significant at a reasonable level of significance. Likewise, the coefficient values of population, household income (GDP) and transport cost are statistically significant at a 5% level of significance in the long-run. It signifies that population, income and transport costs have a considerable influence on the built-up areas in Karachi in both periods: short-term and long-term.

Co-integrating Form				
Variable	**Coefficient**	**Std. Error**	**t-Statistic**	**Prob.**
D(BU (-1))	-0.550	0.134	-4.110	0.001
D(BU(-2))	-0.351	0.141	-2.491	0.026
D(HI)	0.009	0.005	1.870	0.083

D(HI(-1))	-0.016	0.006	-2.799	0.014
D(HI(-2))	-0.016	0.005	-3.035	0.009
D(HI(-3))	-0.019	0.005	-3.902	0.002
D(POP)	-0.597	0.154	-3.888	0.002
D(POP(-1))	-0.871	0.229	-3.798	0.002
D(POP (-2))	-0.510	0.221	-2.308	0.037
D(POP (-3))	-0.326	0.184	-1.766	0.099
D(TC)	-0.008	0.011	-0.714	0.487
D(TC(-1))	-0.031	0.012	-2.496	0.026
D(TC(-2))	-0.038	0.012	-3.075	0.008
D(TC(-3))	-0.047	0.011	-4.138	0.001
CointEq (-1)	-0.310	0.040	-7.820	0.000
Cointeq = BU - (0.0721*HI + 0.9705*POP -0.2215*TC -4.0202)				
Long-Run Coefficients				
Variable	Coefficient	Std. Error	t-Statistic	Prob.
HI	0.072	0.035	2.054	0.059
POP	0.970	0.114	8.532	0.000
TC	-0.222	0.082	-2.690	0.018
C	-4.020	0.757	-5.308	0.000
ARDL Bounds Test- F-statistic	9.513	K=3		
ARDL Cointegrating And Long Run Form, Dependent Variable: BU, Selected Model: ARDL (3, 4, 4, 4)				

Table 5.11: Results of Monocentric Model (Built-Up)

To identify the long-term co-integrating relationship of population density with the population, income (GDP) and transport cost (fuel prices), we have applied the bound testing approach. The results of the bound test in table 5.6 show that the F-statistic value [4.9] is greater than the upper bound value of Pesaran *et al.* (2001) at a 5% level of significance. It confirms the existence of the long-term relationship between the concerned variables. In addition, the short-term dynamics reported in table 5.6 showed that population and income have a significant effect on the population density. The coefficient of the transport cost is incorrectly signed but statistically insignificant. The results of the long-term dynamics showed that only population has a significant effect on the population density, while income and transport costs have no effect on the population density in the long-term.

Cointegrating Form				
Variable	**Coefficient**	**Std. Error**	**t-Statistic**	**Prob.**
D(PD(-1))	0.349	0.171	2.038	0.057
D(PD(-2))	-0.739	0.149	-4.945	0.000
D(PD(-3))	-0.636	0.232	-2.733	0.014
D(HI)	0.017	0.004	4.932	0.000
D(HI(-1))	0.025	0.006	4.417	0.000
D(HI(-2))	0.012	0.004	2.885	0.010
D(HI(-3))	0.014	0.004	3.121	0.006
D(POP)	1.474	0.171	8.601	0.000
D(POP(-1))	0.485	0.272	1.783	0.092
D(POP(-2))	0.052	0.137	0.383	0.707
D(TC)	0.008	0.007	1.174	0.256
CointEq (-1)	-.529	0.200	-5.139	0.000
Cointeq = PD - (-0.0041*HI + 0.9944*POP + 0.0070*TC - 3.4937)				
Long Run Coefficients				
Variable	Coefficient	Std. Error	t-Statistic	Prob.
HI	-0.004	0.005	-0.797	0.436
POP	0.994	0.017	57.547	0.000
TC	0.007	0.008	0.887	0.388
C	-3.494	0.108	-32.297	0.000
Bound Test-F-statistic	4.963	K=3		

Table 5.12: Results of Monocentric Model (Population Density)

ARDL Co-integrating and Long-Run Form, Dependent Variable: PD, Selected Model: ARDL (4,4,4)

Table 5.7 presents the results of the monocentric model when urban sprawl is used as the dependent variable. The results, based on the bound testing approach, indicate a long-term relationship between urban sprawl and include explanatory variables such as population, household income, and transport cost. The findings of the long-run ARDL model suggest that all three variables: population, household income and transport cost, have considerable effects on the urban sprawl in the long- run as the coefficient values of all three variables are statistically significant at a reasonable level of significance. The results of the short-term dynamics showed that population, household income and transport cost have no effect on the urban sprawl. These results signify that urban sprawl is a long-term phenomenon, and population, household income, and transport cost considerably contribute to the sprawl in Karachi.

Cointegrating Form				
Variable	**Coefficient**	**Std. Error**	**t-Statistic**	**Prob.**
D(SP(-1))	0.525	0.192	2.734	0.014
D(HI)	0.113	0.094	1.197	0.240
D(POP)	-1.325	0.913	-1.451	0.157
D(TC)	-0.162	0.202	-0.801	0.429
CointEq (-1)	-.429	0.179	-5.764	0.000
Cointeq = SP - (0.1088*HI -0.9081*POP -0.3163*TC + 6.5763)				
Long Run Coefficients				
Variable	Coefficient	Std. Error	t-Statistic	Prob.
HI	0.109	0.054	2.0185	0.053
POP	0.908	0.335	2.711	0.011
TC	-0.316	0.147	-2.153	0.039
C	6.576	2.133	3.083	0.004
ARDL Bound Test- F-statistic	5.964	K=3		

Table 5.13: Results of Monocentric Model (Sprawl)

ARDL Co-integrating And Long-Run Form, Dependent Variable: SP, Selected Model: ARDL (1,0,0).

5.7. Local Fiscalization

The monocentric model was analyzed using local fiscalization variables: revenue of Karachi Metropolitan Corporation (KMC) and vacant plot tax. The results of the extended model are reported in tables 5.8, 5.9 and 5.10. The results, based on the bound test, in table 5.8 showed that the F-statistics value of the bound test is greater than the upper bound value of Pesaran *et al.* (2001) at a reasonable level of significance. It signifies that there is a long-term relationship between built-up areas and local fiscalization indicators. In addition, the short-term dynamics indicate that KMC revenue and vacant plot tax have significantly correlated with the built-up areas in the short-run. Likewise, the KMC revenue and vacant plot tax have a substantial influence on the built-up areas in the long-run as the long-term coefficient values of both variables are statistically significant. These results suggest that along with the monocentric model variables, KMC revenue and vacant plot tax are the contributing factors in both short- and long-run periods that have a considerable influence on the built-up areas in Karachi.

Cointegrating Form				
Variable	**Coefficient**	**Std. Error**	**t-Statistic**	**Prob.**
D(BU (-1))	-1.087	0.134	-8.105	0.004
D(BU(-2))	-0.991	0.218	-4.543	0.020
D(BU(-3))	-1.298	0.225	-5.779	0.010
D(HI)	-0.019	0.006	-3.216	0.049
D(HI(-1))	0.167	0.020	8.242	0.004
D(HI(-2))	0.140	0.019	7.442	0.005
D(HI(-3))	0.089	0.014	6.492	0.007
D(POP)	-0.092	0.148	-0.621	0.579
D(POP(-1))	-2.866	0.346	-8.285	0.004
D(POP(-2))	-1.644	0.320	-5.140	0.014
D(POP(-3))	-1.339	0.264	-5.078	0.015
D(TC)	0.003	0.009	0.298	0.785
D(TC(-1))	-0.174	0.024	-7.260	0.005
D(TC(-2))	-0.155	0.020	-7.573	0.005
D(TC(-3))	-0.032	0.010	-3.087	0.054
D(KMCR)	0.170	0.019	9.154	0.003
D(KMCR (-1))	0.750	0.097	7.767	0.004
D(KMCR (-2))	0.671	0.083	8.113	0.004
D(KMCR (-3))	0.378	0.058	6.565	0.007
D(VPT)	-0.006	0.001	-6.273	0.008
D(VPT(-1))	-0.026	0.003	-8.776	0.003
D(VPT(-2))	0.016	0.002	7.337	0.005
D(VPT(-3))	-0.007	0.001	-5.479	0.012
CointEq(-1)	-0.591	0.0728	-8.118	0.004
Cointeq = BU - (-0.0769*HI + 2.0608*POP + 0.1310*TC - 0.3548*KMCR -0.0167*VPT -9.8773)				

Long Run Coefficients				
Variable	**Coefficient**	**Std. Error**	**t-Statistic**	**Prob.**
HI	0.077	0.007	10.976	0.002
POP	2.061	0.067	30.556	0.000
TC	0.131	0.018	7.438	0.005
KMCR	-0.355	0.023	-15.224	0.001
VPT	-0.017	0.001	-11.808	0.001
C	-9.877	0.357	-27.684	0.000
Bound Test-F-statistic	3.145	K=5		

Table 5.8: Fiscal Localization (Built-Up)

ARDL Co-integrating And Long-Run Form, Dependent Variable: BU, Selected Model: ARDL (3, 4, 4, 4, 2)

Results of the short- and long-run effect of local fiscalization indicators on population density are reported and summarized in table 5.9. The findings in table 5.9 explicate that the F-statistics value of the Wald test is greater than the upper bound value of Pesaran *et al.* (2001), implying that there is a long-term cointegration association between population density and local fiscalization indicators. Additionally, the results showed that KMC revenue has a significant positive effect on population density as the coefficient of the KMC revenue in both periods is positive and statistically significant. Moreover, the findings in table 5.9 demonstrate that the vacant plot tax has no effect on the population in the short- and long-run as the coefficient of the vacant plot tax is statistically insignificant in both periods. These results imply that along with the population, income and transport cost, the KMC revenue is a contributing factor that has a noticeable influence on the population density in both short- and long-run periods.

Cointegrating Form				
Variable	**Coefficient**	**Std. Error**	**t-Statistic**	**Prob.**
D(PD(-1))	0.570	0.154	3.704	0.001
D(HI)	0.013	0.003	3.897	0.001
D(HI(-1))	0.008	0.004	2.198	0.039
D(POP)	1.099	0.070	15.743	0.000
D(POP(-1))	-0.422	0.144	-2.935	0.008
D(TC)	0.005	0.008	0.688	0.499
D(KMCR)	-0.010	0.011	-0.950	0.353
D(KMCR(-1))	0.036	0.010	3.638	0.002
D(VPT)	0.000	0.001	-0.101	0.921
CointEq(-1)	-1.126	0.181	-6.206	0.000
Cointeq = PD - (0.0034*HI + 1.0568*POP + 0.0044*TC -0.0228*KMCR -0.0004*VPT -3.8813)				
Long Run Coefficients				
Variable	**Coefficient**	**Std. Error**	**t-Statistic**	**Prob.**
HI	0.003	0.002	1.421	0.170
POP	1.057	0.030	34.816	0.000
TC	0.004	0.007	0.638	0.531
KMCR	-0.023	0.009	-2.409	0.025
VPT	-0.000	0.000	-1.516	0.144
C	-3.881	0.179	-21.635	0.000
Bound Test- F-statistic	4.825	K=5		

Table 5.14: Fiscal Localization (Population Density)

Dependent Variable: PD, Selected Model: ARDL (4, 4, 4, 0, 0)

Table 5.10 presents the results of the effect of local fiscalization variables on the sprawl in Karachi. The findings in the mentioned tables indicate that the estimated F-statistic value of the Wald test is greater than the upper bound critical value of Pesaran *et al.* (2001). This result confirms the existence of the long-term relationship between sprawl and local fiscalization variables. Furthermore, the results explicate that the coefficients of all the monocentric model and local fiscalization variables are statistically significant in the short-run. It signifies that along with the monocentric variables, KMC revenue and vacant plot tax have a considerable influence on the sprawl in Karachi. Similarly, KMC revenue has a negative and significant effect on the sprawl in the long-run. These results imply that along with the population, household income and transport cost, KMC revenue and vacant plot tax are the prime factors that have contributed significantly to the sprawl in Karachi.

Cointegrating Form				
Variable	**Coefficient**	**Std. Error**	**t-Statistic**	**Prob.**
D(SP(-1))	-0.181	0.067	-2.709	0.054
D(SP(-2))	-0.921	0.077	-11.970	0.000
D(SP(-3))	-1.085	0.080	-13.596	0.000
D(GDP)	0.483	0.041	11.815	0.000
D(GDP(-1))	-0.122	0.038	-3.220	0.032
D(GDP(-2))	-0.435	0.041	-10.725	0.000
D(GDP(-3))	-0.544	0.035	-15.746	0.000
D(POP)	26.058	2.190	11.900	0.000
D(POP(-1))	-11.140	1.363	-8.174	0.001
D(POP(-2))	-46.183	2.793	-16.535	0.000
D(POP(-3))	-15.494	1.800	-8.606	0.001
D(FP)	-0.927	0.087	-10.644	0.000
D(FP(-1))	1.105	0.090	12.212	0.000
D(FP(-2))	-0.236	0.079	-2.986	0.041
D(FP(-3))	0.965	0.075	12.920	0.000
D(KMCR)	-0.922	0.123	-7.474	0.002
D(KMCR(-1))	-1.169	0.129	-9.078	0.001
D(KMCR(-2))	-0.628	0.138	-4.543	0.011
D(KMCR(-3))	-3.318	0.191	-17.335	0.000
D(VPT)	0.021	0.006	3.716	0.021
D(VPT(-1))	-0.071	0.006	-11.780	0.000
D(VPT(-2))	-0.028	0.005	-5.238	0.006
CointEq(-1)	-.830	0.078	-11.216	0.000
Cointeq = SP - (0.1741*GDP +1.8230*POP +0.9439*FP + 0.4812*KMCR + 0.0364*VPT + 11.8505)				
Long Run Coefficients				
Variable	Coefficient	Std. Error	t-Statistic	Prob.
HI	0.174	0.051	3.425	0.027
POP	1.823	0.601	-3.033	0.039
TC	-0.944	0.152	-6.212	0.003
KMCR	0.481	0.224	2.152	0.098
VPT	0.036	0.009	4.119	0.015
C	11.850	3.358	3.530	0.024
Bound Test- F-statistic	17.469	K=5		

Table 5.15: Fiscal Localization (Sprawl)

ARDL Co-integrating and Long-Run Form, Dependent Variable: SP, Selected Model: ARDL (1, 0, 0, 0, 0)

5.8. Economic Indicators

Economic activities have played a significant in the increase of urbanization for many decades across the globe. To capture the effect of economic activities on the urban sprawl, the current study included the interest rate, average monthly wages and employment opportunities in the monocentric model along with the basic variables of the monocentric model. The results of the short- and long-run dynamics of the economic indicators or activities in the built-up areas are presented in table 5.11. The findings show that the F-statistic value [13.025] of the Wald test is greater than the upper bound critical value of Pesaran *et al.* (2001) at a 1% level of significance. It confirms the existence of the long-term association between built-up areas and economic indicators. Furthermore, the results showed that the coefficients of the interest rate and employment variables were correctly signed in both periods. Employment has a significant effect on the built-up areas both in the short- and long-run, while interest rate has significantly contributed to the built-up areas in the long-run only. In addition, the findings in table 5.11 explicate that the coefficient of average monthly wages is incorrectly signed in both short- and long-run periods but statistically insignificant. These results signify that along with the monocentric model variables, employment opportunities and interest rates considerably contributed to the built-up areas in Karachi.

Cointegrating Form				
Variable	**Coefficient**	**Std. Error**	**t-Statistic**	**Prob.**
D(BU(-1))	-0.800	0.129	-6.162	0.000
D(BU(-2))	-0.859	0.147	-5.840	0.000
D(BU(-3))	-0.568	0.157	-3.606	0.002
D(HI)	-0.007	0.006	-1.070	0.301
D(POP)	-0.785	0.194	-4.046	0.001
D(POP(-1))	-0.851	0.209	-4.059	0.001
D(TC)	0.049	0.018	2.624	0.019
D(TC(-1))	-0.022	0.016	-1.430	0.173
D(IR)	0.010	0.005	1.741	0.102
D(EM)	0.059	0.015	3.827	0.001
D(EM(-1))	-0.029	0.015	-1.890	0.078
D(AMW)	-0.006	0.017	-0.384	0.706
CointEq (-1)	-0.508	0.110	-4.615	0.000
Cointeq = BU - (-0.0145*HI + 0.5477*POP + 0.1115*TC -0.0221*IR + 0.1824*EM -0.0130*AMW -0.9991)				
Long Run Coefficients				
Variable	**Coefficient**	**Std. Error**	**t-Statistic**	**Prob.**
HI	-0.014	0.011	-1.218	0.241
POP	0.547	0.1045	5.236	0.000
TC	0.111	0.039	2.838	0.012
IR	-0.022	0.009	-2.306	0.035
EM	0.182	0.042	4.255	0.000
AMW	-0.012	0.032	-0.399	0.695
C	-0.999	0.616	-1.619	0.126
Bound Test- F-statistic		13.025	K-6	

Table 5.16: Economic Indicator (Built -Up)

Dependent Variable: BU, Selected Model: ARDL (4, 0, 2, 2, 1, 2, 0)

Table 5.12 presents the impact of the economic indicator on the urban sprawl when the population density is used as the dependent variable. The findings in table 5.12 explicate that the F-statistic value of the Wald test is 2.627, which lies between the upper and lower bound values of Pesaran *et al.* (2001) at a 10% level of significance; therefore, the decision about the long-term association between the population density and economic indicators is inconclusive. Moreover, the results explicate that the interest rate and average monthly wages have a statistically significant effect on the population density in both short and long-run periods, as the coefficients of both variables are statistically significant at a 5% level of significance. Additionally, the results show that employment has a considerable effect on population density in the short-run only. These results imply that, along with the population growth, household income and transport cost economic activities have also contributed significantly to the population density in Karachi.

Cointegrating Form				
Variable	**Coefficient**	**Std. Error**	**t-Statistic**	**Prob.**
D(PD(-1))	0.462	0.317	1.454	0.173
D(PD(-2))	0.542	0.353	1.535	0.152
D(HI)	0.011	0.005	2.126	0.056
D(HI(-1))	0.008	0.004	2.006	0.070
D(POP)	0.500	0.197	2.529	0.028
D(POP(-1))	-0.329	0.203	-1.618	0.133
D(POP(-2))	-0.315	0.202	-1.556	0.147
D(TC)	0.032	0.010	3.027	0.011
D(TC(-1))	0.017	0.016	1.047	0.317
D(IR)	-0.020	0.007	-2.914	0.014
D(IR(-1))	-0.004	0.006	-0.647	0.530
D(EM)	0.017	0.0129	1.350	0.204
D(EM(-1))	-0.020	0.013	-1.505	0.160
D(EM(-2))	-0.030	0.014	-2.107	0.058
D(AMW)	0.061	0.018	3.366	0.006
CointEq (-1)	-1.411	0.406	-3.472	0.005
*Cointeq = PD - (0.008*HI + 0.880*POP -0.013*(TC) -0.011*IR + 0.043*EM + 0.043*AMW -2.933)*				
Long Run Coefficients				
Variable	**Coefficient**	**Std. Error**	**t-Statistic**	**Prob.**
HI	0.008	0.006	1.327	0.211
POP	0.880	0.042	20.795	0.000
TC	-0.013	0.017	-0.767	0.459
IR	-0.011	0.006	-1.824	0.095
EM	0.043	0.017	2.465	0.031
AMW	0.043	0.020	2.144	0.055
C	-2.933	0.215	-13.607	0.000
Bound Test- F-statistic 2.627 K -6				

Table 5.17: Economic Indicator (Population Density)

Dependent Variable: PD-Selected Model: ARDL (3, 2, 3, 2, 3, 3, 0)

The results of the short-run and long-run effects of the economic indicators on the sprawl are presented in table 5.13. The findings show that the F-statistic value of the Wald test is greater than the upper bound critical value of Pesaran *et al.* (2001) at a 1% level of significance, implying that there is a co-integrating relationship between sprawl and economic indicators. In addition, the results showed that employment and interest rates have significant effects on the sprawl in both short- and long-run periods. However, the coefficient value of the average monthly wages is statistically insignificant in both short- and long-run periods. These results confirm that, along with the monocentric model, interest rate and employment noticeably contributed to the sprawl in Karachi.

Cointegrating Form				
Variable	**Coefficient**	**Std. Error**	**t-Statistic**	**Prob.**
D(SP(-1))	0.227	0.110	2.052	0.060
D(HI)	0.022	0.055	0.406	0.691
D(HI(-1))	0.081	0.050	1.615	0.130
D(HI(-2))	0.163	0.052	3.100	0.008
D(POP)	1.753	1.326	1.321	0.209
D(TC)	0.090	0.138	0.652	0.525
D(TC(-1))	0.187	0.180	1.040	0.317
D(TC(-2))	-0.716	0.154	-4.638	0.000
D(IR)	-0.487	0.073	-6.633	0.000
D(IR(-1))	-0.258	0.064	-4.037	0.001
D(EM)	0.617	0.134	4.574	0.000
D(EM(-1))	-0.349	0.179	-1.948	0.073
D(AMW)	0.341	0.230	1.480	0.162
CointEq(-1)	-2.170	0.214	-10.117	0.000
Cointeq = SP - (-0.1412*HI -1.0458*POP + 0.2799*TC -0.1189*IR + 0.5558*EM - 0.0633*ANW + 8.4304)				
Long Run Coefficients				
Variable	**Coefficient**	**Std. Error**	**t-Statistic**	**Prob.**
HI	-0.141	0.046	-3.026	0.009
POP	-1.045	0.201	-5.177	0.000
TC	0.279	0.099	2.810	0.014
IR	-0.118	0.043	-2.751	0.016
EM	0.555	0.101	5.496	0.000
AMW	-0.063	0.070	-0.901	0.383
C	8.430	1.185	7.111	0.000
Bound Test- F-statistic 18.328				

Table 5.18: Economic Indicator (Sprawl)

Dependent Variable: SP-Selected Model: ARDL (2, 3, 1, 3, 1, 2, 1)

5.9. Social Indicators

Health and education facilities attract people to migrate to urban cities across the world. To capture the effect of the health and education facilities on the sprawl, we extended the monocentric model by including additional variables: health facility (measured per person per doctor) and education facility (measured by student enrollment) in the model. Table 5.14 presents the results of both the short- and long-run effects of social indicators on the built-up areas in Karachi. The findings in table 5.14 demonstrate a long-term cointegrating relationship between built-up areas and social indicators. In addition, the results explicate that health and education facilities have a substantial influence on the built-up areas as the coefficient values of both variables are statistically significant at a reasonable level of significance. These results imply that social indicators: health and education facilities are also the prime factors along with the monocentric model variables that considerably contributed to the built-up areas in Karachi.

Cointegrating Form				
Variable	**Coefficient**	**Std. Error**	**t-Statistic**	**Prob.**
D(BU(-1))	-0.536	0.083	-6.457	0.000
D(BU(-2))	-0.473	0.085	-5.572	0.001
D(HI)	0.017	0.003	5.676	0.001
D(HI(-1))	-0.033	0.004	-8.368	0.000
D(HI(-2))	-0.021	0.003	-6.938	0.000
D(HI(-3))	-0.024	0.003	-7.523	0.000
D(POP)	-0.406	0.101	-4.035	0.005
D(POP(-1))	-0.382	0.132	-2.885	0.024
D(POP(-2))	0.262	0.109	2.410	0.047
D(POP(-3))	0.528	0.126	4.191	0.004
D(TC)	0.020	0.006	3.102	0.017
D(SE)	-0.011	0.009	-1.294	0.237
D(SE(-1))	0.017	0.008	2.011	0.084
D(SE(-2))	-0.016	0.008	-1.831	0.110
D(PPD)	-0.020	0.004	-4.546	0.003
CointEq (-1)	-0.478	0.034	-13.907	0.000
Cointeq = BU - (0.1167*GDP + 0.0113*POP -0.0374*FP -0.1748*PSE -0.1046*PPD + 2.6614)				
Long Run Coefficients				
Variable	**Coefficient**	**Std. Error**	**t-Statistic**	**Prob.**
GDP	0.117	0.020	5.708	0.001
POP	0.011	0.140	0.081	0.938
TC	-0.037	0.024	-1.531	0.170
PSE	-0.175	0.047	-3.685	0.008
PPD	-0.105	0.016	-6.469	0.000
C	2.661	0.975	2.730	0.029
Bound Test- F-statistic	14.877	K=5		
Dependent Variable: BU, Selected Model: ARDL (2, 3, 3, 0, 2, 0)				

Table 5:19: Social Indicators (Built-Up)

Table 5.15 summarizes the results of the social indicators on the population density. In a specified model, population density is used as the dependent variable, whereas education facility (school enrollment) and health facility (person per doctor), along with the monocentric model variables, are used as explanatory variables in the model. The results, based on the bound testing approach, confirm a cointegrating relationship between population density and social indicators. In addition, the findings explicate that person per doctor has a significant effect on the population density in both short- and long-run periods as the coefficients of the person per doctor are statistically significant in both short- and long-run. Additionally, the results show that the coefficient of school enrollment is statistically insignificant in the short- and long-run. These findings signify that health facilities played a crucial role in increasing the population density in Karachi.

Cointegrating Form				
Variable	**Coefficient**	**Std. Error**	**t-Statistic**	**Prob.**
D(PD(-1))	0.715	0.226	3.170	0.007
D(PD(-2))	-0.514	0.155	-3.312	0.006
D(PD(-3))	-0.711	0.262	-2.708	0.018
D(HI)	0.020	0.004	5.430	0.000
D(HI(-1))	0.025	0.006	4.018	0.002
D(HI(-2))	0.012	0.004	2.813	0.015
D(HI(-3))	0.018	0.005	3.384	0.005
D(POP)	1.517	0.181	8.361	0.000
D(POP(-1))	0.505	0.299	1.688	0.115
D(POP(-2))	-0.011	0.151	-0.071	0.944
D(POP(-3))	-0.482	0.169	-2.851	0.014
D(TC)	0.005	0.007	0.728	0.480
D(SE)	-0.015	0.009	-1.641	0.125
D(PPD)	-0.007	0.006	-1.183	0.258
D(PPD(-1))	0.010	0.005	1.913	0.078
CointEq(-1)	-1.588	0.311	-5.109	0.000
Cointeq = PD - (0.0036*GDP + 0.9676*POP + 0.0012*FP -0.0093*PSE -0.0026*PPD -3.3258)				
Long Run Coefficients				
Variable	Coefficient	Std. Error	t-Statistic	Prob.
GDP	0.968	0.027	35.728	0.000
POP	0.001	0.005	0.221	0.828
TC	-0.009	0.008	-1.202	0.251
PSE	-0.003	0.003	-0.870	0.400
PPD	-3.326	0.175	-19.006	0.000
C	0.004	0.006	0.611	0.552
Bound Test- F-statistic	6.038	K=5		

Table 5.20: Social Indicator (Population Density)

Dependent Variable: PD, Selected Model: ARDL (4, 4, 4, 0, 0, 2)

The results of the short-run and long-run dynamics of social indicators on the sprawl are reported in table 5.16. The findings show that the F-statistic value of the Wald test lies between the upper and lower bound critical values of Pesaran *et al.* (2001); hence, the decision regarding the long-term association between social indicators and sprawl is inconclusive. In addition, the results indicate that coefficients of school enrollment and person per doctor are positive and statistically significant in the short-run. It implies that health and education facilities have positively and significantly contributed to the sprawl in Karachi. Moreover, the results show that the education facility (school enrollment) has a positive effect on the sprawl in the long-run, whereas the coefficient of person per person is statistically insignificant. These results confirm that along with the monocentric variables, health and education facilities are the crucial factors that are noticeably associated with the sprawl in Karachi.

Cointegrating Form				
Variable	**Coefficient**	**Std. Error**	**t-Statistic**	**Prob.**
D(SP(-1))	4.866	0.974	4.995	0.004
D(SP(-2))	3.012	0.665	4.527	0.006
D(SP(-3))	0.878	0.288	3.047	0.029
D(HI)	0.598	0.126	4.769	0.005
D(HI(-1))	-0.754	0.180	-4.188	0.009
D(HI(-2))	-0.528	0.133	-3.964	0.011
D(HI(-3))	-0.251	0.104	-2.422	0.060
D(POP)	11.428	4.294	2.661	0.045
D(POP(-1))	40.204	8.462	4.751	0.005
D(POP(-2))	11.034	4.906	2.249	0.074
D(POP(-3))	-12.863	4.471	-2.877	0.035
D(TC)	-0.341	0.202	-1.690	0.152
D(TC(-1))	2.672	0.563	4.746	0.005
D(TC(-2))	0.639	0.363	1.759	0.139
D(SE)	-0.989	0.287	-3.444	0.018
D(SE(-1))	2.506	0.514	4.876	0.005
D(SE(-2))	1.370	0.430	3.188	0.024
D(SE(-3))	0.768	0.350	2.195	0.080
D(PPD)	0.217	0.155	1.400	0.220
D(PPD(-1))	1.068	0.230	4.638	0.006
D(PPD(-2))	0.756	0.226	3.345	0.020
CointEq(-1)	-0.798	.134	-5.987	0.002
Cointeq = SP - (0.2981*GDP -2.1992*POP -0.5465*FP -0.6307*PSE -0.0563*PPD + 15.7451)				
Long Run Coefficients				
Variable	Coefficient	Std. Error	t-Statistic	Prob.
HI	0.298	0.040	7.472	0.001
POP	-2.199	0.412	-5.341	0.003
TC	-0.546	0.069	-7.965	0.001
PSE	0.631	0.118	5.327	0.003
PPD	-0.056	0.056	-0.998	0.364
C	15.745	2.964	5.312	0.003
Bound Test- F-statistic	2.827	K=5		

Table 5.21: Social Indicator (Sprawl)

Dependent Variable: SP, Selected Model: ARDL (4, 4, 4, 3, 4, 3)

5.10. Utility and Private Transport

Volumetric increase in private transportation significantly contributes to suburbanization in the urban centers. Moreover, the city's expansion on the urban fringe results in more energy consumption. To capture the effect of the utility and transport indicators, the current study extended the monocentric model by including electricity consumption and private vehicles as additional variables. The results of the extended monocentric model are reported and presented in tables 5.17, 5.18 and 5.19. The findings in table 5.17 demonstrate a long-term cointegrating relationship between the built-up areas and utility and transport indicators as the F-statistic value of the Wald test is greater than the upper bound value of Pesaran *et al.* (2001) at a reasonable level of significance. In addition, the results indicate that transport facilities (measured by private vehicles) have no effect on built-up areas in the short run, as the coefficient of private vehicles is statistically insignificant. However, electricity consumption has a positive and significant effect on built-up areas in Karachi. In addition, the results explicate that long-term coefficients of private vehicles and electricity consumption are positive and statistically significant. It signifies that private transport and electricity consumption considerably contribute to the built-up areas in Karachi. Here, it can be concluded that, along with the monocentric model variables, private transport and utility indicators have a substantial influence on the built-up areas in Karachi.

Cointegrating Form				
Variable	Coefficient	Std. Error	t-Statistic	Prob.
D(BU(-1))	0.464	0.134	3.448	0.011
D(BU(-2))	0.729	0.150	4.866	0.002
D(BU(-3))	0.536	0.099	5.394	0.001
D(GDP)	-0.028	0.010	-2.930	0.022
D(HI(-1))	-0.017	0.005	-3.092	0.018
D(HI(-2))	-0.048	0.008	-5.952	0.001
D(HI(-3))	-0.047	0.007	-6.766	0.000
D(POP)	-2.058	0.295	-6.968	0.000
D(POP(-1))	-4.453	0.627	-7.099	0.000
D(POP(-2))	-2.791	0.477	-5.856	0.001
D(POP(-3))	-0.567	0.220	-2.573	0.037
D(TC)	-0.051	0.012	-4.164	0.004
D(TC(-1))	-0.039	0.012	-3.377	0.012
D(TC(-2))	0.077	0.015	5.097	0.001
D(TC(-3))	0.078	0.013	5.972	0.001
D(EC)	0.077	0.038	2.041	0.081
D(EC(-1))	0.010	0.029	0.353	0.734
D(EC(-2))	0.149	0.040	3.753	0.007
D(PVEH)	-0.014	0.025	-0.561	0.592
CointEq(-1)	-1.230	0.173	-7.091	0.000
Cointeq = BU - (-0.0349*HI + 0.9904*POP -0.0217*TC + 0.1766*EC +0.1573*PVEH -4.3334)				
Long Run Coefficients				
Variable	Coefficient	Std. Error	t-Statistic	Prob.
GDP	-0.035	0.019	-1.831	0.110
POP	0.990	0.155	6.392	0.000
TC	-0.022	0.053	-0.413	0.692
EC	0.177	0.082	2.141	0.070
PVEH	0.157	0.044	3.588	0.009
C	-4.333	0.838	-5.174	0.001
Bound Test- F-statistic	4.867	K=5		

Table 5.22 : Utility and Transport (Built -Up)

Dependent Variable: BU, Selected Model: ARDL (4, 4, 4, 4, 3, 1)

Table 5.18 presents the results of the short- and long-run dynamics when the population density is used as the dependent variable. The results indicate that the F-statistic value of the Wald test is greater than the upper bound value of Pesaran *et al.* (2001), implying that there is a significant long-term relationship between population density and utility and private transport indicators. In addition, the findings show that short-term coefficients of the vehicles and electricity consumption are correctly signed and statistically significant. It implies that private transport and electricity consumption have a considerable impact on the population density in the short-run. Contrarily, the long-run coefficients of private vehicles and electricity consumption are statistically insignificant. These results suggest that, along with the monocentric model variables, private transport and electricity consumption are noticeably affected by the population density in Karachi.

Cointegrating Form				
Variable	**Coefficient**	**Std. Error**	**t-Statistic**	**Prob.**
D(PD(-1))	-0.149	0.112	-1.321	0.257
D(PD(-2))	-2.566	0.309	-8.311	0.001
D(PD(-3))	-2.821	0.348	-8.111	0.001
D(HI)	0.089	0.010	9.318	0.001
D(HI(-1))	0.122	0.015	8.063	0.001
D(HI(-2))	0.098	0.012	7.867	0.001
D(HI(-3))	0.084	0.010	8.120	0.001
D(POP)	4.506	0.471	9.557	0.001
D(POP(-1))	5.347	0.646	8.278	0.001
D(POP(-2))	1.380	0.156	8.874	0.001
D(TC)	0.078	0.010	7.948	0.001
D(TC(-1))	-0.176	0.023	-7.790	0.002
D(TC(-2))	-0.197	0.025	-7.959	0.001
D(TC(-3))	-0.062	0.013	-4.721	0.009
D(EC)	-0.028	0.015	-1.865	0.136
D(EC(-1))	-0.375	0.047	-8.066	0.001
D(EC(-2))	-0.415	0.048	-8.578	0.001
D(EC(-3))	-0.137	0.029	-4.689	0.009
D(PVEH)	-0.166	0.026	-6.428	0.003
D(PVEH(-1))	0.144	0.025	5.844	0.004
D(PVEH(-2))	-0.052	0.016	-3.281	0.031
CointEq (-1)	-0.230	0.023	-8.117	0.001
Cointeq = PD - (-0.0247*GDP + 0.1668*POP + 0.2134*FP + 0.3292*EC -0.1513*PVEH + 1.0457)				
Long Run Coefficients				
Variable	**Coefficient**	**Std. Error**	**t-Statistic**	**Prob.**
HI	-0.025	0.024	-1.035	0.359
POP	0.167	0.566	0.295	0.783
TC	0.213	0.145	1.468	0.216
EC	0.329	0.216	1.525	0.202
PVEH	-0.151	0.090	-1.679	0.169
C	1.046	3.160	0.331	0.757
ARDL Bound Test- F-statistic	3.764	K=5		

Table 5.23: Utility and Private Transport (Population Density)

Dependent Variable: PD, Selected Model: ARDL (4, 4, 3, 4, 4, 4)

Table 5.19 presents the effect of private transport and electricity consumption on the sprawl. The results, based on the bound testing, explicate that the F-statistic value of the Wald test lies between the upper and lower bound values of Pesaran *et al.* (2001) at a 10% level of significance; therefore, the decision regarding the long-term association between sprawl and private vehicles, and electricity consumption is inconclusive. In addition, the results show that private vehicles and electricity consumption have a significant effect on sprawl, as the coefficients of both variables are statistically significant. Moreover, the results indicate that private vehicles and electricity consumption have no effect on the sprawl in the long-run. Here, it can be concluded that private transport and utility indicators are the contributing factors, along with the monocentric model variables, that have a considerable influence on sprawl in the short-run in Karachi.

Cointegrating Form				
Variable	Coefficient	Std. Error	t-Statistic	Prob.
D(SP(-1))	-0.933	0.142	-6.566	0.000
D(SP(-2))	-0.530	0.145	-3.658	0.006
D(HI)	-0.363	0.167	-2.169	0.062
D(HI(-1))	-0.326	0.098	-3.315	0.011
D(HI(-2))	-0.128	0.090	-1.427	0.191
D(HI(-3))	-0.298	0.089	-3.337	0.010
D(POP)	-10.342	3.980	-2.599	0.032
D(POP(-1))	-44.568	7.577	-5.882	0.000
D(POP(-2))	-38.406	7.123	-5.392	0.001
D(POP(-3))	-23.018	4.860	-4.737	0.002
D(TC)	-0.791	0.192	-4.118	0.003
D(TC(-1))	2.127	0.433	4.916	0.001
D(TC(-2))	1.362	0.417	3.268	0.011
D(TC(-3))	1.870	0.306	6.109	0.000
D(EC)	-0.092	0.415	-0.221	0.831
D(EC(-1))	5.613	1.101	5.097	0.001
D(EC(-2))	5.633	1.449	3.886	0.005
D(EC(-3))	5.543	0.926	5.986	0.000
D(PVEH)	3.314	0.548	6.051	0.000
CointEq(-1)	-0.183	0.031	-5.863	0.000
Long Run Coefficients				
Variable	Coefficient	Std. Error	t-Statistic	Prob.
GDP	-2.706	16.621	-0.163	0.875
POP	90.643	516.403	0.176	0.865
TC	-19.102	106.409	-0.180	0.862
EC	-33.366	187.777	-0.178	0.863
PVEH	18.973	110.236	0.172	0.868
C	-486.241	2781.070	-0.175	0.866
ARDL Bound Test- F-statistic	3.003	K=5		

Table 5.24: Utility and Transport (Sprawl)

Dependent Variable: SP, Selected Model: ARDL (3, 4, 4, 4, 4, 0)

5.11. Discussion & Interpretation of Research Results

In this section, the interpretation of the results collected from the household survey has been carried out. Since the general purpose of conducting a research study was to answer the questions in a systematic manner, the explanation of results must focus first on the questions which were asked, or anecdotal, in the problem statement (Abbasi, 2015). The results are explained in detail below:

5.11.1. Demography of Survey

Figure 5.7 shows the age groups of the participants involved in this study. As the chart shows, the majority of the respondents belonged to the first age group, ranging from 18 to 25. The number of participants who belonged to the second age group, i.e. (26-35), was also higher, as 30 percent of respondents belonged to this group. 20% of the respondents were aged between 36–45, whereas 9% belonged to the age group of 45–55, and the rest of them were more than 55 years old.

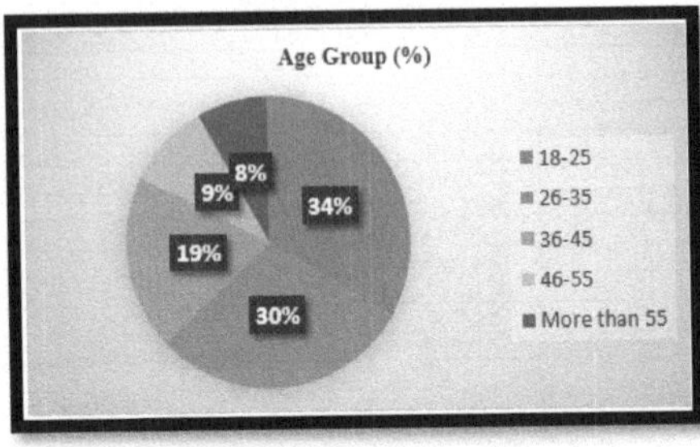

Figure 5.7: Respondent's Demography (a)
Source: Author's Household Survey (2019-20)

Figure 5.8 shows the family size of the respondents. The graph shows that the majority of the participants have around 4-7 family members. The second most significant ratio of participants belonged to the families of 8-10 members. Around 10% of the participants belonged to big families with more than 10 family members, whereas 15% of the respondents were in the first group in which the family had 1–3 members.

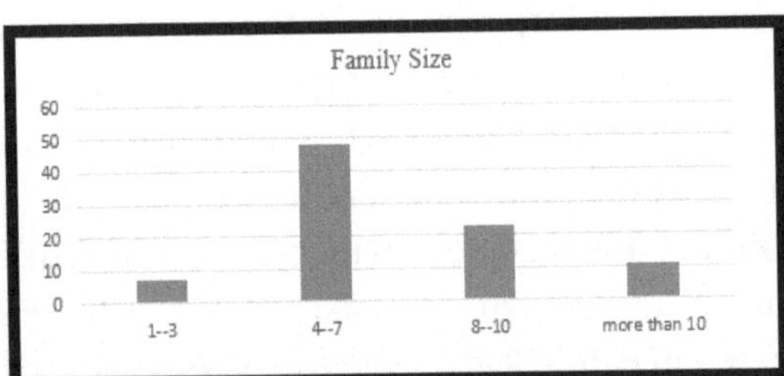

Figure 5.8: Respondent's Demography (b)
Source: Author's Household Survey (2019-20)

Figure 5.9 shows the education level of the participants involved in this study. As shown in the graph, the majority (27%)

of the participants were those who graduated from the university. 17% of the respondents had higher secondary and postgraduate degrees, respectively. The same number of respondents (16%) had secondary education and education below 10th, whereas only a small ratio (7%) of the respondents did not have schooling.

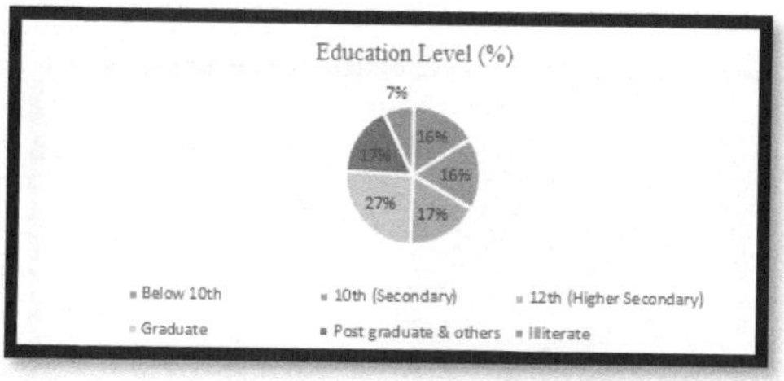

Figure 5.9: Respondent's Demography (c)
Source: Author's Household Survey

Figure 5.10 mentions the number of years the participants have been living in Karachi. According to the statistics, the majority of participants, i.e. 26%, were those who were born in Karachi and have been living there since then. 14% of the participants have been living there for less than ten years, and 25% of the respondents have been living there for 10-20 years. 19% of the respondents have been living for 20-30 years in this city, whereas 16% of the respondents have been living there for the past 30 years.

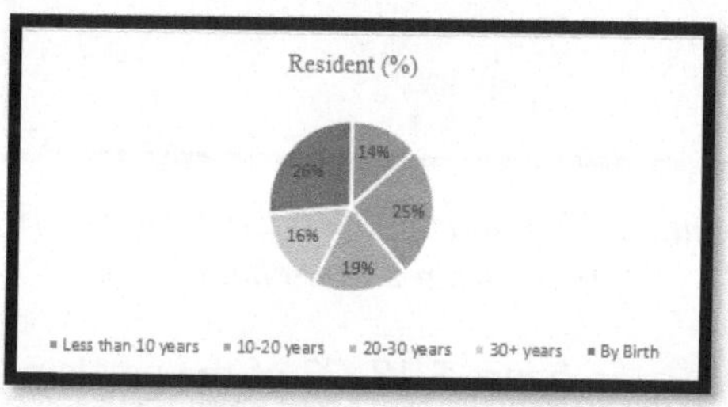

Figure 5.10: Respondent's Demography (d)
Source: Author's Household Survey

5.11.2. Municipal Services Overview

When asked about municipal performance, the majority of the respondents showed satisfaction, whereas 41% were from the "dissatisfied" category and 34% were from the "very much dissatisfied" category. A very small percentage of the responses showed satisfaction regarding this aspect, whereas only 11% were neutral, as shown in Figure 5.11.

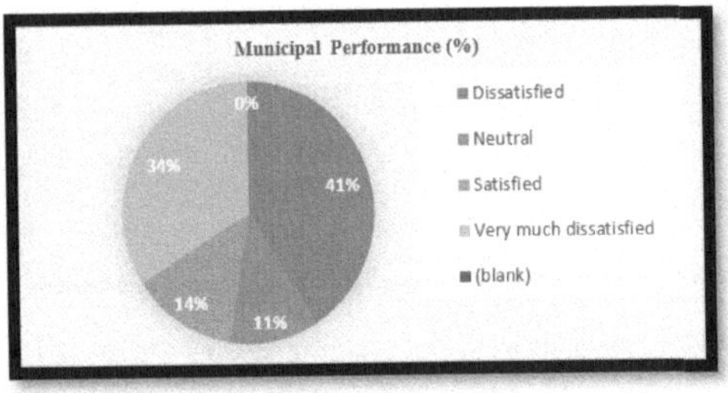

Figure 5.11: Municipal Services Overview (a)
Source: Author's Household Survey

According to the statistics, 35% of the participants said that the level of development in the area has improved, 24.8% said that it declined, whereas 39.6% said that it remained unchanged over the five years, as indicated in figure 5.12.

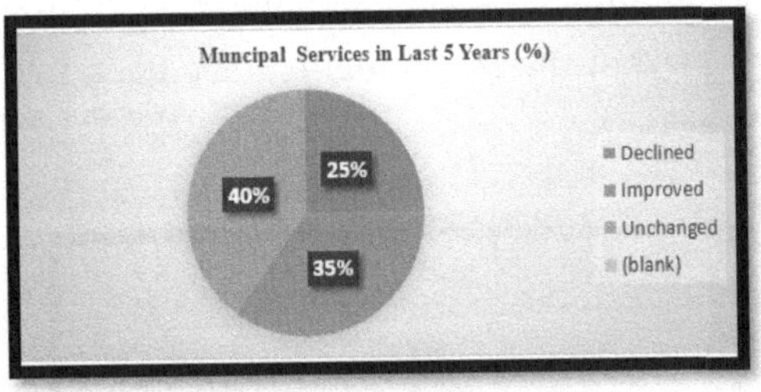

Figure 5.12: Municipal Services Overview (b)
Source: Author's Household Survey

As shown in figure 5.13, 73 of the participants involved in the study said that the major problem faced by people in Karachi is water and sanitation, 31 of the participants said that it is transportation, 12 participants felt that solid waste is the biggest problem, 11 participants said that affording utilities is the major problem. 9 participants reported law and order as a problem, 3 respondents said that owning the house is the biggest problem and the remaining 3 of the respondents chose the "other" category.

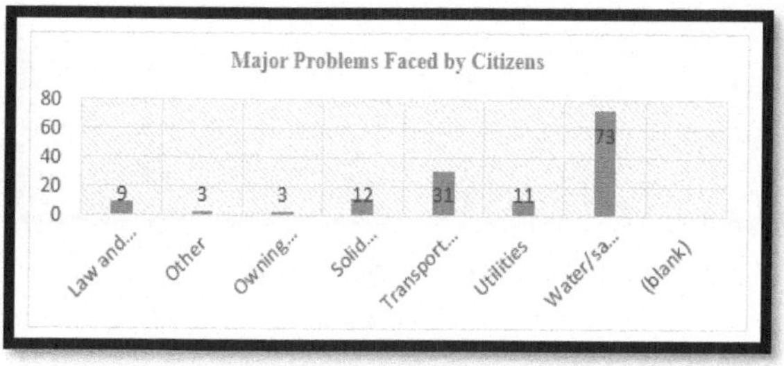

Figure 5.13: Municipal Services Overview (c)
Author's Household Survey

5.11.3. Water & Sanitation

When asked about the question related to water consumption and quality, around 90% of the respondents said that they drink tap water for drinking purposes. In the question regarding the availability of tap water, as presented in figure 5.14 (a), the majority (71.6%) of the respondents said that they do have the supply, but 13.8% said that they don't have it, whereas 6.9% said that it does not operate and 7.6% said that it is disconnected. About the regular supply of water, as given in figure 5.14 (b), 38% of participants said that they get the supply every day, 34.5% said that they get it every week, a small ratio of them said that they get it few days a month, 14.8% of them said that very rarely they get the supply, whereas 7% said that they get no supply. It was also seen that 7.7% said that they don't get water or that there is no supply of tap water in their area.

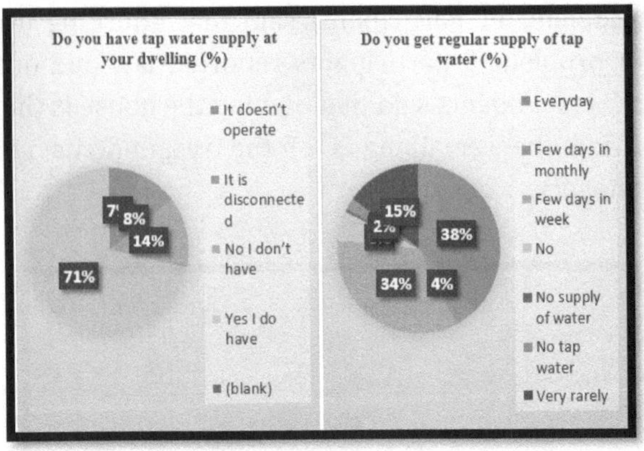

Figure 5.14: Water & Sanitation (a) and (b)
Source: Author's Household Survey

Questions were also asked about the quality of the water. Figure 5.15 indicates that 29.6% and 2.1% of the respondents were satisfied and very much satisfied, respectively, whereas 13.4% and 31.7% of the participants were dissatisfied or very dissatisfied about the quality of water. In addition, around 23% of the respondents were from the neutral category.

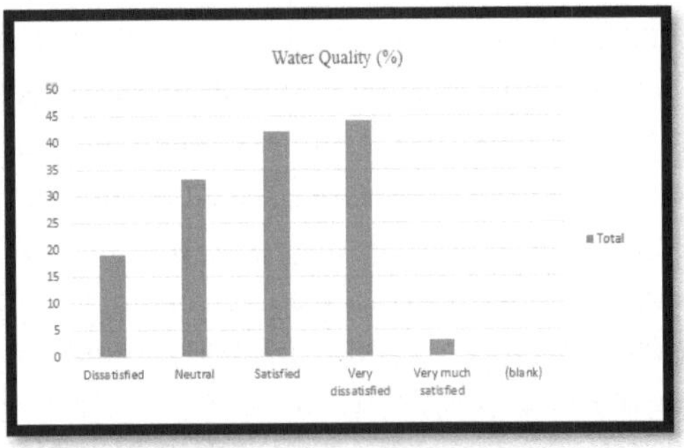

Figure 5.15: Water Quality
Source: Author's Household Survey

It was also explored during the study how many tankers are used for the supply of water. Figure 5.16 shows that the majority (66.7%) of the participants said that they don't use tankers, whereas around 32% said that they do.

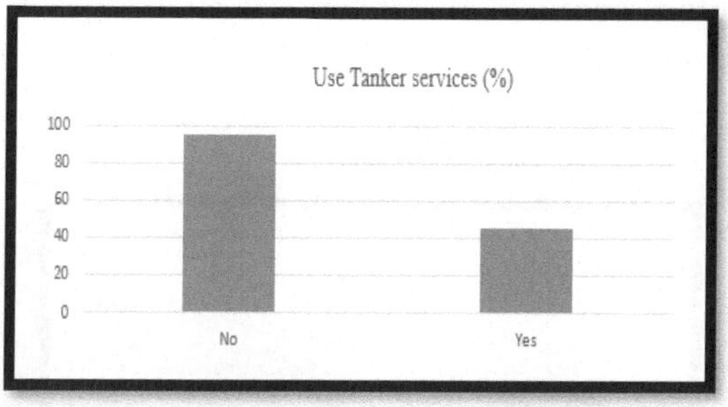

Figure 5.16: Tankers Service Usage (a)
Source: Author's Household Survey

They were also asked how many tankers they use in a month. As exhibited in figure 5.17, the majority of the answers ranged from 1 to 3, as 30.5%, 38.7%, and 19.5% of the total participants use 1 to 3 tankers in a month for the supply of water, whereas the rest said that they use more than 3 tankers in a month for the provision of water.

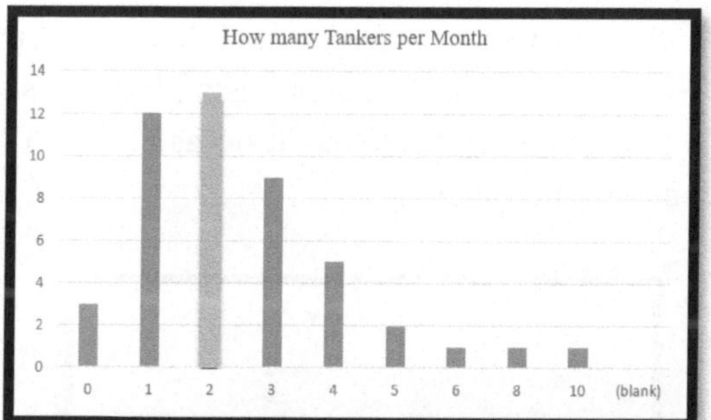

Figure 5.17: Tankers Service Usage (b)
Source: Author's Household Survey

When asked about the price of the tankers, as indicated in figure 5.18a, some of the participants (39.2%) feel that they don't charge high prices, but the majority (51.2%) of them said that they operate like a mafia, whereas a small ratio (8.0%) said that they charge reasonably.

Figure 5.18b indicates that 33.1% of the respondents reported that because of tankers, their budget is affected, whereas around 17% said that they have to manage it as it is a necessity.

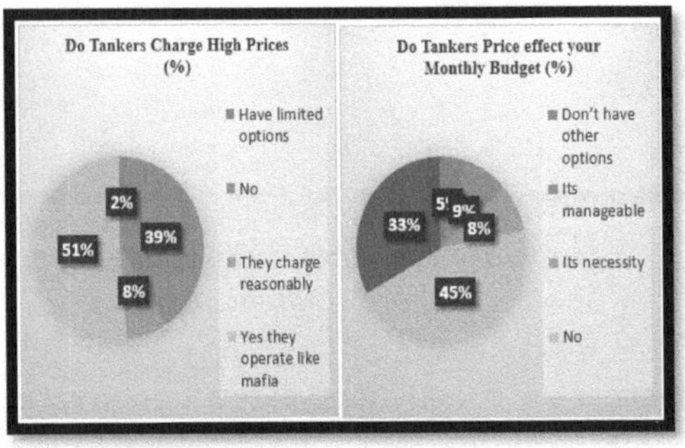

Figure 5.18: Tanker Prices (a) & (b)
Source: Author's Household Survey

5.11.4. Transportation

Questions were also asked to determine how many participants use public transport. As indicated in figure 5.19, other than 23%, almost all the participants reported that they use public transport. Some use it on a regular basis (18.6%), some use it most of the time (18.9%), some use it occasionally (17.6%), and some use it always (16.9%).

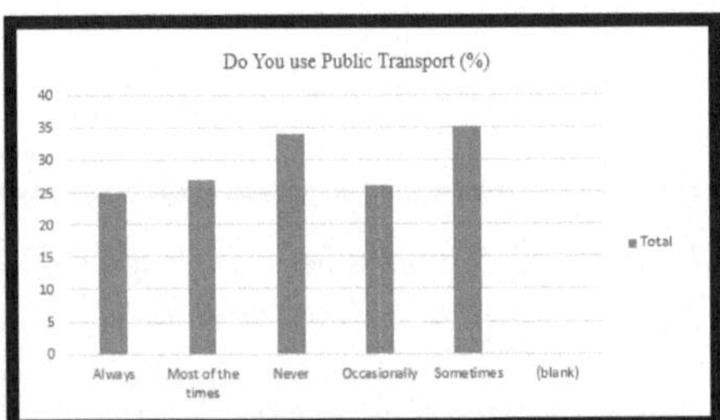

Figure 5.19: Transportation (a)
Source: Author's Household Survey

When asked about their experience of travelling on public transport, the majority of people, as revealed in figure

5.20, showed dissatisfaction with the bus service, 28.4% rated this experience as "very much dissatisfied," and 33.8% rated it as "dissatisfied." Only a small number of respondents, 8.1%, said that they were satisfied with the experience, 1.4% were very much satisfied, while 12.2% of participants remained neutral in this category.

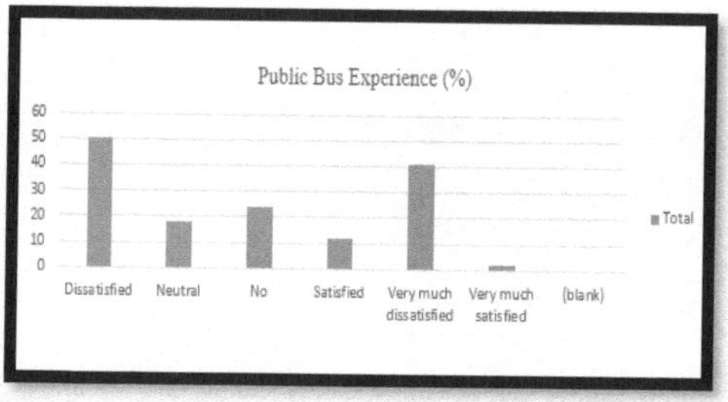

Figure 5.20: Transportation (b)
Source: Author's Household Survey

The majority of the participants (25%) reported that the condition of the buses is very bad; 19.4% rated the condition of the buses as outdated and said that they have gone worse (45.8%) than before, as shown in figure 5.21.

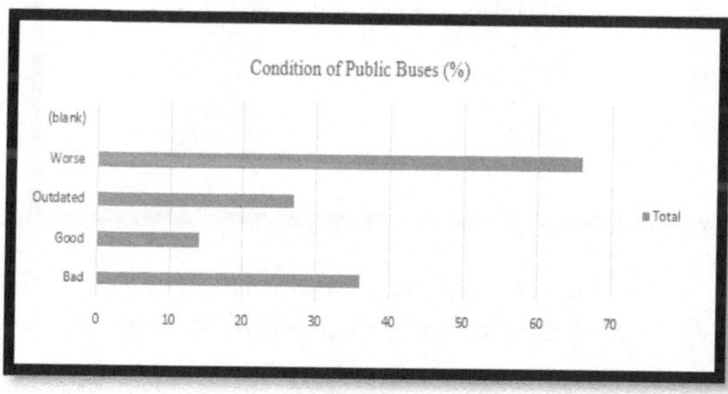

Figure 5.21: Transportation (c)
Source: Author's Household Survey

The participants were also asked, as exhibited in figure 5.22, whether they reach their destination on time through public transport. 37.2% said that they never reach on time,

26.2% said that they sometimes reach on time, 7.6% said that they occasionally reach on time, 9.7% said that they reach on time most of the time, whereas only a small number of respondents (2.1%) said that they always reach on time.

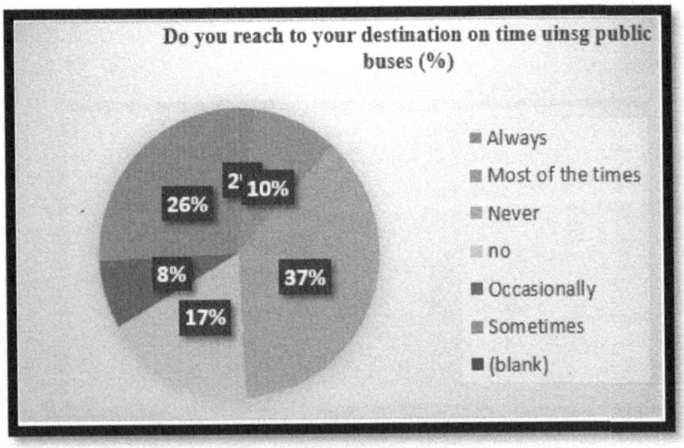

Figure 5.22: Transportation (d)
Source: Author's Household Survey

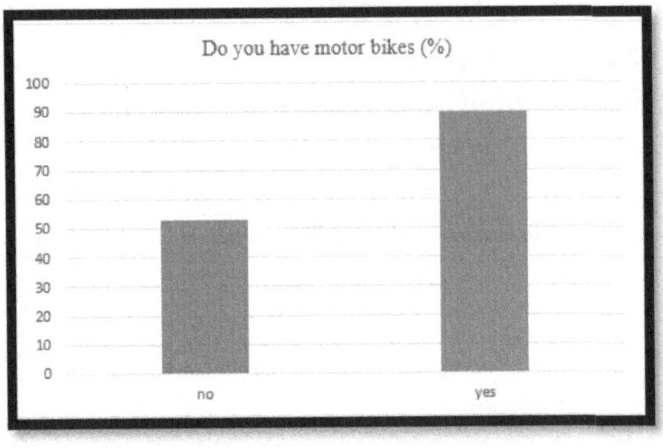

Figure 5.23: Transportation (e)
Source: Author's Household Survey

Participants were also asked whether they own motorbikes and are stuck in traffic jams. In response to that, around 62.5% said that they do own motorbikes, whereas the rest of them (37.5%) said that they don't have bikes, as evident in figure 5.24.

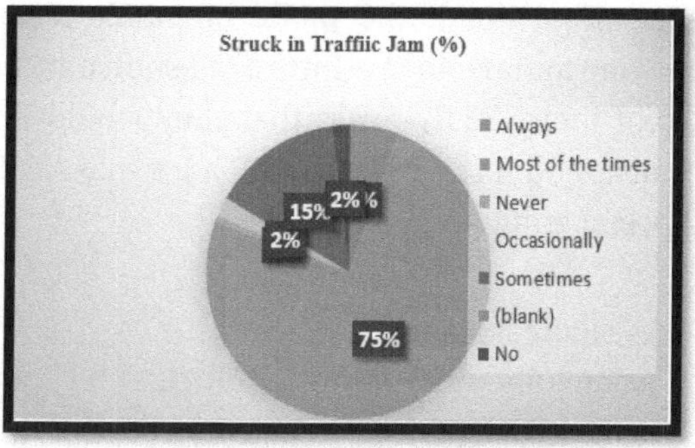

Figure 5.24: Transportation (f)
Source: Author's Household Survey

As far as traffic jams are concerned, the majority (77.3%) of the participants, as evident from figure 5.24, mentioned that they were stuck in traffic most of the time; a very small percentage (7%) of the participants said that they never got caught in traffic; other than them, almost all the participants said that they had been stuck in traffic at some point.

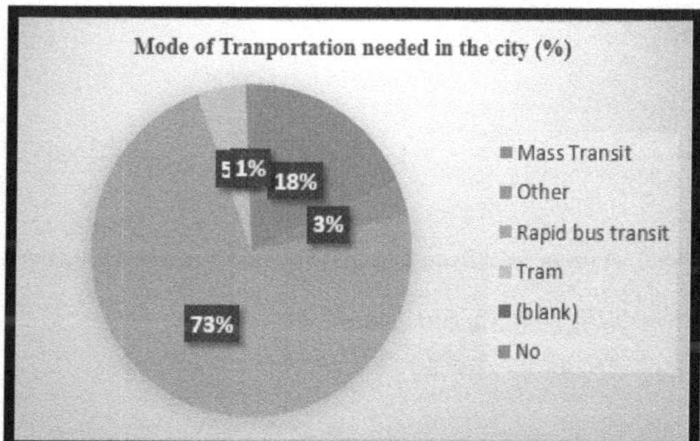

Figure 5.25: Transportation (g)
Source: Author's Household Survey

When asked about the mode of public transportation they would want to have in the future, as shown in figure 5.25, the majority of them, 73.8%, said that they would like to have rapid bus transit and mass transit (17.9%), while 4.8% said that they would prefer tram.

5.11.5. Solid Waste Management

When asked about the KMC/DMC/CANNT performance regarding waste disposal, the majority of the participants (around 51.7%), as mentioned in figure 5.26, said that they live in a clean neighborhood as more than 50% of the total participants rated their neighborhood clean, whereas 48.3% responded in an opposite category as 30.8% said that it is very rare that the area gets cleaned; otherwise, it is always dirty as reported by 33.3% of the respondents.

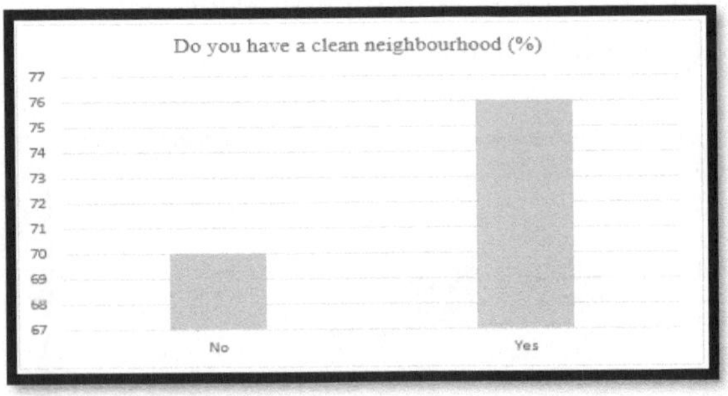

Figure 5.26: Clean Neighbourhood
Source: Author's Household Survey

About 59.2% of the people involved in this survey said that the KMC or DMC municipal service does not fulfill its responsibilities, 13.6% said it is incompetent, whereas 27.2% feel that it fulfils its responsibilities, as reflected in figure 5.27.

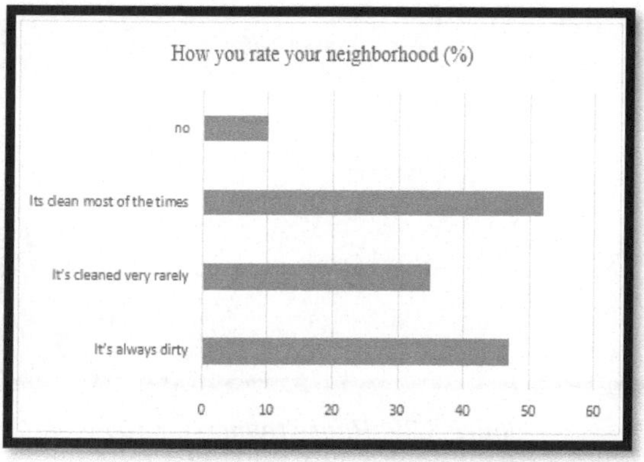

Figure 5.27: Rating of Neighbourhood
Source: Author's Household Survey

When asked about disposal removal, as shown in figure 5.28, the majority of people (63%) mentioned that municipal authorities don't remove garbage from their neighborhoods.

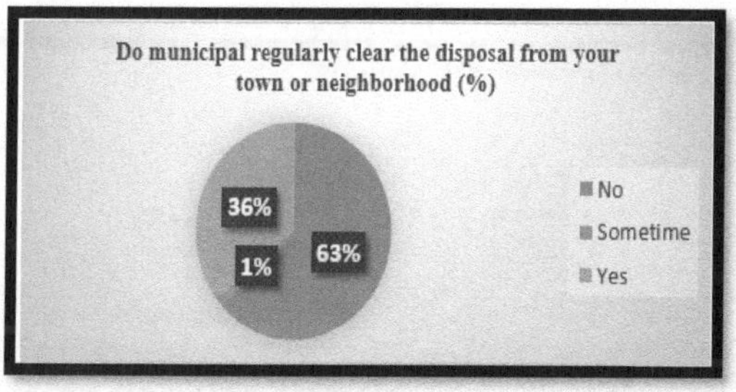

Figure 5.28: Disposal Removal
Source: Author's Household Survey

When asked about house ownership, as reflected in figure 5.29, 62% of the total participants affirmed ownership, whereas 38% said that they live in a rented house.

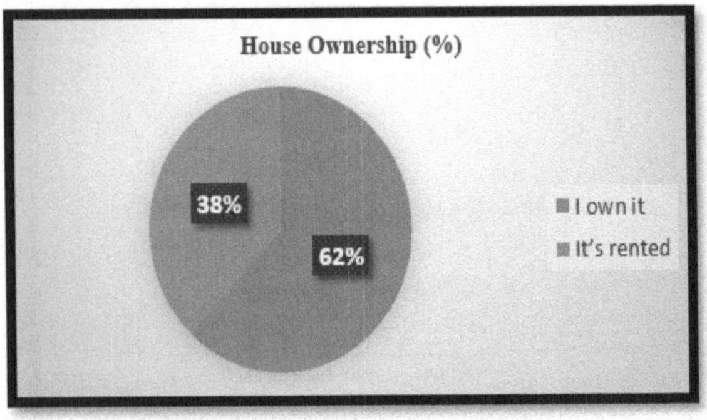

Figure 5.29: House Ownership (a)
Source: Author's Household Survey

According to figure 5.30, the majority of the participants mentioned the affordability issue as the reason for not owning a house, 46.2% said that they live in a rented place and cannot afford the house, 41.5% said that the land is expensive, and 12.3% said that the houses are expensive.

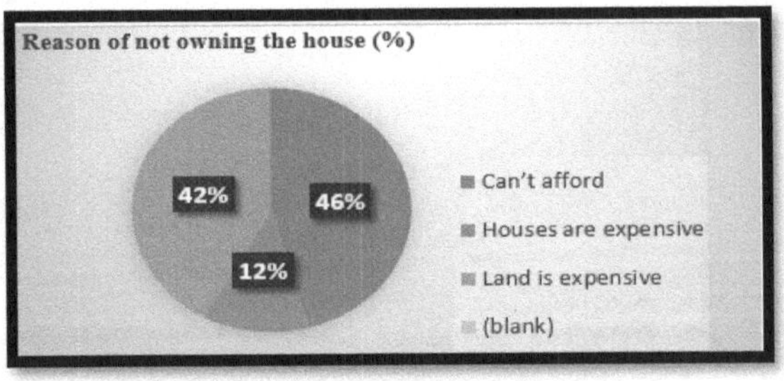

Figure 5.30: House Ownership (b)
Source: Author's Household Survey

Figure 5.31 mentions that the majority (62.5%) of people live in a joint family, whereas 37.5% have adopted a nuclear family system.

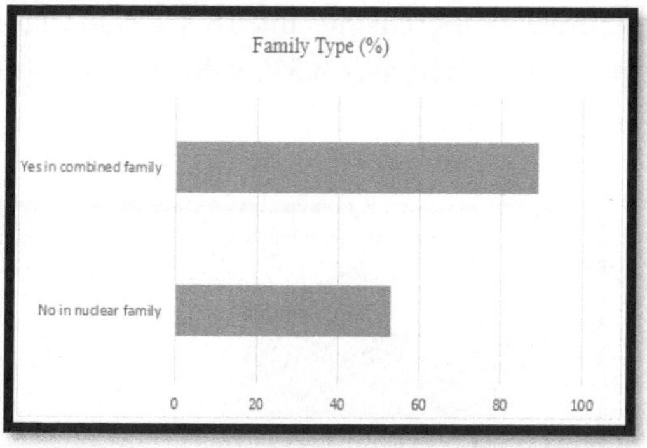

Figure 5.31: Family Classification
Source: Author's Household Survey

About 72.4% of the participants, as mentioned in figure 5.32, replied they would very much be interested in a low-cost housing scheme system, and 12.4% said they would love these schemes as a necessity, whereas 15.2% said they were not interested.

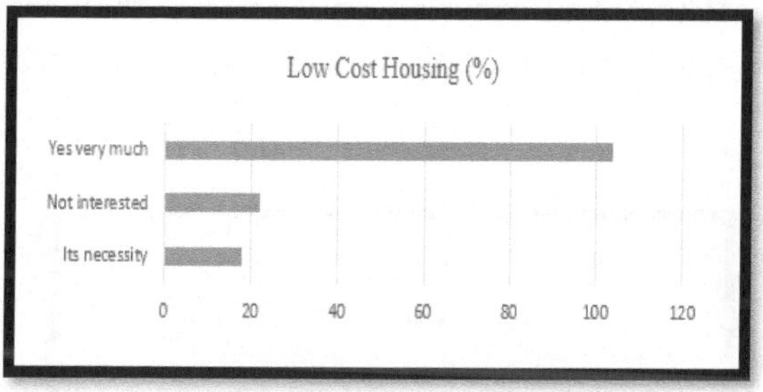

Figure 5.32: Demand for Low Cost Housing
Source: Author's Household Survey

5.11.6. Law and Order

When asked about the law and order situation, 66.4% of the participants, as shown in figure 5.33, said that it has improved, 24.7% said that it is better than before, while 8.2% said that it got worse. According to the majority of the participants (49.6%), one of the causes of crime is poverty; 28.4% think that it is the failure of law enforcement agencies that crime rates are increasing, and 18.4% said that it occurs due to economic issues, whereas 3.5% said that it happens because of a lot of other issues.

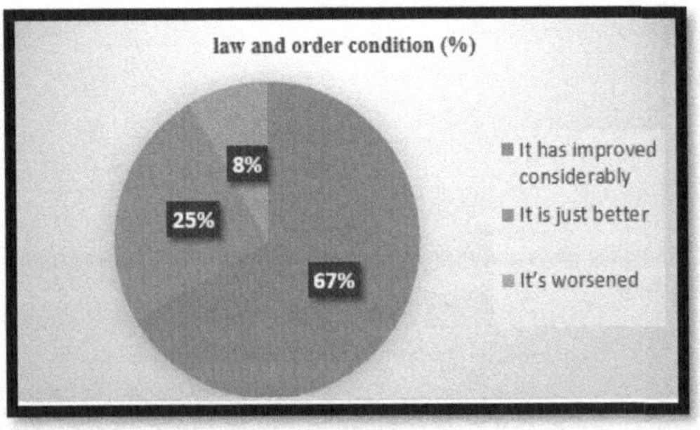

Figure 5.33: Law & Order Situation
Source: Author's Household Survey

When participants were asked, as given in figure 5.34, if any of them had experienced street crimes, only 33.1% of the participants said that they had never experienced street crimes, 7% said that they had experienced it once in their whole lives, and the rest said that they had been a victim of street crimes more than once.

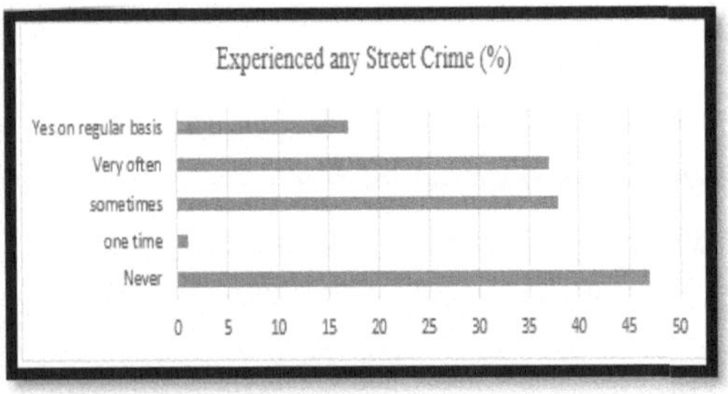

Figure 5.34: Incidence of Street Crimes
Source: Author's Household Survey

Regarding the supply of electricity, as shown in figure 5.35, about 8.7% of participants said that they have a regular supply of electricity, 5.5% complained that they don't get a regular supply of electricity, whereas 7.5% reported that they don't have a connection. Of those who have a regular supply, 36.5% shared that there has been zero load shedding in their areas, 25.5% said that they experience 2-5 hours of load shedding, while 37.9 reported that they have to bear more than 5 hours of load shedding.

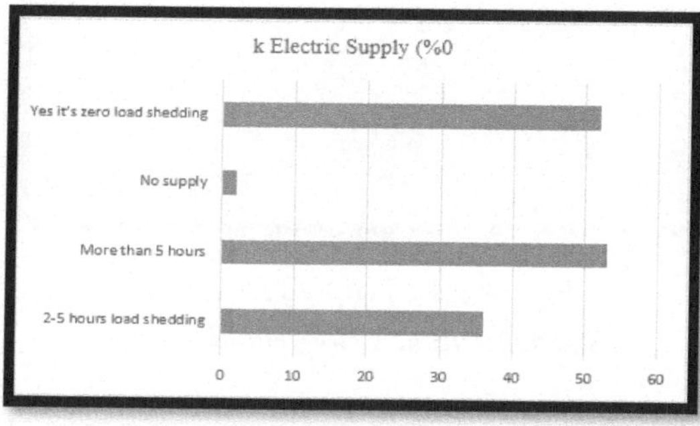

Figure 5.35: K-Electric Performance
Source: Author's Household Survey

The survey reveals in figure 5.36 that more than 80% of the respondents have a gas connection, whereas the remaining don't have such a facility.

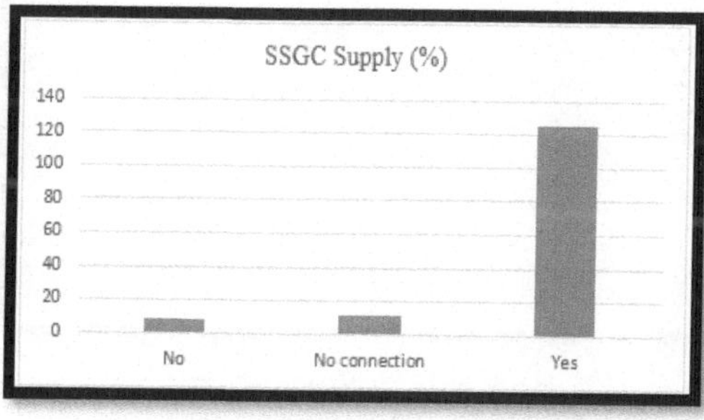

Figure 5.36: Gas Utility
Source: Author's Household Survey

5.11.7. Satisfaction with Local Government Institutions

According to the statistics, 78.1% of participants, as mentioned in figure 5.37, reported that they were not satisfied with the local government institutions in Karachi, while 21.9% showed satisfaction in this aspect.

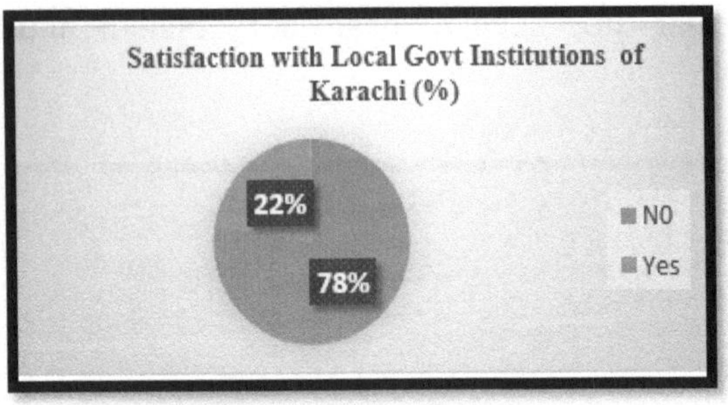

Figure 5.37: People's Feedback
Source: Author's Household Survey

43.4% of the survey participants, as mentioned in figure 5.38, rated the experience of living in Karachi as "nice and livable", 24.8% said that it is getting messier and more disorganized, 11% think it is shabby and dirty, whereas 20% said that the conditions are getting worse and making it difficult to live in the city.

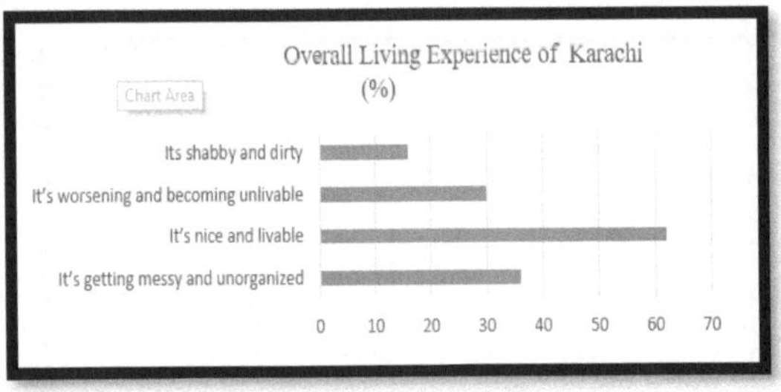

Figure 5.38: Karachi's Living Experience
Source: Author's Household Survey

The survey at the end had open-ended questions for any feedback, which was also well received by the respondents. Those who responded emphasized overhauling the system, empowering the government at the local level, and demanding sound policy-making to improve the overall livability of the city.

Chapter 6| Discussion

The Karachi metropolitan area has witnessed a massive influx and natural population growth from 1981 to 2017, as stated in the official records, as well as the settlement of the people on the urban fringe. The conversion of rural lands for development purposes at a phenomenal speed indicates sprawling trends in the city. The study highlights the causes, effects, and consequences of the prevailing urban structure of the city. The study confirms a significant increase in urban areas due to continuous growth and settlement of the people.

The phenomenal increase in Karachi's population from 1981 to 1998, with official figures of 9.3 million, according to the 2017 census, reflects accumulated figures of 1.49 million into metropolitan limits, indicating a massive influx of people. The huge inflow of people due to multiple reasons necessitates the new development in the form of residential areas, commercial areas, service centers and other infrastructure facilities. The need to cater to a large population results in the replacement of residential facilities with commercial facilities in the core of the city, thereby continuously creating a demand for new houses, satellite towns, gated communities, unregulated houses, and slums. Therefore, sprawl is not confined in a linear direction, as shown in the case of Karachi; it is not localized specifically but is rapidly growing in all directions.

Urban sprawl identification and monitoring revealed that the built-up area rapidly increased in Karachi. Herold (2006) lists further arguments that prove the fitness of remote sensing data in analyzing land cover changes and show that the data are usually historically and spatially consistent. The spatial distribution of built-up areas demonstrated fast growth, disorientation, low efficiency, and scattered spatial distribution characteristics, which clearly suggests a typical tendency toward urban sprawl. The manifold increase in built-up confirms the presence of uncontrolled sprawl, resulting in a considerable decrease in bare and cultivable lands. This phenomenon of land transformation has been labeled as urban sprawl (Bhatta, 2010; Sudhira, 2008; Arbury, 2005). This will immensely compromise the food security and sustainability of the whole process.

A newly developed built-up area expanded in multi-direction from the inner core. Outward expansion of built-up areas from the inner city was observed during the study period. Several satellite towns were developed with the passage of time. Most of the suburbs and urban fringes underwent massive urbanization. The districts of south, east, center, and Korangi have already attained developed status, but there are visible signs of infill development and densification in these areas.

However, the abundance of cheap land in the western and Malir districts is paving the way for low-density, scattered and horizontal development. Low-density land consumption, on the one hand, increases per capita urban land and, on the other hand, overburdens the limited resources, as observed in this study and confirmed by Black (1996) and Downs (1999). This study observed faster land consumption at the urban fringe, which confirmed another essential feature of urban sprawl (Freeman, 2001; Montaigne, 2000).

Moreover, there is an important transformation from vegetation cover to fragmented urban areas located in the periphery of Karachi. In the case of Karachi, the pattern of conversion from agriculture and bare land to built-up land has immensely been observed due to the rapid growth of population and sprawling activities. There are numerous factors driving this growth, and as evident from Karachi, expensive land within the core limits of the city has played a major role in urban sprawl development. As found in this study, this outward development encroaches on agricultural lands and consumes green spaces, leading towards food insecurity and ecological crises. The findings suggest that peripheral growth at the urban fringe will negatively affect the whole ecosystem (Guiliano & Narayan, 2003; Garcia & Riera, 2003; Anderson et al., 1996; Kenworthy, Newman & Vintila, 1995).

This dissertation validated the use of satellite imageries along with the combined use of geographic information systems, remote sensing techniques, landscape metrics, and urban change modelling as an effective method to monitor, identify and assess the urban sprawl in the case of Karachi for the period under observation (Frenkel & Ashkenazi, 2008; Galster et al., 2001; Barnes et al., 2010; Siedentop & Fina, 2008). These tools employed in the study provided essential information regarding sprawling in Karachi, its features, patterns, urban planning and its overall impact on the urban ecosystem.

The study also evaluated and explored the determinants, causal relationships and consequences of sprawling in Karachi. Generally, urban growth is an irreversible process. Therefore, it has undesirable effects on the city's structure, causing a disordered pattern different from the original one. It is important to explore the driving forces to understand the dynamic growth process. Migration, investment, terrorism, political conflict, street crimes and city safety are important factors that emerged from the study.

Moreover, the immigrants are not able to afford houses within the inner region of the city, which forces them to settle down in suburban (periphery) areas. Compared to the center of the city, the suburban areas have limited public amenities. Also, the provision of services and infrastructure has not been able to keep pace, resulting in degraded urban life. The findings of the study established that urban growth promotes social segregation, fragmentation and ghettoization and adversely impacts the public health of the citizens (Gillham, 2002; Hillman, 1996; Sturm & Cohen, 2004; Song & al., 2004; Duany et al., 2001).

Moreover, the study demonstrated that the organic pattern around the city center is surrounded by a disordered pattern. In the late 1960s, this type of disorder pattern occurred and was represented as a connecting area between organic and geometric patterns. The geometric pattern resembles the suburbanization of the city. Due to the expansion of the city boundary, areas that were previously villages or areas near the boundary of the city have constituted the current structure of sprawled areas in the city. Besides the suburban pattern, village patterns near the vicinity of urban areas have been included in the sprawled area. Consequently, some arrangements have also been observed that cannot be classified by the aforementioned patterns. Consequently, energy inefficiency, disparity in wealth, loss of farmland, poor quality of urban life, and inflated infrastructure are the other significant consequences of urban sprawl.

This study observed considerable changes in the urban structure of Karachi from 1947 to 2019. Recently, dramatic growth has been earmarked on the urban fringe in the likes of Bahria Town, DHA City and other satellite towns. The results of this study indicate that the causes of the rapid and uncontrolled urban growth from 1960 are multiple and mutually exclusive. The factors associated with urban sprawl related to Karachi have been exposed to a considerable extent, providing quality input and useful information to policymakers in both the public and private sectors for making informed decisions.

The study established that the rapid, exponential and uncontrolled sprawling growth of Karachi has led towards land fragmentation, social fragmentation and prone to environmental shocks. This urban degeneration is caused due to weak enforcement and lack of applicable laws but can be tackled through comprehensive urban planning and effective monitoring systems (McLaren, Coleman, & Mayunga, 2005). This is further confused by complicated land ownership rights creating room for land profiteers, encroachers, mafias and black marketers, leading towards informal settlements, slums and expansion of the city at the urban fringe, as observed in the case of Karachi.

Additionally, this study assessed the causative factors as guidance to prevent urban ecosystem loss and other socio-ecological consequences derived from spontaneous urban growth. It was assumed that the variables associated with the Monocentric City Model would provide relatively solid explanations for spatial extension. The results led to the inference that the model can be applied to explain spatial development in big urban centers like Karachi. The monocentric city model was further extended based on socio-economic, utility, transportation, and local fiscalization factors to assess the impact of multiple factors on the urban development of Karachi.

The analysis of the study was built on a set of independent variables associated with the monocentric city model but extended it further with variables that capture the changes in the socio-economic structures. Generally, the same set of socio-economic variables yields good results in explaining the three variables: built-up area (PBA), sprawl and population density (PD). An urban built-up area is an important indicator of urbanization and an intuitive reflection of a city's expansion and development. The urban built-up area is extracted based on the impervious surface.

Impervious surfaces are promoted as useful environmental indicators (Arnold & Gibbons, 1996; Barnes, Morgan, & Roberge, 2001) and one environmental condition that impervious surfaces clearly indicate is urbanization. Regardless of how it is defined and evaluated, sprawl is a response to often bewildering sets of economic, social, political, and physical forces (Pendall, 1999). Sprawl increases land consumption and is visible as a transformation of land use (Kline, 2000; Herold, 2006; Loibl & Toetzer, 2003; Burchfield, 2006). Population density is another measure to confirm the compact and scattered growth of any urban area. The presence of the low-density population in urban centers is labelled as an important feature of sprawling. Often, sprawl refers to low-density settlements (Ewing, 1997; Lopez & Hynes, 2006; McGrath, 2005; Burchfield, 2006; Paulsen, 2012).

It is suggested that sprawl be treated as a process, not as a pattern, while quantifying the dynamic process of urban growth. The study confirms land consumption at a faster rate as the population shifts from urban areas to suburban fringes (Porter & England, 2000; Kahn, 2000; Dwyer & Childs, 2004). The causative factors involved in this study are also included in the studies by Brueckner and Fansler (1983) and McGrath (2005) and are derived from the theoretical model that is able to provide basic explanations of urban expansion in the Monocentric City Model (Kraus, 2006), which has long been the standard economic approach to studying the development of urban areas (Anas et al., 1998; Burchfield, 2006).

The robustness of the Muth-Mills Monocentric City Model is confirmed, among others, by McGrath (2005), Wassmer (2008), Spivey (2008), and more recently by Paulsen (2012, 2013). The validity of the model indicates that it captures the most important economic forces for urban growth and thus, as McMillen (2006) argues, in its simple form, stays informative and useful. Beginning with the contribution of Brueckner and Fansler (1983) and continuing among others with McGrath (2005), Wassmer (2008), Spivey (2008), Paulsen (2012, 2013), Polyzos et al. (2013), a number of papers have extended and modified the Monocentric City Model.

Similar to the Monocentric City Model, the results of the predictor variable (population) are consistent and indicate that increased population numbers have contributed immensely to the sprawling of Karachi in all directions. The simple reasoning is that accommodating more people leads towards the expansion of urban areas by creating pressure for more construction activities. The growth of the urban population results from the natural increase in urban population and migration to urban settlements. The various migratory factors, including the 1st Afghan War, rural-urban migration and better economic opportunities, have played a major role in the settlement of people in Karachi, causing rapid urban development. However, Minallah et al. (2016) and Choon et al. (2011) in their studies demonstrated that population and economic conditions represented by population and socio-economic statistical data may not directly influence urban expansion; instead, other factors in the form of topography, hydrology, policies, land availability and satellite cities surrounding the metropolis are important factors but are difficult to quantify. In the case of Karachi, its accessibility, connectivity and infrastructure are prime factors for the settlement of people from upcountry, as demonstrated in this study. The relationship of population is consistent with all explanatory variables.

The increase in income levels (Per capita) raises the purchasing power parity of households (variable of the Monocentric City Model), thereby allowing residents to purchase larger houses. These residents relocate to inexpensive, spacious, suburban and ex-urban areas generally located at the outskirts of metropolitan areas (Carruthers & Ulfarsson, 2002). It is evident from Karachi that better economic prospects, speculative investments, desire for second homes away from the city center, and low interests, among other reasons, have significantly contributed to development and construction at the urban fringe. It is further confirmed by Weilenmann and Schulz (2014) that high income causes sprawl and that big cities are surrounded by a certain type of agglomeration municipalities that swallow commuters and have developed low-density, mostly single-family dwellings. Expansion of the economic base (higher per capita income and an increase in the number of working persons) creates demand for new housing or more housing space for individuals (Boyce, 1963; Giuliano, 1989; Bhatta, 2009). It is observed in the case of Karachi that rapid development of housing and other urban infrastructure often produces a variety of discontinuous unrelated developments. Rapid development has significantly contributed to the unplanned and haphazard growth of Karachi. The increase in per capita income is positively correlated with the extent of built-up area and negatively correlated with population density.

The Monocentric City Model assumes that higher commuting costs prevent spatial extension. The operationalization of commuting costs seems to be a consistent debate in the literature, and researchers have found it difficult (McGrath, 2005; Wassmer, 2008; Spivey, 2008). However, in the case of Karachi, fuel cost was used as a proxy variable for commuting costs. In the case of Karachi, transportation routes have opened the accessibility of the city to the countryside and are responsible for the linear type of development. The study observed an inverse relationship of transportation cost with the variables of sprawl and built-up, whereas it is positively correlated with population density, consistent with the extant literature.

The local fiscalization variables denote great importance for sprawl choices. The larger presence of local governments in an urban area would generate competition among them for new development, fueling land use decisions at the fringe of an urban area with a greater focus on the fiscal bottom line supplemented by property taxation or sales/gross receipts in the urbanized area's state (Wassmer, 2008). The study demonstrated that KMC revenues are positively correlated with sprawl, built-up and population as more revenue targets provided compelling ground for the expansion of metropolitan city. However, the results of taxation on vacant plots have some inconsistencies over the short and long term for unknown reasons.

The study included economic indicators as an extension of the Monocentric City Model to check the causal relationship between measures of urban sprawl in Karachi. The city of Karachi, as shown in the literature, is the prime economic hub of Pakistan, providing enormous growth and employment opportunities. Considering the Pakistan context, results show a strong face validity. On the one hand, Pakistan's economy is undergoing a major transformation and structural changes with a further shift away from agriculture, as exemplified by the number of people employed in the agriculture sector continuously falling, and agricultural lands are being encroached to make way for urban transformation.

The increase in income and the number of employed people through economic growth creates demand for housing and better housing with more living space in a better location. Better employment opportunities, attributed to natural evolution theory, significantly contributed to increasing urban footprint over the long-run, along with interest rates. Furthermore, the relationship of population density with predictor variables showed mixed trends. The relationship between employment opportunities and interest rates is statistically significant, with urban sprawl in Karachi occurring over the short and long-term.

The study incorporated social indicators to evaluate the causal relationship. In the case of Karachi, a study observed that better social indicators had pushed people to migrate and avail themselves of better infrastructure facilities in terms of health and education. Social and economic reasons are claimed to be important drivers of urban and suburban sprawl, which happened earlier in North America. The social indicators comprising school enrolment and advanced health facilities showed a positive relationship with built-up over the short and long-run. The relationship of social indicators with population density was found to be statistically significant, implying a positive relationship. Consequently, the relationship between social indicators and sprawling was found inconclusive in the long-term but was significant over a shorter period.

The Monocentric City model was further extended with utility and transport indicators to evaluate causal relationships in Karachi. The electricity consumption (Utility Indicator) and private vehicles (Private Transport) were incorporated in the model and were found statistically significant over the long run against built-up. The presence of utility infrastructure provides impetus to residential and commercial activities and paves the way for rapid urban expansion. Since the sprawl is automobile-dependent, the construction of highways facilitated the movement of people from farther distances to the city, thus opening these areas for residential development. Karachi consists of 10000 km of roads, making way for auto-dependent sprawl. The study found an inconclusive relationship between utility and transport indicators over the long-term compared to the short-term, where the relationship was statistically more significant. However, when checked with the variable of sprawl, the results of electricity consumption (utility indicator) and private vehicles (private transport indicator) were found to be inclusive in the long-term but were found statistically significant over the short run.

The study revealed that urban households of Karachi are generally experiencing the deterioration of municipal services, and the city is fast approaching a stage where the cost of urban development is alarmingly high. The study elucidated the rapid pace of urban development that has resulted in a severe strain on the existing urban infrastructure in terms of access to basic housing, transportation, law and order, drinking water, sewerage and solid waste management. There is evidence of ever-growing vehicular traffic, which, apart from congestion and supplemented by industrial pollution, is found to destroy the ecology of the city as the green cover has alarmingly eroded.

This study demonstrated that an undesired and unplanned spatial growth of Karachi entails serious policy implications as it is not adequately supported by efficient infrastructure, regulatory framework and institutional mechanism. Also, there is a dearth of policy dynamism and urban vision to contain this phenomenon of sprawling, which is endlessly spreading in all directions. This dissertation presents a reference point to experts framing urban growth policies, particularly to those developers and realtors who are attracted by the availability of low-cost lands at the urban fringe. To sum up, it is safe to assume that Karachi has been growing at a sporadic dimension.

Chapter 7| Conclusion

This research focuses on the patterns and extents of change in urban growth of the Karachi metropolitan area from 1975 to 2016, which can be useful in terms of directing prospective urban plans and policies for Karachi. The results indicate that the presence of urban dispersion and sprawl has increased with time. The study also highlights the sprawling trends, causative factors, and consequences for urban dwellers in Karachi. It is demonstrated from the study that the causes of physical expansion due to a large concentration of people in a city can turn into a mess if it is inadequately planned or poorly governed due to a lack of policies in or between the provinces.

The study thoroughly investigated the city's physical expansion in all directions through remotely sensed data and GIS tech-nique. Remote sensing technology is essential for dealing with dynamic phenomena like urban sprawl, as it helps monitor and estimate the urban sprawl over a time period, especially for the elapsed periods. Urban sprawl was identified and assessed by applying the popular Shannon's entropy model and using built-up area and population data. The methods in the study evolved to identify the advantages and signifi-cance of analytical models for urban growth assessment. Moreover, using population data combined with built-up area data can be considered a very good tech-nique to measure urban sprawl as a process and pattern.

The study was further supplemented by empirical methods of quantifying the causative factors through time series data to identify the factors that affect and drive the city's territorial expansion. The qualitative method, through in-depth interviews, was adopted to understand the opinions of urban experts related to the urban phenomenon, its variables, and their interchangeable relationships with urban expansion. The tail end of the study presents the results of the participant survey conducted among residents to evaluate and record their responses and perceptions regarding the quality of life in Karachi.

The study pinpoints urban sprawl as one of the leading challenges to sustainable development. Moreover, urban planning with effective resource utilization, allocation of natural resources and infrastructure initiatives are key concerns. Accounting for urban infrastructure is essential for accurately estimating the demands of the urban population and turning the city into a livable place. The study also highlights that the endless expansion with a continuous influx of people will create a demand and supply gap in the provision of basic services, which could only be bridged with smarter solutions coupled with technological advances and a holistic approach required from the authorities. The study shows that many issues in sprawling could hamper economic growth and future planning for cities. Therefore, policy-making should be done at an earlier level for smooth development.

Also, the pattern of agglomerated concentration of development in the cities, especially Karachi, reflects the present demand-led forces. As an outcome, land is acquired and developed through an authoritative nexus between private land developers, politicians and bureaucrats. This nexus has contributed towards the propagation of squatter settlements and ill-planned densification of the city. The institutional mechanism of the city, due to their sheer incompetence and political cloud, has immensely contributed towards crippling infrastructure, bad aesthetics and environmental stresses. The uneven spatial distribution of the resources presents special problems for peripheral regions, especially those segregated by weak urban transport infrastructure.

The study clearly indicates that unguided expansion in the growth of Karachi affects the pattern of land use in the city and its surrounding settlements. There were incompatible conversions of land uses and undue encroachment into green areas in the adjoining settlements due to the favorable economic situations and the massive industrialization in the city during the stated period. The city also witnessed a major influx of people soon after independence, and it continued on the back of better economic prospects. Moreover, Karachi's administrative status and concentration of establishments were key determinants for investors and inward migrants to seek green pastures. As a matter of fact, the city's vegetation in the surroundings was removed to make way for further development in the form of new residential development, informal settlements and encroachment. The natural and regional connectivity of the city had greatly influenced the direction of the expansion as the city in the first phase spread out along the fairly flat areas of the north-western part of the city, which appeared to be more favorable for human settlements before it began to diffuse to other areas.

The findings of the study show that urban sprawl is expanding in developing countries, but there are some differences between its characteristics and specifications compared to sprawling in developed countries as well as the dispersal of settlements seen in the region (Ebrahimpour-Masoumi, 2012). The causative factors of sprawl vary from location to location depending on various factors that contribute to the expansion of the cities. This study has demonstrated that socio-economic factors, natural growth of population and focalization of finances are strong drivers of urban sprawl in the Karachi Metropolitan. The study finds that causes related to development policies and planning have much higher efficiency and are the real sprawl drivers. Most of the researchers have confused causality with correlation; however, more in-depth multilayered investigations are needed to clarify the historical and socio-economic aspects of the sprawl drivers and the background of their emergence.

There is no doubt that urban sprawl exists in most of the cities nowadays. However, this study has extensively described the growing concern about the social and environmental impacts of sprawling development patterns. The methods suggested in this study can be used as a benchmark to measure the outward growth of cities in different parts of the world. When crafting policies to address sprawl, policymakers must recognize that the potential market failures involved in urban expansion are of secondary importance compared to the powerful, fundamental forces that underlie this expansion. A more cautious approach, which recognizes the damage done by urban sprawl, should be adopted for the preparation of plans and policies. The focal point of urban growth should concentrate on the sustainable and compact growth of a town or a city.

The governance failure and abdication of state services in the city have not only dented the availability of basic amenities but also facilitated the mushroom growth of the informal sector. We find evidence that economic inequalities are stark realities of the urban phenomenon in Karachi. The city needs to bridge the urban divide. Otherwise, the destruction of urban society would be inevitable. Inequality is neither predetermined nor destined but a result of policies, preferences, choices and power interplay within a society. It must be tackled by making structural adjustments and reshaping socio-economic policies by investing in infrastructure for sustainable development.

The leapfrog urban development in Karachi poses a serious challenge to policymakers as rural areas of the upcountry are underdeveloped, prone to frequent natural disasters and unabated terrorism, and lack industrial activities. Accordingly, the government needs to revisit its policies and work on an urban growth strategy by addressing the financial constraints of the metropolitan city. Hence, the government needs to work with all stakeholders to create a prosperous and inclusive city, and for that, they must frame policies that will make a difference in the lives of the urban poor.

In today's modern era of information technology and artificial intelligence, it is imperative for policy-makers to have vast resources of information management systems for better planning of urban centers. The exponential growth of Karachi as a main center of the country requires well integrated information warfare to counter and mitigate the risks of sprawl. The megacities across the globe are being threatened by catastrophic climatic changes, thereby increasing the risk profile of the residents. Natural disasters in the form of hurricanes, floods and earthquakes are posing an existential threat to urban residents. This necessitates monitoring and analyzing urban areas to control megacities and evaluate their disaster risk management. It is mandatory for planners to have a detailed outlay of spatial information about urban land cover and land use, population distributions and density, socio-economic characteristics and any related information regarding citizens for the perusal of better urban policies.

The study by Herold (2006) emphasizes proper collection and mining of the data for scaling up its uses at the operational level in a more structured way. The data constraints can easily be addressed through a Geo-spatial information system because of its availability and accuracy in understanding the complexities and dynamism involved in the urban processes. The Remotely sensed (RS) data can also be used and combined with other variables to visualize and predict urban growth scenarios for local planning decisions of local governments and can identify potential seismic zones for emergency planning in case of a disaster.

Urban policy-makers come across vast challenges to ensure the sustainable development and advancement of cities. It is a common practice in cities to observe high rates of land and energy consumption, the severity of air pollution and ongoing social fragmentation contravening the aims of sustainable development. Sustainable policies emphasize better utilization of resources to cope with growing risks and challenges faced by urban citizens. Karachi as an urban center presents a bleak picture wrecked with uncoordinated expansion, messy urbanization, and lack of urban planning, missing of key infrastructure facilities and ordeal of black market due to informality and weak enforcement of relevant rules and regulations.

Studies show that adopting sustainable development policies requires a holistic approach and the participation of all key stakeholders in producing desired results. The sustainable development approach demands a decentralized structure focusing on density, a combination of different land uses, polycentrality, and the provision of mass transit systems and public facilities. These are the prerequisites for putting urban sustainability into practice. The research fills the gap between urban sprawling and hazardous consequences by introducing sustainable development policies.

Density is a critical typology in determining sustainable urban forms. The study by Mosk (2000) defines density as an integral part of sustainable cities because it conserves resources and leads towards compactness that encourages social interaction. The increase in density lowers automobile ownership and automobile travel, thereby increasing the transit mode for commute purposes from one point to another. The people living in denser environments use walking, bicycling, or a combination of both for their travelling needs.

There is a general consensus among planners and scholars that mixed land use has an important role in achieving sustainable urban form. Mixed land use indicates the diversity of functional land uses such as residential, commercial, industrial, institutional, and those related to transportation. The recent past has witnessed rigid zoning-based planning resulting in cities with less diversity in local areas and more traffic, as well as reduced safety and diminished attractiveness of local streets (Newman & Thornley, 1997).

The study shows that greening of the city, or green urbanism, appears to be an important design concept for the sustainable urban form. Green spaces contribute immensely to improving the urban ecosystem (Swanwick, Dunnett, & Woolley, 2003). The city of Karachi, which has a dearth of green spaces, needs to emulate a greening model for better liveability. The clean and green Karachi will bring more appeal and aesthetics to the city's environment. Beatley (2000) exemplifies green urbanism if:

- It strives to live within its ecological limits,
- It is designed to function in ways analogous to nature,
- It strives to achieve a circular rather than a linear metabolism,
- It strives toward local and regional self-sufficiency,
- It facilitates more sustainable lifestyles, and
- It emphasizes a high quality of neighborhood and community life.

The elements of a sustainable city are exhibited in figure 9.2.

Moreover, by looking at Karachi's urban compact strategy, it can be seen that development in terms of infrastructure results in better outcomes and economic returns. There is a crucial need to encourage inward development and define certain nodes where urban development is prioritized. The scattered pattern of urban development makes it extremely difficult for municipalities to provide infrastructure and services all over the developed areas. The cities, in terms of spatial capacity, carry significant areas of vacant land parcels within existing quarters. It is remarkably observed that from the core of the city to the urban fringe, there exist large parcels of abandoned land, which need to be developed on the principles of infill development.

Furthermore, if we look into the city dynamics, the expensive and unaffordable land within the existing urban areas of Karachi is the major impediment to infill development. The free market dynamics and concentration of speculators in the property market have skyrocketed prices within the closest vicinity of the city. However, regulatory frameworks, fiscal tools, and taxation measures can help regulate and intervene in the land market in the interest of genuine buyers. It is prudent to revise the planning and building regulations already favoring the low-density development to harmonize with the objectives of compact city solutions. The research highlights that the technical expertise of local authorities needs to be upgraded, and lessons from successful models need to be drawn for the effective implementation of compact city plans.

The growth boundaries of the city need to be marked, and strict compliance is needed to forbid any development outside that particular area. However, field observations indicate that builders, with the connivance of government authorities, have largely misused the laws and infringed on the fertile agricultural lands at the urban fringe, thus lowering the probability of compaction. Implementing an efficient compact city policy requires revisiting the existing land use plan and focusing on the concept of mixed land use.

The study concludes that providing infrastructure consisting of transport, energy, communication, utilities, drinking water purification, sewerage purification, and waste treatment in cities can contribute to the development of a sustainable urban ecosystem, resulting in economic integration and social cohesion among urban residents. The rapidly expanding cities of the developing world, along with budgetary constraints, have miserably failed to provide these fundamental services.

Moreover, the literature helped further to know that the pressure of an ever-growing population becomes a burden on the limited civic amenities, which are nearly failing (Rafiee et al., 2012). The growth of infrastructure has not kept pace with the growth of the population, resulting in disequilibrium in the level of development (Tali & Murthy, 2012). Karachi, being the prime urban center and a major contributor to the public exchequer, is devoid of basic services and presents a gloomy picture as witnessed in the field observations with heaps of garbage, litter, water theft, clogged drainage, open sewers, broken roads and out-dated buses. The uncontrolled and peripheral growth of the city has further downgraded the quality of public infrastructure as residents are aware that no construction will be demolished as a kind of penalty, thus encouraging them to construct houses beyond the urban growth boundary.

Also, Karachi, with 16 million populations, is in dire need of a robust public transport system. Due to its topography, weather, road infrastructure and social fabric, the sprawling metropolis lacks cycling and pedestrian walking as a spread mode of daily commuting. The major commuting, as per this study, is carried out through private transport. The systematic extension of public transit systems (e.g. subways and buses) is an essential requirement of urban dwellers in Karachi. A rail transit network with different speed levels and high capacities, passenger transit pivots and parking lots are important elements of an efficient mass transit system; for example, Shanghai has designed an urban transportation plan, which consists of high-speed rail lines, urban metro lines and urban light railways to limit the quantum of cars, motorcycles and powered bicycles. The experts stressed the role of the municipality to introduce a simple and efficient transport system. Transportation routes can be used as an essential tool in guiding the urban development towards favorable planning locations.

The dissertation shows that Karachi lacks a clear and integrated housing policy. The land belongs to different civil and defence institutions, making the process of securing affordable land more complicated. The moving out of residents on the urban fringe results from unaffordable and expensive land in the core of the city, thereby intensifying the process of urban sprawl in the form of illegal encroachments and the formation of slums and squatter settlements. The city has a chronic housing deficit, which is being temporarily mitigated by sprawling trends on the outskirts of the city. Policy-makers need to devise an effective and affordable mechanism to address this issue, as urban sprawl is an undesired pattern of urban development.

Moreover, the authorities need to formulate a financing plan to fund the infrastructure projects at a large scale. The main problem is to mobilize new external resources to finance gradual improvements of the urban infrastructure and maintain and rehabilitate existing infrastructure to avoid pilferages and deficiencies. Policy-makers need to prioritize whether to finance and manage existing facilities or invest in future facilities. There can be innovative means of funding, especially public-private partnerships (PPPs), which can bring efficiency gains and cost-effectiveness to bridge the financing gaps.

Apart from financial plans, researchers and experts were of the view that good governance is an important component of poverty eradication and sustainable development. Good governance steers the actions of several actors at all levels, including government, ministries, international organizations, NGOs, research institutes, universities and finance institutions. Urban sprawl poses a serious challenge to policy-makers as it demands better management through decentralized and digitalized governance backed by strong institutional mechanisms.

The study concludes that Karachi has suffered tremendously due to the sheer incompetence of federal, provincial and local governments. No tier of government is ready to take ownership of the city and resolve the basic issues of the residents. The city has experimented with different local government systems under civilian and military rules with agonizing results. It would be fair to comment that the last military government had introduced local government, empowering its mayor to make decisions and lead new initiatives for the development of the city. The citizens' issues were largely addressed under that system, and marked improvement was witnessed in the city's infrastructure.

The empowered local governments can be emulated by the London Metropolitan Corporation, backed by a powerful local system to attend to the basic issues of the people at the local level, a trend followed in the megacities of the world as they have to co-ordinate their activities through local units. In the case of Karachi, it is strongly recommended that local government at the street and ward levels be empowered to improve service quality and delivery and end the existing confusion matrix among different tiers of provincial and federal governments.

The extant literature strongly postulates that participatory governance is being practised in many countries to improve urban living conditions by addressing needs as directly as possible and enabling urban dwellers to participate in city matters. The decentralizing process can balance internal socio-political concerns and develop a viable strategy for the megacity on a massive scale.

Also, empowered local governments will not find solutions until and unless they are equipped with technical expertise and the required financial resources. The technical expertise can be upgraded through capacity building and the adoption of smart technologies. It has been observed in Karachi Metropolitan Corporation that due to inadequate mobilization of local resources, the managers have not been able to produce the desired results. Local tax levying capacities are poor due to the lack of any organized collection and control system. Taxation methods are often discretionary and do not encourage taxpayers to comply with them. Therefore, the entire tax system has to be progressive and overhauled to keep pace with economic and social development.

The city needs to have proper mechanisms to mitigate the climatic risks, heat waves, urban flooding and typhoons. The availability of a rapid response system fully equipped with modern tools will reduce the effects of any disaster. However, past events suggest that competent authorities of the city miserably failed in the face of adversity, costing valuable lives triggered by prolonged heat waves and torrential rains.

The local government needs to prioritize its economic and budgetary policies depending on its land use planning strategy, financial policy, credit regulations, education, health policy, and tax legislation. No foreign model of decentralization can be replicated entirely, but one can learn from best practices and experiences. It would be appropriate to design local models of governance and management to yield the desired results.

Chapter 8| Recommendations

8.1. Strict Policies and Measures to Control Urban Sprawling

- The study showed that strict policies and measures can control urban sprawling in Karachi. Strong policy-making and implementation can significantly control sprawling.
- The government needs an effective mechanism to control the influx of migrants from the country and overseas for better management of the city.
- A mechanism needs to be developed for local people to build better housing, create social infrastructure, and improve living conditions in rural areas to mitigate the burden on urban areas of Pakistan.
- The economic profile of the people needs to be improved for better livelihoods, which would reduce the overcrowding of people in urban areas.

8.2. Better Housing Schemes

- Giving housing schemes to low-income women and children can help people settle in the suburbs as well as rural areas. Most low-income households cannot afford subsistence; therefore, they may shift to urban areas for better living facilities.
- The government should initiate a framework for allocating vacant plots. The study finds a large number of vacant plots in the city center, which can be better planned for the benefit of Karachi and its citizens.
- The incremental housing can improve the morphology of the city as it would lessen the slums and informal housing.
- Improved financing from formal channels will help tremendously to bridge the housing deficiency while limiting the city's limitless growth.

- The vertical housing plan will also be a source of containing the sprawl and saving infrastructure costs as well.

8.3. Political Will

- Political will, along with an integrated approach, can lead to sustainable development.
- Adopting a balancing approach in economic, social and policy-making can further develop and maintain a well-planned future.
- Urban sprawling might result in poor, unplanned, and unorganized livelihoods that can adversely impact citizens. In this case, the department should plan extensively, considering 'a sustainable development approach'.
- Much of the sprawling may weaken the overall ecosystem, damaging nature and community growth. Unfortunately, in Karachi, there are few mechanisms for growth and urban development. Therefore, an effective planning mechanism is needed to address these issues.

8.4. Better Infrastructure Facilities

- For sustainability, economic integration, and social cohesion, the provision of infrastructure, including transport, energy, communication, utilities, drinking water purification, sewerage purification, and waste treatment, should be prioritized equally in rural and urban areas.
- Better schooling and improved health facilities in rural areas can prevent a mass exodus of people, thus lessening the burden on urban areas.
- The systematic extension of public transit systems (e.g., subways and buses) is an essential requirement for urban dwellers in Karachi. This will prevent motorization, which is an important component of people's movement in suburban areas.

- Urban policy-makers can adopt the Public-Private Partnership (PPP) model to bridge financing gaps and implement sound urban policy that limits unending expansion.
- It is imperative for policy-makers to have vast resources of information management systems for better urban center planning.
- The exponential growth of Karachi necessitates monitoring and analyzing urban areas to control the megacity and evaluate its disaster risk management using modern information technology and artificial intelligence.

8.5. Smart Growth and Planning

- There is a crucial need to encourage inward development and define certain nodes where urban development should be prioritized. The scattered pattern of urban development makes it extremely difficult for the authorities to provide infrastructure and services throughout the developed areas.
- The growth boundaries of the city need to be marked, and strict compliance is needed to forbid any development outside that particular area.
- A country like Pakistan needs to spend on research and development for smart growth and new urbanism.
- The new urbanism can also support and improve the standard of people living in Karachi.
- Friendly pedestrian areas can also decrease the volumetric growth of traffic.

8.6. Areas of Further Research

The study is targeted at the urbanized cities of the country, and it is suggested that the sprawling trends of other big and midsized cities of the country be checked to check their connotation and relevance with the sprawling dynamics of Karachi. The academia needs to research further in terms of the environmental and ecological effects of the sprawling city in relation to Karachi specifically. The studies must be conducted to pinpoint in detail the urban decay being caused by the rapid and unplanned sprawling of the megapolis. Studies have to be conducted to find the correlation between sprawl and the degrading public health of the citizens in the context of Karachi.

In today's modern era, population growth, immigration, changing lifestyles, and changes in the composition of economic activities supported by the spread of ICT have altered the dynamics and outlook of many urban regions across the globe, which needs to be investigated for the future course of action. It is imperative for urban policy-makers to steer an agenda combining accessibility with sustainability and competitiveness with equity.

Urban-related research, which mainly covers physical and social order, has been explicitly dealt with within the context of large cities (Kloosterman, 1996). Cities in the advanced world dominate the urban research agenda, which cannot be used solely to predict the urban landscape in the developing world. It is necessary to conduct and evaluate the status of growing cities in the developing world, contribute to the extent of literature, and then carry out comparative studies to reach a consensus for the best urban practices to make cities more livable and attractive for their residents.

Urban planners in the developing world need to investigate the causative factors that lead to limitless sprawl in their cities. These factors may be the same as those mentioned in this study but can be different altogether. The causative factors must be evaluated scientifically for the purposes of better planning and resource allocation. The causative factors need to be linked with consequences to ensure the sustainability and competitiveness of cities by enabling them to emerge as hubs of innovation, commercialization, and entrepreneurship.

Policy-makers in the developing world need to come up with Indigenous models for addressing and containing the urban sprawl because of differences in economic, social, cultural and technological structures compared to the developed world. The localized solutions would bring far-reaching effects on the urban ecosystem of developing countries. The planners are required to adapt the best methods after going through trial and error, leading towards alternative models of sprawl best suiting the cities of developing countries.

Urban planners are supposed to frame policies for addressing growing inequalities among different segments of the urban population because of sprawl and address social exclusion as it would lead to deviation, ultimately creating chaos in urban societies. The work on urban poverty needs to be accelerated to find out the determinants of chronic poverty prevailing in urban areas and mechanisms to overcome it. The research world must give coverage to popular economics, informal economy and their role in complex urban economics.

Future studies must highlight the role of weak institutional hierarchies and political economy, which play an important role in expanding the physical boundaries of metropolitan areas. The local governance structure in developing countries, particularly in Pakistan, is badly inefficient, dysfunctional, inept, and centralized. The studies must explore in detail the key reasons behind the malfunctioning of local institutions and should come up with solid evidence to strengthen the local bodies to contain sprawling trends in the cities.

Pakistan, an emerging country, needs to form a strong basis for urban development because it is urbanizing at a very alarming speed, and if corrective measures are not taken, that may lead towards ever-expanding physical limits of the cities at the urban fringe, depleting the fertile land resources of the country and jeopardizing its food security. Policy-makers need to put an act together and come up with action research to address the growing complexities of urban Pakistan.

Social scientists and researchers must highlight the better theoretical grasp of the development of polycentric urban regions because of the growing sprawl in Karachi and then compare it with the other cities within the country and other cities of the world for discussions related to different dimensions of urban sprawl. The studies should investigate changes in the physical forms, types of governance, and functional relationships between the elements of the polycentric urban region and its identity and representation. Research should then try to establish links between these different sets of changes and their interactions with one another (Rijsberman & van de Ven, 2000). This will serve as a platform to understand whether there is a scope for regional policies with respect to, for instance, competitiveness, sustainability, social polarization and exclusion, ICT and the rise of network society, or whether more traditional urban policies will still dominate.

This study should strongly motivate the researchers to carry out research and study different dimensions of sprawling cities across Pakistan. It should also generate concrete evidence and innovative solutions to address and contain urban sprawl, making our cities more sustainable and livable by improving their livability index.

- Informed Consent Statement: Informed consent was obtained from all subjects involved in the study.
- Data Availability Statement: The data presented in this study are available on request from the corresponding author.

- Acknowledgments: The authors would like to thank the anonymous reviewers and the editors for their insightful comments and suggestions.

- Conflicts of Interest: The authors declare no conflict of interest.

References

1. Acioly C, and Davidson F. (1996). Density in Urban Development. Building issues, Lund Centre for Habitat Studies, Lund University, vol 8(3), 3–25.
2. Adams, C. F., Fleeter, H. B., Kim, Y., Freeman, M., & Cho, I. (1996). Flight from blight and metropolitan suburbanization revisited. *Urban Affairs Review, 31*(4), 529-543.
3. Adams, E. (2010). The joys and challenges of semi-structured interviewing. *Community Practitioner, 83*(7).
4. ADB (Asian Development Bank). (2012). The Asian Development Bank (ADB). Key Indicators for Asia and the Pacific Region 2012, Green Urbanization in Asia.
5. Afsar, S. (2001). Application of Remote Sensing for Urban Growth Monitoring and Landcover/Land Use Mapping for Change Detection in Karachi. *Unpublished M. Phil Thesis, Department of Geography, University of Karachi: Karachi.*
6. Afshan, A., Mujeeb, S., & Gill, E. K. A. (2016). 265. Dynamics of Karachi as a Megapolis: Issues and Challenges.
7. Agénor, P. R., & Moreno-Dodson, B. (2006). *Public infrastructure and growth: New channels and policy implications*. The World Bank.
8. Aguirre, B. (2002). "Sustainable development" as collective surge. *Social Science Quarterly.* 83(1), 101-18.
9. Ahmad, K. (1994). Road traffic noise and its control. *J Engineering Research, 1*(1), 73-78.
10. Ahmed, N. (2013, June). Options for improving water supply to low-income communities in Karachi. In *Proceedings of the Institution of Civil Engineers-*

Municipal Engineer (Vol. 166, No. 2, pp. 139-146). Thomas Telford Ltd.

11. Akhtar, S., & Dhanani, M. R. (2013). Urban sprawl in Karachi. *Sindh University Research Journal-SURJ (Science Series)*, *45*(3).
12. Alam, S. (2010). Globalization, poverty and environmental degradation: Sustainable development in Pakistan. *Journal of Sustainable Development*, *3*(3), 103.
13. Aldous, T. (1992). *Urban Villages—A concept for creating mixed-use urban developments on a sustainable scale.* London: Urban Villages Group.
14. Ali, A., Iqbal, S., Amin, N. U., & Malik, H. L. (2015). Urbanization and disaster risk in Pakistan. *Acta Technica Corviniensis-Bulletin of Engineering*, *8*(3), 161.
15. Alkan, M., Oruç, M., Yildirim, Y., Seker, D. Z., & Jacobsen, K. (2013). Monitoring spatial and temporal land use/cover changes; a case study in Western Black Sea Region of Turkey. *Journal of the Indian Society of Remote Sensing*, *41*(3), 587-596.
16. Allmendinger, P., (2002). Towards a Post-Positivist Typology of Planning Theory, Planning Theory, Vol. 1, No.1, 77-99.
17. Alonso, W. (1964). Location and land use. Toward a general theory of land rent. *Location and land use. Toward a general theory of land rent.*
18. Al-sharif, A., Pradhan, B., Shafri, H., & Mansor, S. (2013). Spatio-temporal Analysis of Urban and Population Growths in Tripoli using Remotely Sensed Data and GIS. *Indian Journal of Science and Technology*, *6*(8), 5134-5142.
19. Anas, A., Arnott, R., & Small, K. A. (1998). Urban spatial structure. *Journal of economic literature*, *36*(3), 1426-1464.

20. Anderson, W. P., Kanaroglou, P. S., & Miller, E. J. (1996). Urban form, energy and the environment: a review of issues, evidence and policy. *Urban Studies, 33*(1), 7-35.

21. Andrews, R. (2003). *Research questions.* Bloomsbury Publishing.

22. Angrist, J. D., & Krueger, A. B. (2001). Instrumental variables and the search for identification: From supply and demand to natural experiments. *Journal of Economic Perspectives, 15*(4), 69-85.

23. Ansari, S. F. (2005). *Life after partition: migration, community and strife in Sindh: 1947-1962/Sarah Ansari.* Oxford University Press.

24. Anwar, N. H., Viqar, M. S., Sawas, M. A., Iqtidar, H., Nausheen, H., Amiera, M., & Sawas, D. (2014). Urbanization, Gender & Violence in Millennial Karachi: A Scoping Study.

25. Arabani, M. & Amani, B. (2007). Evaluating the Parameters Affecting Urban Trip-Generation, *Iranian Journal of Science & Technology,* Transaction B, Engineering, Vol. 31, No. B5, pp. 547-560.

26. Araya, Y. H., & Cabral, P. (2010). Analysis and modeling of urban land cover change in Setúbal and Sesimbra, Portugal. *Remote Sensing, 2*(6), 1549-1563.

27. Arbury, J. (2005). From Urban Sprawl to Compact City – An analysis of urban growth management in Auckland. Published thesis. University of Auckland in Geography and Environmental Science.

28. Archer, R. W. (1973). Land Speculation and Scattered Development: Failures in the Urban-Fringe Market. *Urban Studies* 10(3), 367-72.

29. Arif, G. M., & Hamid, S. (2009). Urbanization, city growth and quality of life in Pakistan. *European Journal of Social Sciences, 10*(2), 196-215.

30. Arnfield, A. J. (2003). Two decades of urban climate research: a review of turbulence, exchanges of energy

and water, and the urban heat island. *International Journal of Climatology: a Journal of the Royal Meteorological Society, 23*(1), 1-26.

31. Aronson, M. F., Lepczyk, C. A., Evans, K. L., Goddard, M. A., Lerman, S. B., MacIvor, J. S., ... & Vargo, T. (2017). Biodiversity in the city: key challenges for urban green space management. *Frontiers in Ecology and the Environment, 15*(4), 189-196.
32. Audirac, I., & Shermyen, A. (1994). An evaluation of neotraditional design's social prescription: Postmodern placebo or remedy suburban malaise. *Journal of Planning Education and Research.*13, 161-73.
33. Audirac, I., Shermyen, A. H., & Smith, M. T. (1990). Ideal urban form and visions of the good life Florida's growth management dilemma. *Journal of the American Planning Association, 56*(4), 470-482.
34. Azad, M. (2007). Tree less, smoke more, declining tail.BBC Urdu Karachi. (In Urdu)
35. Aziz, A., & Bajwa, I. U. (2004). Energy and pollution control opportunities for Lahore. *WIT Transactions on The Built Environment, 75.*
36. Aziz, J. A. (2006). Towards establishing air quality guidelines for Pakistan. *EMHJ-Eastern Mediterranean Health Journal, 12 (6), 886-893, 2006.*
37. Bahmani-Oskooee, M., & Oyolola, M. (2007). Export growth and output growth: an application of bounds testing approach. *Journal of Economics and Finance, 31*(1), 1-11.
38. Baillie, J., & Groombridge, B. (1996). Red list of threatened animals. *IUNC: Gland, Switzerland.*
39. Balogun, I. A., Adeyewa, D. Z., Balogun, A. A., & Morakinyo, T. E. (2011). Analysis of urban expansion and land use changes in Akure, Nigeria, using remote sensing and geographic information system (GIS)

techniques. *Journal of Geography and Regional Planning*, *4*(9), 533-541.

40. Bank, S. (2018). Integrated Annual Report 2018.
41. Barnes, K. B., Morgan III, J. M., Roberge, M. C., & Lowe, S. (2001). Sprawl development: Its patterns, consequences, and measurement. *Towson University, Towson*, 1-24.
42. Barnes, K. B., Morgan, J., & Roberge, M. (2001). Impervious surfaces and the quality of natural and built environments. *Baltimore: Department of Geography and Environmental Planning, Towson University*.
43. Barnes, K., & Morgan, J., & Roberge, M., & Lowe, S. (2010). Sprawl Development: Its Patterns, Consequences, and Measurement. *Center for Geographic Information Sciences*. Towson University.
44. Barredo, J. I., Kasanko, M., McCormick, N., & Lavalle, C. (2003). Modelling dynamic spatial processes: simulation of urban future scenarios through cellular automata. *Landscape and urban planning*, *64*(3), 145-160.
45. Basit, M., Sajjad, S. H., Khan, M. I., Ali, A., & Kurshid, S. K. (2018). Spatio-temporal trends of urban population in Pakistan. *Asian Journal of Multidisciplinary Studies*, *6*(8), 21-26.
46. Batty, M. (2005). Agents, cells, and cities: new representational models for simulating multiscale urban dynamics. *Environment and Planning A*, *37*(8), 1373-1394.
47. Batty, M., Xie, Y., & Sun, Z. (1999). Dynamics of urban sprawl.
48. Beatley, T. (2000). Preserving biodiversity: challenges for planners. *Journal of the American Planning Association*, *66*(1), 5-20.

49. Beatley, T., & Manning, K. (1997). *Ecology of place: Planning for environment, economy, and community*. Washington, DC: Island Press.

50. Becker, J. Ö. R. G., & Heller, W. I. L. F. R. I. E. D. (2009). Migration without integration? Polish seasonal labour migrants in today's Germany'. *Revue Roumaine de Géographie/Romanian Journal of Geography, 53*(1), 19-32.

51. Bell, D. V., & Cheung, Y. K. A. (Eds.). (2009). *Introduction to Sustainable Development-Volume I*. EOLSS Publications.

52. Belzer, D., & Autler, G. (2002). *Transit-oriented development: moving from rhetoric to reality* (pp. 06-15). Washington, DC: Brookings Institution Center on Urban and Metropolitan Policy.

53. Benfield, F. K. (1999, October). Once there were greenfields. In *Forum for Applied Research and Public Policy* (Vol. 14, No. 3, p. 6). University of Tennessee, Energy, Environment and Resources Center.

54. Benfield, F. K., Raimi, M. D., & Chen, D. D. (1999). Once There Were Greenfields: How Urban Sprawl is Undermining America's Environment. *Policy project. J. Am. Plan. Associate, 2*(4), 11-23.

55. Bengston, D. N., Potts, R. S., Fan, D. P., & Goetz, E. G. (2005). An analysis of the public discourse about urban sprawl in the United States: Monitoring concern about a major threat to forests. *Forest Policy and Economics, 7*(5), 745-756.

56. Berry, D., & Plaut, T. (1978). Retaining agricultural activities under urban pressures: a review of land use conflicts and policies. *Policy Sciences, 9*(2), 153-178.

57. Berry, H. (2007). '"Crowded suburbs" and "killer cities": A brief review of the relationship between urban environments and mental health', *New South Wales Public Health Bulletin* 18(12), 222–227.

58. Besl, J. (2000). Suburban sprawl advances. Indiana Business Journal 75(2): 5-8.

59. Besussi, E., & Chin, N. (2003). Identifying and measuring urban sprawl. ESRI Press.

60. Besussi, E., & Chin, N., & Batty, M., & Longley, P. (2010). The Structure and Form of Urban Settlements. *Remote Sensing of Urban and Suburban Areas.* 13-31.

61. Bhatta, B. (2009). Modelling of urban growth boundary using geoinformatics. *International Journal of Digital Earth, 2*(4), 359-381.

62. Bhatta, B., Saraswati, S., &Bandyopadhyay, D. (2010). Urban sprawl measurement from remote sensing data. *Applied Geography, 30*(4), 731-740.

63. Bhatta. B. (2010). Causes and Consequences of Urban Growth and Sprawl. *Analysis of Urban Growth and Sprawl from Remote Sensing Data.* Berlin. Germany.

64. Bihamta, N., Soffianian, A., Fakheran, S., & Gholamalifard, M. (2015). Using the SLEUTH urban growth model to simulate future urban expansion of the Isfahan metropolitan area, Iran. *Journal of the Indian Society of Remote Sensing, 43*(2), 407-414.

65. Birabi, A.K., (2007). International Urban Conservation Charters as Catalytic or Passive Tools of Urban Conservation Practices among Developing Countries? City & Time, Vol.3, No.2, 39-53.

66. Birch, E. L., &Wachter, S. M. (2011). *Global urbanization*. University of Pennsylvania Press.

67. Birkmann, J. (2006). Indicators and criteria for measuring vulnerability: Theoretical bases and requirements. *Measuring vulnerability to natural hazards: Towards disaster resilient societies*, 55-77.

68. Bjorvatn, K. (1999). Third World regional integration. *European Economic Review, 43*(1), 47-64.

69. Black, J. (1996). The economics of sprawl. Urban Land 55(3): 6.

70. Blair, R., & Wellman, G. (2011). Smart growth principles and the management of urban sprawl. *Community Development, 42*(4), 494-510.

71. Blakely, E., & Snyder, M. (1997). *Fortress America: gated communities in the United States.* Brookings Institute Press. Washington DC.

72. Blanc, J. Arthur, S. and Wright G. (2012). Natural Flood Management (NFM) Knowledge System: Part 1 – Sustainable Urban Drainage Systems (SUDS) and Flood Management in Urban Areas – Final Report. CREW – Scotland's Centre of Expertise for Waters, Edinburgh, UK.

73. Bloom, D. E., Canning, D., & Fink, G. (2008). Urbanization and the wealth of nations. *Science, 319*(5864), 772-775.

74. Boarnet, M., & Crane, R. (1997). LA story: A reality check for transit-based housing. *Journal of the American Planning Association.* 63 (2), 189-204.

75. Bogart, W. T. (1998). *The economics of cities and suburbs.* Prentice Hall.

76. Borsdorf, A., & Hidalgo, R. (2008). The urban sprawl in Europe and Latin America. A comparison of the growth of urban agglomerations. *Mitteilungen Der Osterreichischen Geographischen Gesellschaft, 150,* 229-250.

77. Bougheas, S., Demetriades, P. O., & Manuneas, T. P. (2000). Infrastructure, specialization, and economic growth. *Canadian Journal of Economics, 33,* 506-522.

78. Boyatzis, R. E. (1998). *Transforming qualitative information: Thematic analysis and code development.* Sage.

79. Boyce, R. R. (1963). Myth versus Reality in Urban Planning. *Land Economics 39.* 241-51.

80. Bradford, D. F., & Kelejian, H. H. (1973). An econometric model of the flight to the suburbs. *Journal of Political Economy, 81*(3), 566-589.

81. Brannen, J. (2017). Combining qualitative and quantitative approaches: an overview. In *Mixing methods: Qualitative and quantitative research* (pp. 3-37). Routledge.

82. Braun, V., & Clarke, V. (2006). Using thematic analysis in psychology. *Qualitative research in psychology, 3*(2), 77-101.

83. Breheny, M., & Gent, T. & Lock, D. (1993). *Alternative development patterns: New settlements.* London: HMSO.

84. Brown, A., Collins, C., Frank, T., Haddow, K., Hitchings, B., Parry, S., ... & Wormser, L. The Dark Side of the American Dream: The Costs and Consequences of Suburban Sprawl: The Sierra Club. (1998). *accessible through URL: http://www. sierraclub. org/sprawl/report98.*

85. Brueckner Jan K. & Kim, H. (2003). "Urban Sprawl and the Property Tax," *International Tax and Public Finance* 10, 5-23.

86. Brueckner, J. K. (1987). The structure of urban equilibria: A unified treatment of the Muth-Mills model. *Handbook of regional and urban economics, 2*(20), 821-845.

87. Brueckner, J. K. (2000). Urban sprawl: diagnosis and remedies. *International regional science review, 23*(2), 160-171.

88. Brueckner, J. K. (2003). Strategic interaction among governments: An overview of empirical studies. *International regional science review, 26*(2), 175-188.

89. Brueckner, J. K., & Fansler, D. A. (1983). The economics of urban sprawl: Theory and evidence on the spatial sizes of cities. *The Review of Economics and Statistics*, 479-482.

90. Brueckner, J. K., & Kim, H. A. (2003). Urban sprawl and the property tax. *International Tax and Public Finance, 10*(1), 5-23.

91. Brueckner, J. K., & Pereira, A. M. (1997). Housing wealth and the economy's adjustment to unanticipated shocks. *Regional Science and Urban Economics, 27*(4-5), 497-513.

92. Brunori, D. (2004). The Politics of State Taxation: Corporate Taxes are All the Rage. *State Tax Notes, 31*(10).

93. Buiton, P.J. (1994). A vision for equitable land use allocation. Land Use Policy 12 (1), 63–68.

94. Burchell, R. W. (1992). Impact Assessment of the New Jersey Interim State Development and Redevelopment Plan, Re-port II: Research Findings. *Trenton: New Jersey Office of State Planning*.

95. Burchell, R. W. (1998). The Costs of Sprawl–Revisited, Research Program Report 39.

96. Burchell, R. W., & Downs, A., & McCann, B., & Mukherji, S. (2005). *Sprawl Costs: Economic Impacts of Unchecked Development.* Island Press. The USA.

97. Burchell, R. W., & Mukherji, S. (2003). Conventional development versus managed growth: the costs of sprawl. *American Journal of Public Health, 93*(9), 1534-1540.

98. Burchell, R. W., Listokin, D., & Galley, C. C. (2000). Smart growth: More than a ghost of urban policy past, less than a bold new horizon. *Housing policy debate, 11*(4), 821-879.

99. Burchell, R. W., Shad, N. A., Listokin, D., Phillips, H., Downs, A., Seskin, S., ... & Gall, M. (1998). *The costs of sprawl-revisited* (No. Project H-10 FY'95).

100. Burchfield, M., Overman, H. G., Puga, D., & Turner, M. A. (2006). Causes of sprawl: A portrait from space. *The Quarterly Journal of Economics, 121*(2), 587-633.

101. Burgess, P. (1998). Revisiting "Sprawl": Lessons from the Past. The Urban Center Publications, Cleveland State University. Cleveland, OH.

102. Burgess, R. (1998). Urban violence: the next agenda. *Centre for Development and Emergency Practice (CENDEP) Newsletter*, 7-8.

103. Burki, S. J. (2011). *Exploding Karachi.* Institute of South Asian Studies, National University of Singapore.

104. Buttenheim, H. S., & P.H. Cornick. (1938). Land reserves for American cities. The Journal of Land and Public Utility Economics 14: 254-265.

105. Cabral, P., Feger, C., Levrel, H., Chambolle, M., & Basque, D. (2016). Assessing the impact of land-cover changes on ecosystem services: A first step toward integrative planning in Bordeaux, France. *Ecosystem Services, 22*, 318-327.

106. Camhis M., (2006).*Sustainable Development and Urbanization.* Keiner (editor) .The future of Sustainability. Dordrecht: Springer.

107. Campbell Collaboration. (2014). Campbell systematic reviews: Policies and guidelines. *Campbell Systematic Reviews, 1.*

108. Carruthers, J. I. (2002). Evaluating the Effectiveness of Regulatory Growth Management Programs An Analytic Framework.*Journal of Planning Education and Research, 21*(4), 391-405.

109. Carruthers, J. I., & Ulfarsson, G. F. (2003). Urban sprawl and the cost of public services. *Environment and Planning B: Planning and Design, 30*(4), 503-522.

110. Carruthers, J. I., &Ulfarsson, G. F. (2002). Fragmentation and sprawl: Evidence from interregional analysis. *Growth and change, 33*(3), 312-340.

111. Carruthers, J. I., &Ulfarsson, G. F. (2003). Urban sprawl and the cost of public services. *Environment and Planning B: Planning and Design, 30*(4), 503-522.

112. CEC, C. P. (2006). Cities: the urban contribution to growth and jobs in the regions. *Communication from the Commission to the council and parliament, COM, 385*.

113. Cheema, A., Khwaja, A. I., & Khan, A. (2005). Decentralization in Pakistan: Context, content and causes.

114. Cheema, Ali, Aijaz, Asim, Adnan, Khawaja (2005) `Local Government Reforms in Pakistan: Context, Content and Causes`, KSG Working Paper No. RW/P05-034. Kennedy School of Government, WP

115. Chen, C., LeGates, R., Zhao, M., & Fang, C. (2018). The changing rural-urban divide in China's megacities. *Cities, 81*, 81-90.

116. Chen, S., Claramunt, C., & Ray, C. (2014). A spatio-temporal modelling approach for the study of the connectivity and accessibility of the Guangzhou metropolitan network. *Journal of Transport Geography, 36*, 12-23.

117. Cheng, J., & Masser, I. (2003). Urban growth pattern modeling: a case study of Wuhan City. PR China. *Landscape and Urban Planning*. 62(4), 199-217.

118. Choon, S. W., Siwar, C., Pereira, J. J., Jemain, A. A., Hashim, H. S., & Hadi, A. S. (2011). A sustainable city index for Malaysia. *International Journal of Sustainable Development & World Ecology, 18*(1), 28-35.

119. Christens, B. (2004). *Regional sprawl in the Northern Colorado Front Range.* MS Thesis:

120. Christiansen, P., & Loftsgarden, T. (2011). Drivers behind urban sprawl in Europe. *TØI Report, 1136*, 2011.

121. Cirtautas, M. (2013). Urban sprawl of major cities in the Baltic States.

122. City District Government Karachi, C. D. G. K. (2007). Karachi strategic development plan 2020.

123. Clark, W. and J.L. Onaka. (1983). "Life-Cycle and Housing Adjustment as Explanations of Residential-Mobility," *Urban Studies* 20 :(1) 47.
124. Clawson, M. (1962). Urban sprawl and speculation in suburban land. *Land economics, 38*(2), 99-111.
125. Club, S. (1998). Sprawl: The dark side of the American dream. *Sierra Club Sprawl Report.*
126. Colantoni, A., Ferrara, C., Perini, L., & Salvati, L. (2015). Assessing trends in climate aridity and vulnerability to soil degradation in Italy. Ecological Indicators, 48, 599–604.
127. Colbeck, I., Nasir, Z. A., & Ali, Z. (2010). The state of ambient air quality in Pakistan—a review. *Environmental Science and Pollution Research, 17*(1), 49-63.
128. Coq-Huelva, D., & Asián-Chaves, R. (2019). Urban sprawl and sustainable urban policies. A review of the cases of Lima, Mexico City and Santiago de Chile. *Sustainability, 11*(20), 5835.
129. Couch, C., Leontidou, L., & Petschel-Held G. (2007). Urban Sprawl in Europe: Landscapes. Land-Use Change and Policy. Blackwell Publishing Ltd.
130. Cowherd, R., & Heikkila, E. (2002). Orange County, Java: Hybridity, social dualism and an imagined West. *Southern California and the world*, 195-220.
131. Creswell, J. W., & Clark, V. L. P. (2017). *Designing and conducting mixed methods research*. Sage publications.
132. Cutsinger, J., Galster, G., Wolman, H., Hanson, R., & Towns, D. (2005). Verifying the multi-dimensional nature of metropolitan land use: Advancing the understanding and measurement of sprawl. *Journal of Urban Affairs, 27*(3), 235-259.
133. Czech, B., Krausman, P. R., & Devers, P. K. (2000). Economic associations among causes of species endangerment in the United States: associations among causes of species endangerment in the United

States reflect the integration of economic sectors, supporting the theory and evidence that economic growth proceeds at the competitive exclusion of nonhuman species in the aggregate. *BioScience, 50*(7), 593-601.

134. Dantzig, G., & Saaty, T. (1973). Compact City: Plan for a Livable Urban Environment. San Francisco: W.H. Freeman & Co.

135. Daramola, A., & Ibem, E. O. (2010). Urban Environmental Problems in Nigeria: Implications for Sustainable Development. *Journal of Sustainable Development in Africa* .12(1).

136. Davis, D. E. (2005). Cities in global context: A brief intellectual history. *International Journal of Urban and Regional Research, 29*(1), 92-109.

137. De Leeuw, E. D. (2008). Choosing the method of data collection.

138. Deal, B., &Schunk, D. (2004). Spatial dynamic modeling and urban land use transformation: a simulation approach to assessing the costs of urban sprawl. *Ecological Economics, 51*(1), 79-95.

139. Declaration, R. (1992). Rio declaration on environment and development. Retrieved 10 January, 2013 from: http://www.un.org/esa/dsd/agenda21/.

140. Deka, J., Tripathi, O. P., & Khan, M. L. (2011). Urban growth trend analysis using Shannon Entropy approach - A case study in North-East India. *International Journal of Geomatics and Geosciences, 2*(4), 1062-1068.

141. Dempsey, N. (2010). Revisiting the Compact City? *Built Environment* .36(1).

142. Deng, X., Huang, J., Rozelle, S., & Uchida, E. (2008). Growth, population and industrialization, and urban land expansion of China. *Journal of Urban Economics, 63*(1), 96-115.

143. Deng, X., Huang, J., Rozelle, S., & Uchida, E. (2010). Economic growth and the expansion of urban land in China. *Urban studies, 47*(4), 813-843.

144. Deuskar, C., Baker, J. L., & Mason, D. (2015). *East Asia's changing urban landscape: Measuring a decade of spatial growth.* World Bank Publications.

145. Dewan, A. M., & Corner, R. J. (2014). Spatiotemporal analysis of urban growth, sprawl and structure. In *Dhaka megacity* (pp. 99-121). Springer, Dordrecht.

146. Dieleman, F., & Wegener, M. (2004). Compact city and urban sprawl. *Built Environment, 30*(4), 308-323.

147. Dixon, J., & Fallon, L. (1989). The Concept of Sustainability: Origins, Extensions and Usefulness for Policy. *Society and Natural Resources.* 2, 73–84.

148. Doan, P., & Oduro, C. Y. (2012). Patterns of population growth in peri-urban Accra, Ghana. *International Journal of Urban and Regional Research, 36*(6), 1306-1325.

149. Dokko, Y., Edelstein, R., Lacayo, A., & Lee, D. (1999). Real estate income and value cycles: A model of market dynamics. *Journal of real estate research, 18*(1), 69-95.

150. Dosch, J. (2009). Vietnam in 2008: Foreign Policy Successes but Daunting Domestic Problems. *Southeast Asian Affairs*, 373-388.

151. Downs, A. (1999). Some realities about sprawl and urban decline. *Housing policy debate, 10*(4), 955-974.

152. Downs, A. (2005). Smart Growth: Why We Discuss It More than We Do It. *Journal of the American Planning Association.* 71(4).

153. Downs, A. (2017). Using the lessons of experience to allocate resources in the community development program. In *Housing Urban America* (pp. 522-535). Routledge.

154. Drexhage, J., & Murphy, D. (2010). Sustainable development: from Brundtland to Rio 2012. *United Nations Headquarters, New York, 2010*, 9-13.

155. Duany, A., & Plater-Zyberk, E., & Speck, J. (2000). *Suburban Nation: the rise of sprawl and the decline of the American dream.* North Point Press. New York.

156. Duany, A., and E. Plater-Zyberk. (1998). The Traditional Neighborhood and Suburban Sprawl: Attributes and Consequences.

157. Duany, A., Plater-Zyberk, E., & Speck, J. (2001). *Suburban nation: The rise of sprawl and the decline of the American dream*. Macmillan.

158. Duensing, E. (1977). *Suburban Shopping Centers versus the Central Business District: A Bibliography.* Monticello, IL: Vance Bibliographies.

159. Duncan, J. E. et al. (1989). *The Search for Efficient Urban Growth Patterns.* Tallahassee: Florida Department of Community Affairs.

160. Dwyer, J. F., & Childs, G. M. (2004). Movement of people across the landscape: a blurring of distinctions between areas, interests, and issues affecting natural resource management. *Landscape and urban planning*, *69*(2-3), 153-164.

161. Dye, R. F., & McGuire, T.J. (2000). "Property Taxes, Schools, and Sprawl," State Tax Notes, (May 29). 905.

162. Ebrahimpour-Masoumi, H. (2012). Urban sprawl in Iranian cities and its differences with the western sprawl. *Spatium*, (27), 12-18.

163. Ebrahimpour-Masoumi, H. (2014). Neo-traditional neighbourhood design concepts based on the urban form of the historical cities of central Iran. *International Journal of Sustainable Society*, *6*(3), 264-286.

164. EEA. (2011b). 'Land take' (http://www.eea.europa.eu/ data-and-

maps/indicators/land-take-2) accessed 12 August 2015.

165. El Nasser, H, & Overberg, P. (2001). What you don't know about sprawl. USA Today 19(112:1).

166. Elkin, T., Mc Laren, D., Hillman, M. (1991). Reviving the City: Towards Sustainable Urban Development. Friends of the Earth, London.

167. Elliot (2012). *A Better Way to Zone: Ten Principles to Create More Livable Cities.* Island Press.

168. Engelen, E., Froud, J., Johal, S., Salento, A., & Williams, K. (2016). *How cities work: a policy agenda for the grounded city* (No. 141, p. 115). CRESC Working Paper.

169. Engle, R. F, & Granger, C.W. (1987). C0-integration and error correction: representation, estimation, and testing. Econometrica, 55(2), 251-276

170. European Environment Agency. (2006). Urban Sprawl in Europe, the Ignored Challenge. European Commission: Joint Research Center. 23, 5– 24. European Environment Agency Report 10. Office for Official Publications of the European

171. Ewing, R. (1997). Is Los Angeles-style sprawl desirable? *Journal of the American Planning Association, 63*(1), 107-126.

172. Ewing, R. H. (2008). Characteristics, causes, and effects of sprawl: A literature review. In *Urban Ecology* (pp. 519-535). Springer, Boston, MA.

173. Ewing, R., & Pendall, R., & Chen, D. (2002). *Measuring sprawl and its impact: the character & consequences of metropolitan expansion.* Washington DC: Smart Growth America.

174. Fahrig, L., & Pedlar, J. H., & Pope, S. E., & Talyor, P. D., &. Wegner, J. F. (1995). Effect of road traffic on amphibian density. *Biological Conservation.* 15,177–182.

175. Falconer, R. (2008). *Living on the Edge: transport sustainability in Perth's Liveable Neighbourhoods* (Doctoral dissertation, Murdoch University).
176. Fan, D. P., Bengston, D. N., Potts, R. S., & Goetz, E. G. (2005). The rise and fall of concern about urban sprawl in the United States: an updated analysis. *United States department of agriculture forest service general technical report nc, 265*, 1.
177. Fan, Y., Yu, G., He, Z., Yu, H., Bai, R., Yang, L., & Wu, D. (2017). Entropies of the Chinese land use/cover change from 1990 to 2010 at a county level. *Entropy, 19*(2), 51.
178. Farkisch, H., Che-Ani, A. I., Ahmadi, V., Surat, M. (2012). Sense of Territoriality and Revitalization of Neighborhood Centers in Boshrooyeh City", *World Academy of Science, Engineering and Technology*, Vol. 67, pp. 670-675.
179. Farkisch, H., Che-Ani, A. I., Ahmadi, V., Surat, M., Tahir, M. M. (2011). "Sense of Community through Neighborhood Center", *Journal of Design+Built*, Vol. 4.
180. Feitelson E. (1993). The Spatial Effects of Land Use Regulations: A Missing Link in Growth Control Evaluations. J. Amer. Planning Assoc., 4: 461-72.
181. Ferrara, A., Salvati, L., Sabbi, A., & Colantoni, A. (2014). Urbanization, soil quality and rural areas: Towards a spatial mismatch? Science of the Total Environment, 478, 116–122.
182. Fischel, W. (1985). *The Economics of Zoning Laws: A Property Rights Approach to American Land Use Controls*. Baltimore: Johns Hopkins University Press.
183. Forman, R. T. T. (2002). *Road ecology: science and solutions*. Island Press. Washington, DC. The USA.
184. Forys, E., & Allen, C. (2005).The Impacts of Sprawl on Biodiversity: the Ant Fauna of the Lower Florida Keys. *Ecology and Society*. 10(1).

185. Fragkias, M., &Seto, K. C. (2007). Modeling urban growth in data-sparse environments: A new approach. *Environment and Planning B: Planning and Design*, 34, 858-883.

186. Frank, J. E. (1989). *The Costs of Alternative Development Patterns: A Review of the Literature.* Washington, DC: Urban Land Institute.

187. Freeman, L. (2001). The effects of sprawl on neighborhood social ties: An explanatory analysis. Journal of the American Planning Association 67: 69-77.

188. Freestone, R., ed. (2000). Urban Planning in a Changing World: The Twentieth Century Experience, E&FN Spon, London; New York.

189. Freilich, R., & Bruce, G. (1997). *The Social Costs of Sprawl.* The Urban Lawyer 29. 2, 183-198.

190. Frenkel, A., & Ashkenazi, M. (2008). Measuring urban sprawl: how can we deal with it? *Environment and Planning B: Planning and Design, 35*(1), 56-79.

191. Frumkin, H. (2002). Urban Sprawl and Public Health. *Public Health Reports.* Association of Schools of Public Health.

192. Fuguitt, G. V., & Brown, D. L. (1990). Residential preferences and population redistribution: 1972–1988. *Demography, 27*(4), 589-600.

193. Fujita, M., Thisse, J. F., & Zenou, Y. (1997). On the endogenous formation of secondary employment centers in a city. *Journal of Urban Economics, 41*(3), 337-357.

194. Fulton, G. (1992). Future designs for small towns in Canada. *Plan Canada.* 35, 29-30.

195. Gabriel, S. A., Faria, J. A., & Moglen, G. E. (2006). A multi-objective optimization approach to smart growth in land development. *Socio-Economic Planning Sciences, 40*(3), 212-248.

196. Gaffron, P., Benecke, J., & Flämig, H. (2007). Hinterland traffic of the Port of Hamburg-keeping the gateway open. In *Proceedings of the European Transport Conference (etc.) 2007 held 17-19 October 2007, Leiden, the Netherlands.*

197. Gaffron, P., Schubert, U., Skala, F. and Wagner, T. (2007), Planning Urban Structures for Sustainable Transport. In Land Use and Transport - European Research Towards Integrated Policies, Marshall S. and Banister D. (eds.), p. 71-103. Oxford: Elsevier.

198. Galea, S., Freudenberg, N., & Vlahov, D. (2005). Cities and population health. *Social science & medicine*, *60*(5), 1017-1033.

199. Galster, G. (2001). On the nature of neighborhood. *Urban Studies*, *38*(12), 2111-2124.

200. Galster, G., & Hanson, R., & Wolman, H., & Coleman, S., & Freihage, J. (2001). Wrestling Sprawl to the Ground: Defining and Measuring an Elusive Concept. *Housing Policy Debate 12*. 681-717.

201. Garcia, D., & Riera, P. (2003). Expansion versus density in Barcelona: A valuation exercise. *Urban Studies*, *40*(10), 1925-1936.

202. Garreau, J. (1992). *Edge city: Life on the new frontier*. Anchor.

203. Gaston, K.J., Ávila-Jiménez, M.L. & Edmondson, J.L. (2013). Managing urban ecosystems for goods and services. *Journal of Applied Ecology*, 50, 830– 840.

204. Ghani, E. (2012). Urbanization in Pakistan: challenges and options. *Pakistan Institute of Development Economics (PIDE) Working Paper*.

205. Ghauri, B., Lodhi, A., & Mansha, M. (2007). Development of baseline (air quality) data in Pakistan. Environmental Monitoring and Assessment, 127(1-3), 237-252.

206. Giles-Corti, B., Foster, S., Shilton, T., & Falconer, R. (2010). The co-benefits for health of investing in

active transportation. *New South Wales Public Health Bulletin, 21*(6), 122-127.

207. Gill, J. (2008). *The Effect of Urban Sprawl on Sydney's Peri-Urban Agricultural Region.* Society. Environmental Policy and Sustainability.

208. Gillham, O. (2002). *The limitless city: a primer on the urban sprawl debate.* Washington. D. Island Press.

209. Gin, A., & Sonstelie, J. (1992). The streetcar and residential location in nineteenth-century Philadelphia. *Journal of Urban Economics, 32*(1), 92-107.

210. Giuliano, G. (1989). New Directions for Understanding Transportation and Land Use. *Environment and Planning A.* 21, 145-159.

211. Glaeser, E. L., & Kahn, M. E. (2003). Sprawl and urban growth. *Handbook of regional and urban economics, 4,* 2481-2527.

212. Glaeser, E. L., & Kahn, M. J. Rappaport. (2000). "Why do the poor live in cities?" *NBER Working Paper, 7636*(20), 99-114.

213. Glaeser, E. L., & Sacerdote, B. (1999). Why is there more crime in cities? *Journal of Political Economy, 107*(S6), S225-S258.

214. Glaeser, E. L., La Porta, R., Lopez-de-Silanes, F., & Shleifer, A. (2004). Do institutions cause growth? *Journal of Economic Growth*, 9(3), 271-303.

215. Glaeser, Edward L., and Matthew E. Kahn. (2003). "Sprawl and Urban Growth," *Harvard Institute of Economic Research Discussion Paper,* Number 2004.

216. Goetz, S. (2002, February). Impacts of Housing Development and Sprawl on Selected Economic and Health Outcomes. In *Conference Proceedings. Land Use Research Workshop, Orlando, Florida.*

217. Goldberg, D. (1999). *Covering Urban Sprawl: Rethinking the American Dream.* Washington: RTNDF.

218. Gordon, P., & Richardson, H. W. (1997). Are compact cities a desirable planning goal? *Journal of the American Planning Association, 63*(1), 95-106.

219. Gordon, P., & Richardson, H. W. (2000). *Critiquing sprawl's critics*. Washington, DC: Cato Institute.

220. Gore, Al. (1998). Remarks as Delivered by Vice President Al Gore at the Brookings Institution. The Brookings Institution, Washington DC.

221. Grahn, P. and Stigsdotter, U. (2003). 'Landscape planning and stress', *Urban Forestry & Urban Greening*2 (1), 1–18.

222. Grimm, N. B., Grove, J. G., Pickett, S. T., & Redman, C. L. (2000). Integrated approaches to long-term studies of urban ecological systems: Urban ecological systems present multiple challenges to ecologists—pervasive human impact and extreme heterogeneity of cities, and the need to integrate social and ecological approaches, concepts, and theory. *BioScience, 50*(7), 571-584.

223. Großmann, K., Bontje, M., Haase, A., & Mykhnenko, V. (2013). Shrinking cities: Notes for the further research agenda. *Cities, 35*, 221-225.

224. Gruebner, O., Rapp, M. A., Adli, M., Kluge, U., Galea, S., & Heinz, A. (2017). Cities and mental health. *Deutsches Ärzteblatt International, 114*(8), 121.

225. Guest, G., MacQueen, K. M., & Namey, E. E. (2012). Validity and reliability (credibility and dependability) in qualitative research and data analysis. *Applied thematic analysis. London: Sage Publications*, 79-106.

226. Gülersoy, N.Z., Ayrancı, İ., (2011). Management Plan for Conservation Areas, ITU, Urban and Environmental Planning and Research Center, Cenkler Publishing, Istanbul.

227. Gunay, B. (2007). Car following theory with lateral discomfort. *Transportation Research Part B: Methodological, 41*(7), 722-735.

228. Günay, E. (2007). Interaction of urban fringe and transportation system: Istanbul case. *Published thesis in the İzmir Institute of Technology*. Turkey.

229. Gupta, R., & Sen, A. (2008). Monitoring physical growth of Ranchi City by using geoinformatics techniques. *ITPI journal, 5*(4), 38-48.

230. Gurin, D. (2003). *Understanding Sprawl: A Citizens' Guide*. Vancouver: David Suzuki Foundation.

231. Haber, W. (2007). Energy, food, and land—the ecological traps of humankind. *Environmental Science and Pollution Research-International, 14*(6), 359-365.

232. Habibia, S., & Asadib, N. (2011) .Causes, results and methods of controlling urban sprawl. International Conference on Green Buildings and Sustainable Cities. *Procedia Engineering*. 21, 133 – 141.

233. Haider, M., & Haider, I. (2006). Urban development in Pakistan. *Urbanisation and Sustainability in Asia: Case Studies on Best Practice Approaches to Sustainable Urban and Regional Development*, 245-272.

234. Halbert, L., Henneberry, J., & Mouzakis, F. (2014). The financialization of business property and what it means for cities and regions. *Regional Studies, 48*(3), 547-550.

235. Hale, M. L., &. Lurz, P. W. W., & Shirley, M. D. F., & Rushton, S., & Fuller, R. M., & K. Wolff. (2001). Impact of landscape management on the genetic structure of red squirrel populations. *Science*. 293, 2246– 2248.

236. Hall, E. (2006). Divide and sprawl, decline and fall: A comparative critique of Euclidean zoning. *U. Pitt. L. Rev., 68*, 915.

237. Hameed, M., Moradkhani, H., Ahmadalipour, A., Moftakhari, H., Abbaszadeh, P., & Alipour, A. (2019). A review of the 21st century challenges in the food-

energy-water security in the Middle East. *Water, 11*(4), 682.

238. Hartig, T., Mang, M. and Evans, G. W., (1991). 'Restorative effects of natural environment experiences', *Environment and Behavior* 23(1), 3–26.

239. Harvey, A. S., & Clark, S. (1973). *Descriptive Analysis of Halifax Time Budget Data*.

240. Harvey, R. O., & Clark, W. A. (1965). The nature and economics of urban sprawl. *Land Economics, 41*(1), 1-9.

241. Harvey, R. O., &. Clark, W. A. V. (1971). The nature and economics of urban sprawl. *In Internal Structure of the City*, ed. L. S. Bourne. New York: Oxford University Press. 475-482.

242. Hasan, A. (1999). Planning for Karachi: An agenda for citizen and NGOs. *Karachi: OPP-RTI.*

243. Hasan, A., & Raza, M. (2009). *Migration and small towns in Pakistan* (Vol. 15). IIED.

244. Hasan, A., & Raza, M. (2011). The evolution of the microcredit programme of the OPP's Orangi Charitable Trust, Karachi. *Environment and Urbanization, 23*(2), 517-538.

245. Hasan, A., Ahmed, N., Raza, M., Sadiq, A., Ahmed, S. U., & Sarwar, M. B. (2015). *Karachi: the land issue*. Karachi: Oxford University Press.

246. Hasan, A., Mohib, M. (2003). Urban Slums Reports: The case of Karachi, Pakistan. In: UN-Habitat. Global Report on Human Settlements 2003, The Challenge of Slums, Earthscan, London; Part IV: 'Summary of City Case Studies'. p. 195-228.

247. Hasan, A., Pervaiz, A., & Raza, M. (2017). Drivers of climate change vulnerability at different scales in Karachi. *International Institute for Environment and Development (IIED) Working Paper. IIED London, 10.*

248. Hashmi, S. S. (1965). The people of Karachi's demographic characteristics.

249. Hassan, A. A. M. (2011, September). Changes in the urban spatial structure of the greater Cairo metropolitan area, Egypt. In *UDMS 2011: 28th Urban Data Management Symposium, Delft, The Netherlands, September 28-30, 2011*. Urban Data Management Society; OTB Research Institute for the Built Environment; Delft University of Technology.

250. Hassan, A. J., Arsalan, M. H., & Fatima, H. (2016). Assessment of Urban Growth of Karachi: From A Tiny Town to A Meta City of the World. *Karachi, Pakistan: Institute of Space and Planetary Astrophysics. University of Karachi.*

251. Hassan, A. J., Arsalan, M. H., & Fatima, H. (2017). Assessment of Urban Growth of Karachi: From A Tiny Town to A Meta City of the World.

252. Hasse, J. E., & Lathrop, R. G. (2003). Land resource impact indicators of urban sprawl. *Applied Geography, 23*(2), 159-175.

253. Hatab, A. A., Cavinato, M. E. R., Lindemer, A., & Lagerkvist, C. J. (2019). Urban sprawl, food security and agricultural systems in developing countries: A systematic review of the literature. *Cities, 94*, 129-142.

254. Haughton, G. (1999). Environmental justice and the sustainable city. *In Sustainable Cities*, ed. D. Satterthwaite. London: Earthscan. 62-79.

255. Haughton, G., & Hunter, C. (1994). Sustainable Cities (Jessica Kingsley, London).

256. Heberle, L. (2008*). Sustainable Urban Development: Local Strategies as Global Solutions.* Local Sustainable Urban Development in a Globalized World.

257. Heilburn, J. (1987). Urban Economics and Public Policy. New York: St. Martin's Press.

258. Heimlich, R. E., & Anderson, W. D. (2001). *Development at the urban fringe and beyond:*

Impacts on agriculture and rural land (No. 1473-2016-120733).

259. Heinrich, D., Nuissl, H., & Rodriguez S, C. (2009). Urban sprawl and new challenges for (metropolitan) governance in Latin America: The case of Santiago de Chile. *Revista Latinoamericana de Estudios Urbano Regionales-EURE*, (104), 29.
260. Henderson, V., & Mitra, A. (1996). The new urban landscape: Developers and edge cities. *Regional Science and Urban Economics, 26*(6), 613-643.
261. Heng Sun, Wayne. F and Nigel. W. (2007). "Modeling Urban Land Use Change and Urban Sprawl: Calgary, Alberta, Canada", Netw Spat Econ7, 353–376.
262. Henslin, J. M. (2005). Sociology: A down-to-earth approach, (7th international edition).
263. Herold, M. (2006). Urban Patterns and Processes: a Remote Sensing Perspective, PFG 4/2006, pp. 265-276.
264. Herold, M., Goldstein, N. C., & Clarke, K. C. (2003). The spatiotemporal form of urban growth: measurement, analysis and modeling. *Remote sensing of Environment, 86*(3), 286-302.
265. Herold, M., Mayaux, P., Woodcock, C. E., Baccini, A., & Schmullius, C. (2008). Some challenges in global land cover mapping: An assessment of agreement and accuracy in existing 1 km datasets. *Remote Sensing of Environment, 112*(5), 2538-2556.
266. Hess, G., Daley, S. S., Dennison, B. K., Lubkin, S. R., McGuinn, R. P., Morin, V. Z., ... & Wrege, B. M. (2001). Just what is sprawl, anyway? *Carolina Planning, 26*(2), 11-26.
267. Hikichi, L. (2003). New urbanism and transportation. *University of Wisconsin-Milwaukee*, 1-28.

268. Hill, R and Kim, J. (2000). Global cities and developmental states: New York, Tokyo and Seoul. Urban Studies 12(37), 2241–2256.

269. Hill, R. C. (2004). Cities and nested hierarchies. *International Social Science Journal, 56*(181), 373-384.

270. Hillier, J. & Healey, P., eds. (2010). Research Companion to Planning Theory: Conceptual Challenges for Spatial Planning, Ashgate, Farnham; Surrey, UK.

271. Hillier, J., & Healey, P. (2008). *Critical essays in planning theory. Vol. 1, Foundations of the planning enterprise.* Ashgate.

272. Hillman, M. (1996). 'In Favor of the Compact City', in Jenks, M., Burton, E. and Williams, K. (eds.). *The Compact City: A Sustainable Urban Form?* E & FN Spoon, London: 36-44.

273. Hirt, S. (2007). The Compact versus the Dispersed City: History of Planning Ideas on Sofia's Urban Form. Virginia Polytechnic Institute and State University. *Journal of Planning History*, 6(2), 138-165.

274. Holcombe, R. G., Pope, C., & Bast, J. B. (1999). Urban sprawl: pro and con. *Defense of Urban Sprawl. Property and Environment Research Center Reports, Disponível em: http://www. perc. org/articles/article356. php.*

275. Hu, P. E. N. G., & Huapu, L. U. (2007). Study on the impacts of urban density on the travel demand using GIS spatial analysis. *Journal of Transportation Systems Engineering and Information Technology, 7*(4), 90-95.

276. Huang, J., Lu, X. X., & Sellers, J. M. (2007). A global comparative analysis of urban form: Applying spatial metrics and remote sensing. *Landscape and urban planning, 82*(4), 184-197.

277. Hurley, R. E. (2009).Studying Sustainability in Urban Environments. *Published thesis in University of Delaware.* Delaware.

278. Hussain, S. I., & Mazhar, U. (2018). Estimated export demand and supply functions for Pakistan: A disaggregated analysis. *Pakistan Business Review, 20*(1), 222-234.

279. Imran, M., & Low, N. (2005). Sustainable urban transport in Pakistan: threats and opportunities. *Management of Environmental Quality: An International Journal.*

280. Information and communication technologies (ICT). (2003). Retrieved 10 January 2013 from international summit for information and communication technology: www.moneoman.gov.om.

281. Ingram, G. (1998). 'Patterns of metropolitan development: What have we learned?', *Urban Studies.* 35(7), 1019–1035.

282. Inman, R. P. (Ed.). (2009). Making *cities work: Prospects and policies for urban America.* Princeton University Press.

283. Inskeep, S. (2011). *Instant City, Life & Death in Karachi.* Penguin Press HC.

284. Irvine, K. N., Warber, S. L., Devine-Wright, P., & Gaston, K. J. (2013). Understanding urban green space as a health resource: A qualitative comparison of visit motivation and derived effects among park users in Sheffield, UK. *International journal of environmental research and public health, 10*(1), 417-442.

285. Ishrat, H. (2014). Deregulating the economy. Retrieved from: http://ishrathussain.iba.edu.pk.

286. Iyer, N. K., Kulkarni, S., & Raghavaswamy, V. (2007, June). Economy, population and urban sprawl: A comparative study of urban agglomerations of Bangalore and Hyderabad, India using remote sensing and GIS techniques. In *PRIPODE workshop on urban*

population, development and environment dynamics in developing countries (pp. 1-37).

287. Jabareen, Y. (2006). Sustainable Urban Forms: Their Typologies, Models, and Concepts. *Journal of Planning Education and Research.* 26(1), 38-52.
288. Jackson, K. T. (1987). *Crabgrass frontier: The suburbanization of the United States.* Oxford University Press.
289. Jacquin, A., Misakova, L., & Gay, M. (2008). A hybrid object-based classification approach for mapping urban sprawl in peri-urban environment. *Landscape and Urban Planning, 84*(2), 152-165.
290. Jaeger, J. A., Bertiller, R., Schwick, C., & Kienast, F. (2010). Suitability criteria for measures of urban sprawl. *Ecological Indicators, 10*(2), 397-406.
291. Jaeger, J.A.G., & Schwick, C. (2014). Improving the measurement of urban sprawl: Weighted Urban Proliferation (WUP) and its application to Switzerland. Ecological Indicators, 38, 294–308.
292. Jamil, S. (2018). Politics in a Digital Age: The Impact of New Media Technologies on Public Participation and Political Campaign in Pakistan's 2018 Elections–A Case Study of Karachi. *Global Media Journal, 16*(31), 1-9.
293. Jarvis, D.; Lambie, H. and Berkeley, N., (2009). Creative Industries and Urban Regeneration, Journal of Urban Regeneration and Renewal, Vol. 2, No.4, 364-374.
294. Jaspar, J. (2008). Teaching for Sustainable Development: Teachers' Perceptions. *Published thesis in the University of Saskatchewan*, Saskatchewan.
295. Jat, M. K., Garg, P. K., & Khare, D. (2008). Monitoring and modelling of urban sprawl using remote sensing and GIS techniques. *International Journal of Applied Earth Observation and Geoinformation, 10*(1), 26-43.

296. Jiang, F., Liu, S., Yuan, H., & Zhang, Q. (2007). Measuring urban sprawl in Beijing with geo-spatial indices. *Journal of Geographical Sciences, 17*(4), 469-478.

297. Jieli, C., Manchun, L. I., Yongxue, L. I. U., Chenglei, S., & Wei, H. U. (2010, June). Extract residential areas automatically by new built-up index. In *2010 18th International Conference on Geoinformatics* (pp. 1-5). IEEE.

298. Jingnan Huang, X. X. Lu., Jefferey M. Sellers. (2007). "A global comparative analysis of urban form: Applying spatial metrics and remote sensing," Landscape and Urban Planning, 82, 184-197.

299. Johnson, M. P. (2001). Environmental impacts of urban sprawl: a survey of the literature and proposed research agenda. *Environment and Planning A, 33*(4), 717-735.

300. Jokilehto, J. I., (1986). History of Architectural Conservation: The Contribution of English, French, German and Italian Thought towards an International Approach to the Conservation of Cultural Property, PhD Dissertation, Institute of Advanced Architectural Studies, The University of York, UK.

301. Jones, C., & Kammen, D. M. (2014). Spatial distribution of US household carbon footprints reveals suburbanization undermines greenhouse gas benefits of urban population density. *Environmental science & technology, 48*(2), 895-902.

302. Kahn, L. M. (2000). Wage inequality, collective bargaining, and relative employment from 1985 to 1994: Evidence from fifteen OECD countries. *Review of Economics and Statistics, 82*(4), 564-579.

303. Kahn, M. E., & Schwartz, J. (2008). Urban air pollution progress despite sprawl: the "greening" of the vehicle fleet. *Journal of Urban Economics, 63*(3), 775-787.

304. Kain, J. F. (1968). Housing segregation, Negro employment, and metropolitan decentralization. *The quarterly journal of economics, 82*(2), 175-197.

305. Kärrholm, M. (2008).*Setting the Scale of Sustainable Urban Form – Some scale-related problems discussed in the context of a Swedish urban landscape.* Retrieved 3 January 2013 from Conference Architectural Inquiries: http://www.tintin.arch.chalmers.se.

306. Kasarda, D. (1990). City Jobs and Residents on a Collision Course: The Urban Underclass Dilemma. *Economic Development Quarterly* .4(4), 313-19.

307. Kasarda, J. (1985). Urban change and minority opportunities. *The new urban reality.*

308. Kasarda, J. D. (1988). Jobs, migration, and emerging urban mismatches. *Urban change and poverty*, 148-198.

309. Kasarda, J. D. (1989). Urban industrial transition and the underclass. *The Annals of the American Academy of Political and Social Science, 501*(1), 26-47.

310. Katz, B. and J. Bradley. (1999). Divided we sprawl. The Atlantic Monthly 284(6): 26.

311. Kazmi, S. J. H., Mehdi, R., & Arsalan, M. H. (2008). Karachi: Environmental challenges of a mega city. *South Asian Mega Cities. Cambridge University Press, New Delhi, India*, 23-36.

312. Kazmi, S.J.H. (1995). Applications of Remote Sensing Techniques for Monitoring of Desertification: An Appraisal of Malir Valley, Proceedings of the Second Asia-Pacific Conference on Multilateral Cooperation of Space Technology (APC-MCSTA), Islamabad. p. 196-203.

313. KDA. (1991). Karachi Development Plan 2000, Master Plan and Environmental Control Department, Karachi Development Authority, Karachi.

314. Ke, S., Song, Y., & He, M. (2009). Determinants of urban spatial scale: Chinese cities in transition. *Urban Studies*, *46*(13), 2795-2813.

315. Keiner, M., & Schmid, W. A. (2003). Urbanisierungstendenzen in Entwicklungsländern: Probleme und Potenziale für nachhaltige Stadtentwicklung. *disP–The Planning Review*, *39*(155), 49-56.

316. Kelbaugh, D. (2008). Toward Neighborhood and Regional Design. *Pioneer America Society Transactions: PAST*, *31*, 77.

317. Kelly E. (1993). Managing Community Growth: Policies, Techniques, and Impacts Praeger, Westport.

318. Kelly, C., Ferrara, A., Wilson, G. A., Ripullone, F., Nolè, A., Harmer, N., & Salvati, L. (2015). Community resilience and land degradation in forest and shrubland socio-ecological systems: Evidence from Gorgoglione, Basilicata, Italy. *Land use policy*, *46*, 11-20.

319. Kendig, H. L. (1984). "Housing Careers, Life Cycle and Residential Mobility: Implications for the Housing Market," *Urban Studies*, 21:271-283.

320. Kenworthy, J. (2006). The eco-city: Ten key transport and planning dimensions for sustainable city development. *Environment and Urbanization.* 18 (1), 67-85.

321. Khan, N. (2010). *Mohajir militancy in Pakistan: violence and transformation in the Karachi conflict.* Routledge.

322. Khuhro, H., & Mooraj, A. (2010). *Karachi: mega-city of our times*. Oxford University Press.

323. Kiran, S., & Joshi, B. (2012). Estimation of variables explaining urbanization concomitant with land-use change: a spatial approach, International Journal of Remote Sensing, vol 34(3), 824–847.

324. Kirtland, D., DeCola, L., Gaydos, L., Acevedo, W., Clarke, K., & Bell, C. (1994). An analysis of human-induced land transformations in the San Francisco Bay/Sacramento area. *World Resource Review ;(United States)*, *6*(CONF-940422--).

325. Kline, J. (2000). Comparing states with and without growth management analysis based on indicators with policy implications comment. Land Use Policy, 17, 349–355.

326. Kloosterman, R. (1996). Mixed experiences: Post-industrial transition and ethnic minorities on the Amsterdam labour market. *Journal of Ethnic and Migration Studies*, *22*(4), 637-653.

327. Knaap G, Talen E, Olshansky R. (2000). Government Policy and Urban Sprawl. Department of Urban and Regional Planning. p. 2.

328. Knaap, G. (1998). The Determinants of Residential Property Values: Implications for Metropolitan Planning. Journal of Planning Literature 12, 3: 267-282.

329. Knaap, G., & Nelson, A. C. (1992). *The regulated landscape: Lessons on state land use planning from Oregon*. Lincoln Institute of Land Policy.

330. Knaap, G., Talen, E., Olshansky, R., & Forrest, C. (2000). Government policy and urban sprawl. *Illinois Department of Natural Resources, Office of Realty and Environmental Planning: Springfield, IL, USA*.

331. Kofmann, T. (1999). Even in Maine? Environment 41(4): 30.

332. Koizumi, Y., Nishimiya, N., & Kaneko, M. (2013). Urban transportation characteristics and urban mass transit introduction in the cities of developing countries. *Journal of the Eastern Asia Society for Transportation Studies*, *10*, 81-99.

333. Kolankiewicz, L., & Beck, R. (2001). Weighing sprawl factors in large US cities. *Analysis of US Bureau of the Census Data on the, 100.*

334. Koslowsky, M., Aizer, A., & Krausz, M. (1996). Stressor and personal variables in the commuting experience. *International Journal of Manpower, 17*(3), 4-14.

335. Kotkin, J., & Cox, W. (2013). The Future of the Affluent American City. *A Journal of Policy Development and Research, 15*(3), 203.

336. Kraus, M. (2006). Monocentric cities: In: Arnott, R.J., McMillan, D.P. (Eds.), A Companion to Urban Economics, Blackwell Publishing, Oxford, 96-108.

337. Kronenfeld, D. A. (2008). Afghan refugees in Pakistan: not all refugees, not always in Pakistan, not necessarily Afghan? *Journal of Refugee Studies, 21*(1), 43-63.

338. Kugelman, M., & Hathaway, R. M. (2011). Pakistan's demographics: Possibilities, perils, and prescriptions. *Reaping the Dividend: Overcoming Pakistan's Demographic Challenges (Wilson Center, 2011).*

339. Kumar, A., Pandey, A. C., Hoda, N., & Jeyaseelan, A. T. (2011). Evaluation of urban sprawl pattern in the tribal-dominated cities of Jharkhand state, India. *International Journal of Remote Sensing, 32*(22), 7651-7675.

340. Kumar, J. A. V., Pathan, S. K. and Bhandari, R. J. (2007). Spatio-Temporal Analysis for Monitoring Urban Growth- A Case Study of Indore City, Journal of the Indian Society of Remote Sensing, Vol. 35, No. 1, pp 11-20.

341. Kunstler, J. H. (1993). The Geography of Nowhere, New York. *Touchstone/Simon & Schuster.*

342. Kunstler, J. H. (1996). (1996a, September). Home from nowhere. The Atlantic Monthly, 278, 43-66.

343. Ladd, H.F. (1998). "Effects of Taxes on Economic Activity," in Ladd, H. (Ed.). "Local Government Tax and Land Use Policies in the United States: Understanding the Links (pp. 82-101), Northampton, MA: Edward Elgar Publishing, Inc.

344. Laghai, H., Loghman, M., & Kolbadi, N. (2010). Strategy for Sustainable Urban Development Guidelines for Tehran."

345. Lagro Jr, James, A. (1994). Population growth beyond the urban fringe: implications for rural land use policy. *Landscape and Urban Planning, 28*(2-3), 143-158.

346. Lambin, E. F., Turner, B. L., Geist, H. J., Agbola, S. B., Angelsen, A., Bruce, J. W., ... & George, P. (2001). The causes of land-use and land-cover change: moving beyond the myths. *Global environmental change, 11*(4), 261-269.

347. Lande, R., & Shannon, S. (1996). The role of genetic variation in adaptation and population persistence in a changing environment. *Evolution.* 50,434–437.

348. Lang, R. E. (2005). Valuing the suburbs: Why some "improvements" lower home prices. Opolis: An International Journal of Suburban and Metropolitan Studies, 1(1), 5-12.

349. Langley, S. K., Cheshire, H. M., & Humes, K. S. (2001). A comparison of single date and multi-temporal satellite image classifications in a semi-arid grassland. *Journal of Arid Environments, 49*(2), 401-411.

350. Langørgen, A. (2007). Sentralisering-årsaker, virkninger og politick Samfunnspeilet nr. 2.

351. Lapalme, L. (2003). The Social Dimension of Sustainable Development and the Mining Industry. Retrieved 3 January 2018 from: www.nrcan.gc.ca.

352. Lassila, K. D. (1999). The new suburbanites. Amicus Journal, 16 – 21.

353. Law, S., & Zhao, Y. (2009). Exploring Multi-layered Hyper Dense Urban Environments through Spatial Analysis. In *Proceedings of the 7th International Space Syntax Symposium, Stockholm: KTH.*

354. Lawrence, B. L. (2005). The context and causes of sprawl. *Nature in fragments: the legacy of sprawl. Columbia University Press, New York*, 3-17.

355. Le Goix, R. (2005). Gated communities: sprawl and social segregation in southern California. *Housing Studies.* 20(2), 323-343.

356. Leao, S., Bishop, I., & Evans, D. (2001). Assessing the demand for solid waste disposal in urban regions by urban dynamics modelling in a GIS environment. *Resources, conservation and recycling*, *33*(4), 289-313.

357. Leccese, M., & McCormick, K. (2000). *Charter of the new urbanism*. New York: McGraw-Hill.

358. Lee, J., Tian, L., Erickson, L. J., & Kulikowski, T. D. (1998). Analyzing growth-management policies with geographical information systems. *Environment and Planning B: planning and design*, *25*(6), 865-879.

359. Lee, J., Tian, L., Erickson, L. J., & Kulikowski, T. D. (1998). Analyzing growth-management policies with geographical information systems. *Environment and Planning B: planning and design*, *25*(6), 865-879.

360. Leichencko, R and Solecki, W. (2005). Exporting the American dream: the globalization of suburban consumption landscapes. Regional Studies 39(2), 241–253.

361. Lessinger, J. (1962). 'The cause for scatteration: some reflections on the National Capitol Region Plan for the Year 2000'. Journal of the American Institute of Planners 28(3): 159-170.

362. Levine N. (1999). The Effects of Local Growth Controls on Regional Housing Production and

Population Redistribution in California. Urban Studies. 12: 2047-68.

363. Lewis, P. G. (2001). Retail politics: Local sales taxes and the fiscalization of land use. Economic Development Quarterly, 15, 21-35.

364. Lewis-Kraus, G. (2006). Disentangled from Redemption.

365. Li, K., Fei, M., Irwin, G. W., & Ma, S. (Eds.). (2007). *Bio-Inspired Computational Intelligence and Applications: International Conference on Life System Modeling and Simulation, LSMS 2007, Shanghai, China, September 14-17, 2007. Proceedings* (Vol. 4688). Springer Science & Business Media.

366. Lin, B.B. & Fuller, R.A. (2013). Sharing or sparing? How should we grow the world's cities? *Journal of Applied Ecology*, 50, 1161– 1168.

367. Litman, T. (2012). *Where We Want To Be Home Location Preferences And Their Implications For Smart Growth*. Retrieved 10 March, 2013 from: Victoria Transport Policy Institute: www.vtpi.org/sgcp.pdf.

368. Liu, X. I. I. I., & Lathrop Jr, R. G. (2002). Urban change detection based on an artificial neural network. *International Journal of Remote Sensing, 23*(12), 2513-2518.

369. Liu, Z. (2002). Foreign direct investment and technology spillover: Evidence from China. *Journal of Comparative Economics, 30*(3), 579-602.

370. Llewellyn, G., Sullivan, G., & Minichiello, V. (2004). Sampling in qualitative research. In *Handbook of research methods for nursing and health science.* Pearson Education Australia.

371. Loibl, W., & Toetzer, T. (2003). Modeling growth and densification processes in suburban regions—simulation of landscape transition with spatial agents. Environmental Modelling & Software, 18(6), 553-563.

372. Lopez, R., & Hynes, H. P. (2006). Sprawl in the 1990s: Measurement, distribution and trends. Urban Affairs Review, 38(3), 325–355.

373. Luck, M., & Wu, J. (2002). A gradient analysis of urban landscape pattern: a case study from the Phoenix metropolitan region, Arizona, USA. *Landscape ecology*, *17*(4), 327-339.

374. MacBurnie, I. (1992). Reconsidering the dream: Alternative design for sustainable development. *Plan Canada.* 35, 19-23.

375. Maier, G., Franz, G., & Schrock, P. (2006). Urban Sprawl. How Useful Is This Concept?

376. Maimbo, S. M., &Ratha, D. (Eds.). (2005). *Remittances: Development impact and future prospects.* World Bank Publications.

377. Maktav, D., & Erbek, F. S. (2005). Analysis of urban growth using multi-temporal satellite data in Istanbul, Turkey. *International Journal of Remote Sensing*, *26*(4), 797-810.

378. Malik, K. (2013). Human Development Report 2013. The rise of the South: Human progress in a diverse world. *The Rise of the South: Human Progress in a Diverse World (March 15, 2013). UNDP-HDRO Human Development Reports.*

379. Malpezzi, S. (1999). *Estimates of the measurement and determinants of urban sprawl in US metropolitan areas* (No. 99-06). University of Wisconsin Center for Urban Land Economic Research.

380. Mann, S. (2009). Institutional causes of urban and rural sprawl in Switzerland. Land Use Policy, 26(4), 919–924.

381. Mansha, M., Javed, S. H., Kazmi, M., & Feroze, N. (2011). Study of rice husk ash as a potential source of acid resistance calcium silicate. *Advances in Chemical Engineering and Science*, *1*(3), 147-153.

382. Mason, J. (2002). Linking qualitative and quantitative data analysis. In *Analyzing qualitative data* (pp. 103-124). Routledge.

383. Masoumi, H. E. (2013). Residential self-selection and its effects on urban commute travels in Iranian cities compared to US, UK, and Germany. *International Journal of Social Sciences, 7*(5), 877-881.

384. Masoumi, H. E. (2014). Urban sprawl in mid-sized cities of MENA, evidence from Yazd and Kashan in central Iran. *Management Research and Practice, 6*(2), 25-41.

385. Mayerhofer R. and Skala F. (2005). Objectives for a Transit Oriented Eco-city Development, Full paper available from: http://www.oekostadt.at/docs/AESOP_Beitrag.doc [Accessed 18 September 2017].

386. McGee, T. G. (1991). The emergence of desakota regions in Asia: expanding a hypothesis. *The extended metropolis: Settlement transition in Asia.*

387. McGrath, D. T. (2005). More evidence on the spatial scale of cities. Journal of Urban Economics, 58,1-10.

388. McKinsey, G. I. (2011). Urban world: mapping the economic power of cities. *Report of the McKinsey Global Institute.*

389. McLaren, R., Coleman, D. and Mayunga, S. (2005). Sustainable Management of Mega Growth in Mega-cities. FIG Working Week 2005 and 8th International Conference on Global Spatial Data Infrastructure (GSDI-8), Cairo, Egypt, 16-21 April 2005.

390. McMillen, D. P. (2006). Testing for monocentricity. *A Companion to Urban Economics. Oxford: Blackwell,* 128-140.

391. McMillen, D. P., & McDonald, J. F. (1998). Suburban subcenters and employment density in metropolitan Chicago. *Journal of Urban Economics, 43*(2), 157-180.

392. Mebratu, D. (1998). Sustainability and Sustainable Development: Historical and Conceptual Review. *Environmental Impact Assessment Review.*18, 493-520.

393. Megahed, Y., Cabral, P., Silva, J., & Caetano, M. (2015). Land cover mapping analysis and urban growth modelling using remote sensing techniques in greater Cairo region — Egypt. *ISPRS International Journal of Geo-Information, 4*(3), 1750-1769.

394. Mehdi, M. R., Kazmi, S. J. H., & Arsalan, M. H. (2002). Spotting noise risk zones in Karachi, Pakistan: A GIS perspective. *Proceedings GISDECO: Governance and the use of GIS in developing countries. ITC Enschede, the Netherlands.*

395. Memon, R. (2005). Determinants and trends of internal migration in Pakistan. *Internal Labour Migration in Pakistan. Institute of Developing Economies, Japan External Trade Organisation, Chiba, Japan.*

396. Menon N (2004). Retrieved July 20, 2011, from World Student Community for Sustainable Development: http://wscsd.org/urban-sprawl/

397. Mensah, A. M., & Castro, L. C. (2004). Sustainable resource use & sustainable development: a contradiction. *Center for Development Research, University of Bonn.*

398. Mieszkowski, P., & Mills, E. S. (1993). The causes of metropolitan suburbanization. *Journal of Economic Perspectives, 7*(3), 135-147.

399. Miles, M. B., & Huberman, A. M. (1994). *Qualitative data analysis: An expanded sourcebook.* sage.

400. Mills, D. E. (1981). Growth, speculation and sprawl in a monocentric city. *Journal of Urban Economics, 10*(2), 201-226.

401. Mills, E. S. (1967). An aggregative model of resource allocation in a metropolitan area. *The American Economic Review, 57*(2), 197-210.

402. Mills, E. S. (1972). Studies in the Structure of the Urban Economy.

403. Millward, H. (2006). Urban containment strategies: A case-study appraisal of plans and policies in Japanese, British, and Canadian cities. *Land Use Policy, 23*(4), 473-485.

404. Minallah, M. N., Ghaffar, A., Rafique, M., & Mohsin, M. (2016). Urban growth and socio-economic development in Gujranwala, Pakistan: a geographical analysis. *Pakistan Journal of Science, 68*(2), 176.

405. Mirmoghtadaee, M. (2012). The Relationship between Land Use, Socio-Economic Characteristics of Inhabitants, and Travel Demand in New Towns - A Case Study of Hashtgerd New Town (Iran), *International Journal of Urban Sustainable Development* 4(1), pp: 39-62.

406. Misczynski, Dean J. (1986). "The Fiscalization of Land Use," in J. Kirlin and D.R. Winkler (Eds.), *California Policy Choices,* Sacramento, CA: School of Public Administration, University of Southern California.

407. Mitchell, J. (2001). 'Urban sprawl' *National Geographic,* 200(1): 48-56.

408. Mobaraki, O., Mohammadi, J., & Zarabi, A. (2012). Urban form and sustainable development: The case of Urmia City. *Journal of Geography and Geology, 4*(2), 1.

409. Mohammadi, J., Zarabi, A., & Mobaraki, O. (2012). "Urban sprawl pattern and effective factors on them: The case of Urmia City, Iran", *Journal of Urban & Regional Analysis,* vol. 4, no. 1, p. 77-89.

410. Monishiya, B. G., & Padmanaban, R. (2012). Mapping and change detection analysis of marine resources in Tuticorin and Vembar group of Islands using remote sensing. *Int. J. Adv. For. Sci. Manag, 1,* 1-16.

411. Montaigne, F. (2000). There goes the neighborhood! Audubon 102(2): 60-70.

412. Moriondo, M., Stefanini, F. M., & Bindi, M. (2008). Reproduction of olive tree habitat suitability for global change impact assessment. Ecological Modelling, 218(1), 95–109.

413. Mosk, C. (2000). *Japanese industrial history: technology, urbanization, and economic growth*. ME Sharpe.

414. Moudon, A. (2009). 'Real noise from the urban environment: How ambient community noise affects health and what can be done about it', *American Journal of Preventive Medicine* 37(2), 167–171.

415. Müller, K., Steinmeier, C., & Küchler, M. (2010). Urban growth along motorways in Switzerland. Landscape and Urban Planning, 98(1), 3–12.

416. Mumford, L. (1961). The City in History: its origins, its transformations, and its Prospects, Harcourt, Brace & World, New York.

417. Muñiz, I., Calatayud, D., & Dobaño, R. (2013). The compensation hypothesis in Barcelona measured through the ecological footprint of mobility and housing. *Landscape and Urban Planning*, *113*, 113-119.

418. Murray, W. E. (2006). Globalizing Economic Geographies," Geographies of Globalization.

419. Muth, R. F. (1961). Economic change and rural-urban land conversions. *Econometrica: Journal of the Econometric Society*, 1-23.

420. Muth, R. F. (1969). Cities and housing; the spatial pattern of urban residential land use.

421. Nachimias, D., & Nachimias, C. (1992). Research methods in the social sciences. New York: St.

422. Nasar, J. (2003). Does neotraditional development build community? *Journal of Planning Education and Research*. 23, 58-68.

423. National Association of Homebuilders (NAH). (2002). Smart growth examples.

424. Navamuel, E. L., Morollón, F. R., & Cuartas, B. M. (2018). Energy consumption and urban sprawl: Evidence for the Spanish case. *Journal of cleaner production, 172*, 3479-3486.

425. Nechyba, T. J., & Walsh, R. P. (2004). Urban Sprawl. Journal of Economic Perspectives, 18(4), 177–200.

426. Nelson, A. C. (1990). Economic critique of US prime farmland preservation policies: Towards state policies that influence productive, consumptive, and speculative value components of the farmland market to prevent urban sprawl and foster agricultural production in the United States.

427. Nelson, A. C., & Duncan, J. B. (1995). *Growth management principles and practices.* American Planning Association.

428. Newburn, D., & Berck, P. (2011). Exurban development. *Journal of Environmental Economics and Management, 62*(3), 323-336.

429. Newman, P. G., & Kenworthy, J. R. (1989). *Cities and automobile dependence: An international sourcebook.*

430. Newman, P., & Kenworthy, J. (1989). Gasoline consumption and cities: A comparison of US cities with a global survey. *Journal of the American Planning Association.* 55, 23-37.

431. Newman, P., & Thornley, A. (1997). Fragmentation and centralization in the governance of London: influencing the urban policy and planning agenda. *Urban Studies, 34*(7), 967-988.

432. Newman, P., Kenworthy, J., & Robinson, L. (1992). *Winning back the cities.*

433. Newton, P. W. (1997). Reshaping cities for a more sustainable future: exploring the link between urban form, air quality, energy and greenhouse gas emissions: report of Task Group 6-Urban

Infrastructure, to the Australian Academy of Technological Sciences and Engineering for the inquiry into urban air pollution in Australia.

434. Niazi, F., & Azad, A. P. (2018). Investigation of Ethnic Diversity in Pakistan: A Case Study of Karachi. *Journal of Basic and Applied Sciences, 14*, 246-253.

435. Nielsen, G. (2001). Den attraktive bilen som byens problem. In: Hompland, A. (ed.) Byens veier: lokal transport- og arealpolitikk. Bergen: Fagbokforlaget.

436. Niemeier, D., Bai, S. & Handy, S. (2011). The Impact of Residential Growth Patterns on Vehicle Travel and Pollutant Emissions, *the Journal of Transport and Land Use*, Vol. 4, No. 3, pp. 65-80.

437. Nijkamp, P., & Pepping, G. (1998). A Meta-analytical Evaluation of Sustainable City Initiatives. *Urban Studies*. 35 (9), 1481-1500.

438. Niwa, D. K. (2012). *UN Agenda 21 "sustainable development."* Retrieved 3 January, 2013 from US Congress: www.narlo.org/una21report.pdf.

439. Njoh, A. J. (2003). Urbanization and development in sub-Saharan Africa. *Cities, 20*(3), 167-174.

440. Novaco, R. W., Stokols, D., & Milanesi, L. (1990). Objective and subjective dimensions of travel impedance as determinants of commuting stress. American journal of community psychology, 18(2), 231-257.

441. Nozzi, D. (2003). *Road to Ruin: An introduction to sprawl and how to cure it.* Praeger. Westport Connecticut.

442. NRDC (National Resources Defense Council). (1996). Environmental Characteristics of Smart Growth Neighborhoods: An Exploratory Case Study. Natural Resources Defense Council, Washington DC. URL=www.nrdc.org/cities/smartGrowth/char/charinx.asp, visited 2001 Jan 16.

443. Nuissl, H., & Rink, D. (2005). The 'production of urban sprawl in eastern Germany as a phenomenon of post-socialist transformation. *Cities, 22*(2), 123-134.

444. Nuissl, H., Rink, D., & Steuer, P. (2005). *The consequences of urban sprawl in a context of decline: The case of Leipzig* (No. 7/2005). UFZ-Diskussionspapiere.

445. Office of Air and Radiation. (1995). *Air Quality Trends-1994: Six Principle Pollutants.* Washington, DC Environmental Protection Agency.

446. Office of Mobile Source. (1993). *Automobiles and Ozone.* Washington DC US Environmental Protection Agency.

447. Oge, M. (1995). *Automotive Emissions: Progress and Challenges.* Presentation to Automotive Management Briefing Session. Traverse City. Mich.

448. Osman, S., & Nawawi, A., & Jamalunlaili, J. (2008). Urban Sprawl and Its Financial Cost: - A Conceptual Framework. *Canadian Center of Education.* 4(10).

449. Osman, T., Arima, T., & Divigalpitiya, P. (2016). Measuring urban sprawl patterns in Greater Cairo Metropolitan Region. *Journal of the Indian Society of Remote Sensing, 44*(2), 287-295.

450. Ottensmann, J. R. (1977). Urban sprawl, land values and the density of development. *Land economics, 53*(4), 389-400.

451. Oueslati, W., Alvanides, S., & Garrod, G. (2013). Determinants of Urban Sprawl in European Cities. SSRN Electronic Journal.

452. Owoeye, J. O., & Ibitoye, O. A. (2016). Analysis of Akure urban land use change detection from remote imagery perspective. *Urban Studies Research, 2016.*

453. Owusu-Ansah J, O'Connor KB. (2010). Housing Demand in the Urban Fringe around Kumasi, Ghana. J. Housing Built Environ. 25(1): 1-17.

454. Padmanaban, R., Kumar, R. (2012). Mapping and Analysis of Marine Pollution in Tuticorin Coastal Area Using Remote Sensing and GIS. Int. J. Adv. Remote Sense 34–48.

455. Pagano, Michael A. (2003). "City Fiscal Structures and Land Development," Washington, DC: The Brookings Institution Center on Urban and Metropolitan Policy.

456. Patacchini, E., Zenou, Y., Henderson, J. V., & Epple, D. (2009). Urban sprawl in Europe. *Brookings-Wharton Papers on Urban Affairs*, 125-149.

457. Patel, P. (2014). Cities without sprawl: A utopian concept. *International Journal of Research, 1*(5), 669-679.

458. Pauleit, S., Ennos, R., & Golding, Y. (2005). Modeling the environmental impacts of urban land use and land cover change—a study in Merseyside, UK. Landscape and Urban Planning, 71(2-4), 295–310.

459. Paulsen, K. (2012). Yet even more evidence on the spatial size of cities: Urban spatial expansion in the US, 1980–2000. Regional Science and Urban Economics.

460. Paulsen, K. (2013). Geography, policy or market? New evidence on the measurement and causes of sprawl (and infill) in US metropolitan regions. Urban Studies, 0(0), 1–17.

461. Pedersen, D., Smith, V. E., & Adler, J. (1999). Sprawling.

462. Peijun, D. U., Xingli, L. I., Wen, C. A. O., Yan, L. U. O., & Zhang, H. (2010). Monitoring urban land cover and vegetation change by multi-temporal remote sensing information. *Mining Science and Technology (China), 20*(6), 922-932.

463. Peiser, R. B., & Chang, A. C. (1999). Is it possible to build financially successful new towns? The Milton Keynes experience. *Urban Studies, 36*(10), 1679-1703.

464. Pendall, R. (1999). Do Land Use Controls Cause Sprawl? Environment and Planning B: Planning and Design 26: 555-571.

465. Perera, R., Permana, A.S. and Charoentrakulpeeti, W. (2007), Promoting Reduction in Travel Demand in Transport Sector of Asian Cities, Air Pollution Control in the Transportation Sector: Third Phase Research Report of the Urban Environmental Management Project, IGES (Hayama), Japan.

466. Persky, J., H. Kurban, and T. Lester. (2000). The Impact of Federal and State Expenditures on Residential Land Absorption: A Quantitative Case Study—Chicago, unpublished working manuscript, University of Illinois-Chicago.

467. Pesaran, M. H., Shin, Y., & Smith, R. P. (1999). Pooled mean group estimation of dynamic heterogeneous panels. *Journal of the American Statistical Association*, *94*(446), 621-634.

468. Pili, S., Grigoriadis, E., Carlucci, M., Clemente, M., & Salvati, L. (2017). Towards sustainable growth? A multi-criteria assessment of (changing) urban forms. Ecological Indicators, 76, 71–80.

469. Pirotte, a., & Madre, J.-L. (2011). Determinants of Urban Sprawl in France: An Analysis Using a Hierarchical Bayes Approach on Panel Data. Urban Studies, 48(13), 2865–2886.

470. Pithawalla, M. B. (1950). *An Introduction to Karachi: Its Environs and Hinterland.* Times Press.

471. Pohanka, M., & Fitzgerald, S. (2004). Urban sprawl and you: how sprawl adversely affects worker health. *Aaohn Journal, 52*(6), 242-246.

472. Polyzos, S., Minetos, D., & Niavis, S. (2013). Driving Factors and Empirical Analysis of Urban Sprawl in Greece. Theoretical and Empirical Researches in Urban Management, 8(1), 5–29.

473. Poormohamadi, M. & Jamekasra, M. (2011), "Analysis of the pattern of uneven development in Tabriz", *Geographical Research*, vol. 25, no. 100, p. 31–54.

474. Porter, B. E., & England, K. J. (2000). Predicting red-light running behavior: a traffic safety study in three urban settings. *Journal of Safety Research*, *31*(1), 1-8.

475. Porter, D.R. (1997). Managing Growth in America's Communities. Washington, DC: Island Press.

476. Pramanik, M. M. A., & Stathakis, D. (2016). Forecasting urban sprawl in Dhaka city of Bangladesh. *Environment and Planning B: Planning and Design*, *43*(4), 756-771.

477. Punia M, and Singh L. (2011). Entropy approach for assessment of urban growth: a case study of Jaipur, India, Journal of the Indian Society of Remote Sensing, vol 40(2), 231–244.

478. Putnam, R.D. (2000). Bowling Alone, Simon and Schuster, New York.

479. Quarrie, J. (Ed.). (1992). *Earth Summit 1992: The United Nations Conference on Environment and Development, Rio de Janeiro*. Regency Press.

480. Qureshi, F. M., Rajabifard, A., & Olfat, H. (2009). Facilitating urban planning and management at the local level through the development of SDI (a case study of Lahore-Pakistan).

481. Qureshi, I. A., & Lu, H. (2007). Urban transport and sustainable transport strategies: A case study of Karachi, Pakistan. *Tsinghua Science and Technology*, *12*(3), 309-317.

482. Qureshi, S., Arsalan, M. H., & Coles, R. (2007). Simulating the socio-metric analysis of landscape changes in GIS framework: An example of the selected town of Karachi metropolis. *Bunce, RGH, Jongman, RHG, Hojas, L., and Weel, S. (eds.)*, *25*, 799-800.

483. Qureshi, S., Breuste, J. H., & Lindley, S. J. (2010). Green space functionality along an urban gradient in

Karachi, Pakistan: a socio-ecological study. *Human Ecology, 38*(2), 283-294.

484. Qureshi, S., Kazmi, S. J. H., & Breuste, J. H. (2010). Ecological disturbances due to a high cutback in the green infrastructure of Karachi: Analyses of public perception about associated health problems. *Urban Forestry & Urban Greening, 9*(3), 187-198.

485. Rafiee, N., Mahesh, T. M., Tali, J. A., & Emtehani, M. R. (2012). The Appropriate Approach to Renewal the Historical Center Of Shiraz City, Iran. *New York Science Journal, 5*(12), 80-5.

486. Rafiq, S., Salim, R., & Nielsen, I. (2016). Urbanization, openness, emissions, and energy intensity: a study of increasingly urbanized emerging economies. *Energy Economics, 56*, 20-28.

487. Rahman, A., Aggarwal, S. P., Netzband, M., & Fazal, S. (2010). Monitoring urban sprawl using remote sensing and GIS techniques of a fast-growing urban centre, India. *IEEE Journal of selected topics in applied earth observations and remote sensing, 4*(1), 56-64.

488. Ramachandra, T. V., Bharath, H. A., & Sowmyashree, M. V. (2014). Urban footprint of Mumbai-the commercial capital of India. *Journal of Urban and Regional Analysis, 6*(1), 71. Rubiera Morollón, F., González Marroquín, V. M., & Pérez Rivero, J. L. (2016). Urban sprawl in Madrid? An analysis of the urban growth of Madrid during the last quarter of the twentieth century. *Letters in Spatial and Resource Sciences.*

489. Raman, N., & Narayanan, D. S. (2008).Impact of solid waste effect on groundwater and soil quality nearer to Pallavaram solid waste landfill site in Chennai. *Rasayan J. Chem, 1*(4), 828-836.

490. Randolph, J. (2004). Land Use Planning for Environmental Management. Chapter 3,

Environmental Land Use Planning and Management. Washington DC Island Press. 36-52.

491. Rathbone, D. B., & Huckabee, J. C. (1999). Controlling road rage: A literature review and pilot study.

492. Rauhala, K. (2007). Promotion of Walking: A Complex Interdisciplinary Task. In Land Use and Transport - European Research Towards Integrated Policies, ed. Marshall S. and Banister D. (eds.), p. 293-311. Oxford: Elsevier.

493. Razin, E. (1998). Policies to control urban sprawl: Planning regulations or changes in the "rules of the game?" *Urban Studies.*35 (2), 321–40.

494. Register, R., (2002), Eco-cities: Building Cities in Balance with Nature, Berkeley Hills Books, Berkeley California.

495. Rejmánek, M. (1989). Invasibility of plant communities. Pages 369–388 in J. A. Drake, H. A. Mooney, F. di Castri, R. H. Groves, F. J. Kruger, M. Rejmánek, and M. Williamson, editors. *Biological invasions, a global perspective.* John Wiley, Chichester, UK.

496. Richardson, H. W. (1987). Whether national urban policy in developing countries? *Urban Studies, 24*(3), 227-244.

497. Rienow, A., Stenger, D., & Menz, G. (2014). Sprawling cities and shrinking regions–forecasting urban growth in the Ruhr for 2025 by coupling cells and agents. *Erdkunde,* 85-107.

498. Rijsberman, M. A., & Van de Ven, F. H. (2000). Different approaches to assessment of design and management of sustainable urban water systems. *Environmental Impact Assessment Review, 20*(3), 333-345.

499. Robinson, J. (2002). Global and world cities: a view from off the map. *International journal of urban and regional research, 26*(3), 531-554.

500. Robinson, L., Newell, J. P., & Marzluff, J. M. (2005). Twenty-five years of sprawl in the Seattle region: growth management responses and implications for conservation. *Landscape and Urban planning*, *71*(1), 51-72.

501. Rodwin, L. (1945). Garden cities and the Metropolis. *The Journal of Land & Public Utility Economics*, *21*(3), 268-281.

502. Romiguer, A. T. (2011).Sustainable Development: Objectives, Enablers and Challenges for Spanish Companies. *Published Thesis in Tampere University of Technology*.

503. Roshan, G. R., Rousta, I., and Ramesh, M. (2009). "Studying the Effects of Urban Sprawl of Metropolis on Tourism - Climate Index Oscillation: A Case Study of Tehran City", *Journal of Geography and Regional Planning*, 2(12), pp. 310-321.

504. Roshan, G., Shahraki, S. Z., & Sauri, D. (2010). Urban sprawl and climatic changes in Tehran. *Journal of Environmental Health Science & Engineering*, *7*(1), 43-52.

505. Rossi, P. (1955). *Why Families Move*, 2nd edition. Sage Publications, Beverly Hills.

506. Rustiadi, E., Pravitasari, A. E., Setiawan, Y., Mulya, S. P., Pribadi, D. O., & Tsutsumida, N. (2021). Impact of continuous Jakarta mega-city urban expansion on the formation of the Jakarta-Bandung conurbation over the rice farm regions. *Cities*, *111*, 103000.

507. Rykwert, J., (1976). The Idea of A Town: The Anthropology of Urban Form in Rome, Italy and The Ancient World, Princeton University Press, Princeton, New Jersey.

508. Sabry, A., & Talaat, H. (2015). Factors Impacting Link Travel Speed Reliability: A Case Study at Cairo, Egypt. *Journal of Traffic and Logistics Engineering Vol*, *3*(1).

509. Saleem, B. M., Farooq, R. Y., & Masood, Z. (2016). Length-weight relationship of Epinephelus diacanthus (family Serranidae; sub-family epinephrine) collected from Karachi fish harbour, Pakistan. *fuuast journal of biology*, *6*(2), 225-229.
510. Saleh, B., & Al Rawashdeh, S. (2007). Study of urban expansion in Jordanian cities using GIS and remote Sensing. *International Journal of Applied Science and Engineering*, *5*(1), 41-52.
511. Salman, A., & Qureshi, S. (2009).*Indicators of sustainable urban development: A review of urban regeneration projects in Karachi, Pakistan*. Retrieved 10 February 2013 from Department of Geography and Geology, University of Salzburg: www.herodot.net.
512. Salvati, L., & Carlucci, M. (2014). Distance matters: Land consumption and the mono-centric model in two southern European cities. Landscape and Urban Planning, 41–51.
513. Saraei, M. H. (2007). Multi-dimensional patterns of physical development of Yazd. *Geographical Research Quarterly, 84*.
514. Saraei, M.H. (2010). "Why were residential transferred lands in the city of Yazd left unused?" *Urban Regional Studies and Research*, vol. 1, no. 3, p. 43–70.
515. Sarantakos, S. (2005). Social Research. (3. Baskı).
516. Saravanan, P., & Ilangovan, P. (2010). Identification of urban sprawl pattern for Madurai region using GIS. *International Journal of Geomatics and Geosciences*, *1*(2), 141.
517. Sarvestani, M. S., Ibrahim, A. L., & Kanaroglou, P. (2011). Three decades of urban growth in the city of Shiraz, Iran: A remote sensing and geographic information systems application. *Cities*, *28*(4), 320-329.

518. Sathar, Z., Singh, S., Shah, Z. H., Rashida, G., Kamran, I., & Eshai, K. (2013). Post-abortion care in Pakistan: A national study.
519. Savini, F., & Aalbers, M. B. (2016). The de-contextualization of land use planning through financialization: Urban redevelopment in Milan. *European Urban and Regional Studies, 23*(4), 878-894.
520. Savitch, H. V. (2003). How suburban sprawl shapes human well-being. *Journal of Urban Health, 80*(4), 590-607.
521. Sawas, A., Mustafa, D., Anwar, N. H., Iqtidar, H., & Viqar, S. (2014). Urbanization, gender and violence in Rawalpindi and Islamabad: a scoping study.
522. Schafer, R. (1975). *Exclusionary Land Use Controls: Conceptual and Empirical Problems in Measuring the Invisible Wall.* Cambridge, MA: Harvard University Press.
523. Schneider, A., & Woodcock, C. E. (2008). Compact, dispersed, fragmented, extensive? A comparison of urban growth in twenty-five global cities using remotely sensed data, pattern metrics and census information. *Urban Studies, 45*(3), 659-692.
524. Schwab, J. (1996). Sustainable Development. Converting Motherhood and Apple Pie into Substance. *Development.* 1–4.
525. Scoging, H. (1993). The assessment of desertification. *Geography, 78*(2), 190-193.
526. Scott, A. J. (2002). Competitive dynamics of Southern California's clothing industry: the widening global connection and its local ramifications. *Urban Studies, 39*(8), 1287-1306.
527. Seidel, S. (1978). *Housing Costs and Government Regulations.* New Brunswick, NJ: Center for Urban Policy Research. Rutgers University.

528. Serra, P., Vera, A., Tulla, A. F., & Salvati, L. (2014). Beyond urban-rural dichotomy: Exploring socio-economic and land-use processes of change in Spain (1991–2011). Applied Geography, 55, 71–81.

529. Serrador, P., & Pinto, J. K. (2015). Does Agile work?—A quantitative analysis of Agile project success. *International Journal of Project Management, 33*(5), 1040-1051.

530. Seto, K. C., Güneralp, B. & Hutyra, L. R., (2012). 'Global forecasts of urban expansion to 2030 and direct impacts on biodiversity and carbon pools', *Proceedings of the National Academy of Sciences of the United States of America* 109(40), 16083–16088 (DOI: 10.1073/ pnas.1211658109).

531. Shaalan, I. (2013). "Sustainable urban transformation in small cities in Egypt. A UN-habitat perspective," *Journal of Cleaner Production*, vol. 50, p. 200–204.

532. Shahraki, S. Z., Sauri, D., Serra, P., Modugno, S., Seifolddini, F., & Pourahmad, A. (2011). Urban sprawl pattern and land-use change detection in Yazd, Iran. *Habitat International, 35*(4), 521-528.

533. Shahraki, S. Z., Seifolddini, F., & Pourahmad, A. (2012). Urban Sprawl and Fertile Agricultural Lands in Iranian Cities-Case Study: Tehran and Karaj. *Journal of Civil Engineering and Architecture, 6*(2), 204.

534. Shaikh, G. H., & Rizvi, S. S. H. (1990). Frequency and other Parametric Analysis of Traffic Nose in Karachi City. *PCSIR Laboratories, Karachi, Pakistan.*

535. Shaikh, H. (2019). Urbanization and Growth.

536. Shalaby, A. (2012). Assessment of urban sprawl impact on the agricultural land in the Nile Delta of Egypt using remote sensing and digital soil map. *International Journal of Environment and Sciences, 1*(4), 253-262.

537. Shanzi, K. (2009). Spread-backwash and Market Area Effects of Urban and Regional Growth in China [J]. *Economic Research Journal, 8,* 85-98.

538. Shao, G., Qian, T., Liu, Y., & Martin, B. (2008). The role of urbanization in increasing atmospheric CO2 concentrations: Think globally, act locally. *The International Journal of Sustainable Development & World Ecology, 15*(4), 302-308.

539. Shen, Q. (1996). Spatial Impacts of Locally Enacted Growth Controls: The San Francisco Bay Area in the 1980s. Environment and Planning B: Planning and Design. 23: 61-91.

540. Shirazi, S. A., & Kazmi, J. H. (2016). Analysis of socio-environmental impacts of the loss of urban trees and vegetation in Lahore, Pakistan: a review of public perception. Ecol Process 5: 5.

541. Shwayri, S. T. (2013). A model Korean ubiquitous eco-city? The politics of making Songdo. *Journal of Urban Technology, 20*(1), 39-55.

542. Siedentop, S., & Fina, S. (2008, September). Urban sprawl beyond growth: from a growth to a decline perspective on the cost of sprawl. In *44th Isocarp Conference, Dalian (China)* (Vol. 13, p. 23).

543. Siedentop, S., & Fina, S. (2012). Who sprawls most? Exploring the patterns of urban growth across 26 European countries. *Environment and Planning A, 44*(11), 2765-2784.

544. Siegel, G. B. (1999). Where are we on local government service contracting? *Public Productivity & Management Review,* 365-388.

545. Silbaugh, K. B. (2007). Women's Place: Urban Planning, Housing Design, and Work-Family Balance. *Fordham L. Rev., 76,* 1797.

546. Simberloff, D. E. (1981). Community effects of introduced species. Pages 53–81 in M. H. Nitecki,

editor. *Biotic crises in ecological and evolutionary time.* Academic Press, New York, New York, USA.

547. Simmie, J. (Ed.). (2001). *Innovative cities.* Taylor & Francis.

548. Sinha, S. (2018). Spatial Metrics: A Tool for Measurement of Urban Growth/Sprawl.

549. Sinha, S. K. (2017). Urban Sprawl in Gautam Budh Nagar, PhD Thesis, Department of Geography, University of Delhi, [Unpublished Thesis].

550. Smart Growth America. (2002). Available at: http://www.smartgrowthamerica.org/sprawlindex/chart.pdf, visited 2019, June 5.

551. Snyder, K., & Bird, L. (1998). Paying the costs of sprawl: using fair-share costing to control sprawl. *Smart Communities Network, 37.*

552. Social, P. (2015). Living Standards Measurement Survey (PSLM) 2013–14 National.

553. Sohn, J., & Choi, S. (2008). Characterizing urban sprawl with accessibility measures. Presented paper 55th annual North American meeting of the Regional Science Association International in Brooklyn (NY).

554. Solon, J. (2009). Spatial context of urbanization: Landscape pattern and changes between 1950 and 1990 in the Warsaw metropolitan area, Poland. *Landscape and Urban Planning, 93*(3-4), 250-261.

555. Song, Y. (2005). Smart growth and urban development pattern: A comparative study. *International Regional Science Review, 28*(2), 239-265.

556. Song, Y., & Knaap, G. J. (2004). Measuring urban form: Is Portland winning the war on sprawl? *Journal of the American Planning Association, 70*(2), 210-225.

557. Song, Y., & Zenou, Y. (2006). Property tax and urban sprawl: Theory and implications for US cities. Journal of Urban Economics, 60(3), 519-534.

558. Soomro, T. A., Soomro, M. A., Laghari, A. N., Bhangwar, D. K., & Soomro, M. A. (2018). Fading legacy of the architectural heritage of the historic core of Karachi. *Engineering, Technology & Applied Science Research*, *8*(2), 2735-2740.

559. South, S. J., & Crowder, K. D. (1997). Escaping distressed neighborhoods: Individual, community, and metropolitan influences. *American Journal of Sociology*, *102*(4), 1040-1084.

560. Southworth, F. (2001). On the potential impacts of land use change policies on automobile vehicle miles of travel. *Energy Policy*, *29*(14), 1271-1283.

561. Sowell, F. (1992). Maximum likelihood estimation of stationary univariate fractionally integrated time series models. *Journal of Econometrics*, *53*(1-3), 165-188.

562. Squires, G. D. (Ed.). (2002). *Urban sprawl: Causes, consequences, & policy responses*. The Urban Institute.

563. Statistics, P. (2017). Of Pakistan Bureau of Statistics.

564. Stephenson, R. B. (1999). A vision of green: Lewis Mumford's legacy in Portland, Oregon. *Journal of the American Planning Association*, *65*(3), 259-269.

565. Stock, J. H., & Watson, M. W. (2007). Why has US inflation become harder to forecast? *Journal of Money, Credit and Banking*, *39*, 3-33.

566. Stoel, T. B. (1999). Reining in Urban Sprawl. *Environment.* 41, 6-16.

567. Stone Jr, B. (2008). Urban sprawl and air quality in large US cities. *Journal of Environmental Management*, *86*(4), 688-698.

568. Sturm, R., & Cohen, D. (2004). Suburban sprawl and physical and mental health. *Public Health*. 118, 488-496.

569. Sudhira, H. (2008). *Studies on Urban Sprawl and Spatial Planning Support System for Bangalore, India.*

Published doctorate thesis, Indian Institute of Science Department of Management Studies.

570. Sudhira, H. S., Ramachandra, T. V., &Jagadish, K. S. (2004). Urban sprawl: metrics, dynamics and modelling using GIS. *International Journal of Applied Earth Observation and Geoinformation*, *5*(1), 29-39.

571. Sullivan III, W. C. (1994). Perceptions of the rural-urban fringe: citizen preferences for natural and developed settings. *Landscape and urban planning*, *29*(2-3), 85-101.

572. Suribabu, C. R. (2012). Heuristic-based pipe dimensioning model for water distribution networks. *Journal of Pipeline Systems Engineering and Practice*, *3*(4), 115-124.

573. Sutro, S. (1990). *Reinventing the village.* American Planning Society Report no. 430. Washington, DC: American Planning Association.

574. Sutton, R. E., & Wheatley, K. F. (2003). Teachers' emotions and teaching: A review of the literature and directions for future research. *Educational psychology review*, *15*(4), 327-358.

575. Swanwick, C., Dunnett, N., & Woolley, H. (2003). Nature, role and value of green space in towns and cities: An overview. *Built Environment (1978-)*, 94-106.

576. Tacoli, C., McGranahan, G., & Satterthwaite, D. (2015). *Urbanization, rural-urban migration and urban poverty*. London: IIED.

577. Taherdoost, H. (2016). Validity and reliability of the research instrument; how to test the validation of a questionnaire/survey in research. *How to Test the Validation of a Questionnaire/Survey in a Research (August 10, 2016)*.

578. Talen, E. (2003).Measuring Urbanism: Issues in Smart Growth Research. *Journal of Urban Design.* 8(3), 303-328.

579. Talen, E., & Ellis, C. (2002). Beyond relativism reclaiming the search for good city form. *Journal of Planning Education and Research, 22*(1), 36-49.

580. Tali, J. A., & Murthy, K. (2012). Impact of demographic and areal changes on urban growth: a case study of Srinagar city. *International Journal of Environmental Sciences, 1*(2), 38-45.

581. Tasan-Kok, T. & Baeten, G., eds., (2011). Contradictions of Neoliberal Planning: Cities, Policies and Politics, Springer, Berlin; New York.

582. Taylor, P. J., Walker, D. R., Catalano, G., & Hoyler, M. (2002). Diversity and power in the world city network. *Cities, 19*(4), 231-241.

583. Tennøy, A. (2012). How and why planners make plans that, if implemented, cause growth in traffic volumes. *Explanations related to the expert knowledge, the planners and the plan-making processes PhD thesis, 1.*

584. Tiebout, C. M. (1956). A pure theory of local expenditures. *Journal of Political Economy, 64*(5), 416-424.

585. Torjman, S. (2000). *The Social Dimension of Sustainable Development.* Retrieved 20 January 2013 from Caledon Institute of Social Policy: www.caledoninst.org/publications/pdf/1-894598-00-8.pdf.

586. Torrens, P. M. (2008). A toolkit for measuring sprawl. *Applied Spatial Analysis and Policy, 1*(1), 5-36.

587. Torrens, P. M., &Alberti, M. (2000). Measuring sprawl. London: Centre for Advanced Spatial Analysis, University College. Working paper no. 27.

588. Tossell, C. J., Schvaneveldt, R. W., & Branaghan, R. J. (2010). Assessing a New Method to Elicit Knowledge Structures Approach. *Cognitive Technology, 15,* 11-19.

589. Transportation Research Board of the National Academy. (1996). *Transit and urban form*. Washington, DC: National Academy Press. 16(2).

590. Tratalos, J., Fuller, R.A., Warren, P.H., Davies, R.G. & Gaston, K.J. (2007) Urban form, biodiversity potential and ecosystem services. *Landscape and Urban Planning*, **83**, 308– 317.

591. Tsai, Y. H. (2005). Quantifying urban form: compactness versus' sprawl'. *Urban Studies*, *42*(1), 141-161.

592. Twumasi-Ankrah, K. (1995). Rural-Urban Migration and Socio-economic Development in Ghana: Some Discussions. J. Soc. Devel. Afri. 10(2): 13-22.

593. Tyagi, N. (2015). Urban Sprawl in Gorakhpur City, Uttar Bharat Boogol Patrika, 45(1):23-42.

594. Tyner, J. A. (2000). Migrant labour and the politics of scale: Gendering the Philippine state. *Asia Pacific Viewpoint*, *41*(2), 131-154.

595. Ud Din Ahmed, S. (2016). *Informal land controls, a case of Karachi-Pakistan* (Doctoral dissertation, Cardiff University).

596. Umair, M., & Naz, L. (2019). The Index Value Trend Analysis of Rural-Urban Migration in Pakistan: The Current and Future Perspectives. *Pakistan Journal of Social Sciences (PJSS)*, *39*(3).

597. UNDP. (2012). World Urbanization Prospects, the 2011 Revision: Highlights. New York. *Online at http://esa.*

598. United Nations Population Fund (UNPF) (1999). *The State of World Population*, United Nations Publication, New York, NY, USA, 1999.

599. United Nations Development Programme (UNDP). (2012). Building Greener City, Singapore.

600. United Nations Population Division (UNPD) (2006). World Urbanization Prospects: The 2005 Revision. New York.

601. United Nations Population Fund (UNFPA) (2007). The State of the World Population 2007. New York.

602. United Nations. Statistical Division. (2010). *International recommendations for tourism statistics 2008* (No. 83). United Nations Publications.

603. US-FHA (Federal Highway Administration). (2001). National Household Travel Survey, 2001. URL= http://www.bts.gov/nhts/, visited 2019, May 3.

604. Van Loon, J. (2016). Patient versus impatient capital: the (non-) financialization of real estate developers in the Low Countries. *Socio-Economic Review, 14*(4), 709-728.

605. Van, T. T. (2008). Research on the effect of urban expansion on agricultural land in Ho Chi Minh City by using remote sensing method. *VNU Journal of Science: Earth and Environmental Sciences, 24*(2).

606. Velibeyoğlu, H. (2004). Development trends of single family housing estates in Izmir metropolitan fringe area. *Published thesis in İzmir Institute of Technology,* Turkey. Vanderbilt University.

607. Verkaaik, O. (2016). Violence and ethnic identity politics in Karachi and Hyderabad. *South Asia: Journal of South Asian Studies, 39*(4), 841-854.

608. Vicenzotti, V., & Qviström, M. (2018). Zwischenstadt as a travelling concept: towards a critical discussion of mobile ideas in transnational planning discourses on urban sprawl. *European Planning Studies, 26*(1), 115-132.

609. Vincent, M. J., Keyes, M. A., & Reed, M. (1994). *Npts urban travel patterns. 1990 nationwide personal transportation survey (npts)* (no. fhwa-pl-94-018).

610. Visalatchi, A., &Padmanaban, R. C. (2012). Land use, land cover mapping, and shoreline change studies in Tuticorin coastal area using remote sensing. *International Journal of Advanced Earth Science and Engineering,* pp-1.

611. Walsh, C. (2012). Territorial agenda of the European Union 2020: towards an inclusive, smart and sustainable Europe of diverse regions.

612. Wang, L., Li, C., Ying, Q., Cheng, X., Wang, X., Li, X., & Gong, P. (2012). China's urban expansion from 1990 to 2010 determined with satellite remote sensing. *Chinese Science Bulletin, 57*(22), 2802-2812.

613. Ward, S.V. (2004). Planning and Urban Change, Thousand Oaks, London; UK and SAGE, California, USA.

614. Wasserman, M. (2000). Urban sprawl. *Regional Review*, (Q1), 9-17.

615. Wassmer, R. W. (2008). Causes of urban sprawl in the United States: auto reliance compared to natural evolution, flight from blight, and local revenue reliance. *Journal of Policy Analysis and Management: The Journal of the Association for Public Policy Analysis and Management, 27*(3), 536-555.

616. Wassmer, R. W., & Bass, M.C. (2004). *Sprawl's Impact on Urban Housing Prices in The United States.* Sacremento: California Senate Office of Research.

617. Watanabe, K., Divigalpitiya, P., Ohgai, A., & Kondo, A. (2005). Evaluation for Sustainable Urban Form in Asian Developing Countries by Cellular Automata Simulation. In *Proceedings of 9th International Conference on Computers in Urban Management and Urban Planning, ref* (Vol. 123).

618. WCED. (1987). *"Report of the World Commission on Environment and Development: Our Common Future"*, Oxford University Press, Oxford.

619. Weber, R. (2010). Selling city futures: The financialization of urban redevelopment policy. *Economic geography, 86*(3), 251-274.

620. Wei Ji, J. M., Rima Wahab Twibell and Karen Underhil. (2006). "Characterizing urban sprawl using multi-stage remote sensing images and landscape metrics",

Computers, Environment and Urban Systems, 30, 861-879.

621. Weilenmann, B., & Schulz, T. (2014). Socio-economic explanation of urban sprawl: Evidence from Switzerland, 1970-2010.

622. Weisbrod, G., Vary, D., & Treyz, G. (2003). Measuring economic costs of urban traffic congestion to business. *Transportation research record, 1839*(1), 98-106.

623. Weng Q. (2001). Remote sensing? GIS evaluation of urban expansion and its impact on surface temperature in the Zhujiang Delta, China, International Journal of Remote Sensing, vol 22(10), 1999–2014.

624. Wheaton, W. C. (1974). A comparative static analysis of urban spatial structure.*Journal of Economic Theory, 9*(2), 223-237.

625. White, J. W. (1998). Old wine, cracked bottle? Tokyo, Paris, and the global city hypothesis. *Urban Affairs Review, 33*(4), 451-477.

626. Whitelegg, J., & Haq, G. (Eds.). (2017). *The Earthscan reader on world transport policy and practice.* Routledge.

627. Wickramasekara, P. (2016). South Asian Gulf migration to the Gulf: a safety valve or a development strategy? Migration and Development, 5(1), 99-129.

628. Williams, B., & Shiels, P. (2000). Acceleration into sprawl: causes and potential policy responses. *Quarterly Economic Commentary,* (June 2000), 37-73.

629. Williams, K., & Burton, E., & Jenks, M. (1996). Achieving the compact city through intensification: An acceptable option. In *The compact city: A sustainable urban form?* ed. Mike, J., & Burton, E., & Williams, K. London: E & FN Spon. 83-96

630. Williams, K., & Burton, E., & Jenks, M. (2000): *Achieving Sustainable Urban Form.* E & FN Spon, New York.

631. Wilson, B., & Chakraborty, A. (2013). The environmental impacts of sprawl: emergent themes from the past decade of planning research. *Sustainability, 5*(8), 3302-3327.

632. Wilson, E. H., Hurd, J. D., Civco, D. L., Prisloe, M. P., & Arnold, C. (2003). Development of a geospatial model to quantify, describe and map urban growth. *Remote sensing of environment, 86*(3), 275-285.

633. Wilson, W. J. (1987). The Truly Disadvantaged: The Inner City. *The Underclass, and Public Policy, 8.*

634. Wisner, B., Blaikie, P. M., Blaikie, P., Cannon, T., & Davis, I. (2004). *At risk: natural hazards, people's vulnerability and disasters.* Psychology Press.

635. Wissen Hayek, U., Jaeger, J. a. G., Schwick, C., Jarne, A., & Schuler, M. (2010). Measuring and Assessing Urban Sprawl: What are the Remaining Options for Future Settlement Development in Switzerland for 2030? Applied Spatial Analysis and Policy, 4(4), 249–279.

636. World Bank Group. (2014). *Doing Business 2015: Going beyond Efficiency: Comparing Business Regulations for Domestic Firms in 189 Economies: a World Bank Group Flagship Report.* World Bank Publications.

637. World Bank. (2006). Pakistan Strategic Country Environmental Assessment.

638. World Bank. (2007). *The World Bank Annual Report 2007.* The World Bank.

639. World Health Organization, & UNICEF. (2010). Progress on sanitation and drinking water: 2010 update. In *Progress on Sanitation and Drinking-water: 2010 Update* (pp. 60-60).

640. Wu, K. Y., Ye, X. Y., Qi, Z. F., & Zhang, H. (2013). Impacts of land use/land cover change and socio-

economic development on regional ecosystem services: The case of fast-growing Hangzhou metropolitan area, China. *Cities, 31*, 276-284.

641. Xu, G., Jiao, L., Liu, J., Shi, Z., Zeng, C., & Liu, Y. (2019). Understanding urban expansion combining macro patterns and micro dynamics in three Southeast Asian mega-cities. *Science of the Total Environment, 660*, 375-383.

642. Yang, G., Bowling, L. C., Cherkauer, K. A., & Pijanowski, B. C. (2011). The impact of urban development on hydrologic regime from catchment to basin scales. *Landscape and Urban Planning, 103*(2), 237-247.

643. Yang, J., & Gakenheimer, R. (2007). Assessing the transportation consequences of land use transformation in urban China. *Habitat International, 31*(3-4), 345-353.

644. Yang, X., & Lo, C.P. (2002). Modelling urban growth and landscape changes in the Atlanta metropolitan area. *International Journal of Geographic Information Science.* 17(5), 463-488.

645. Yanich, D. (2001). Location, location, location: Urban and suburban crime on local TV news. Journal of Urban Affairs, 23(3/4), 221-241.

646. Yanos, P. T. (2007). Beyond "Landscapes of Despair": the need for new research on the urban environment, sprawl, and the community integration of persons with severe mental illness. *Health & Place, 13*(3), 672-676.

647. Yeh, A. G. O, & Li, X. (2001). Measurement and monitoring of urban sprawl in a rapidly growing region using entropy. Photogrammetric Engineering and Remote Sensing, 67, 83–90.

648. Yeh, A. G. O., & Li, X. (1998). Sustainable land development model for rapid growth areas using GIS.

International Journal of Geographical Information Science, 12, 169–189.

649. Yeh, A. G. O., & Li, X. (2001). Measurement and monitoring of urban sprawl in a rapidly growing region using entropy. *Photogrammetric engineering and remote sensing, 67*(1), 83-90.

650. Yokohari, M., Takeuchi, K., Watanabe, T., & Yokota, S. (2000). Beyond greenbelts and zoning: future directions of the environment of Asian mega-cities. *Lands Urban Plan, 47,* 159-171.

651. Yoshino, N., Taghizadeh-Hesary, F., & Otsuka, M. (2017). International remittances and poverty reduction: Evidence from Asian developing countries.

652. Youssef, A. M., Pradhan, B., & Tarabees, E. (2011). Integrated evaluation of urban development suitability based on remote sensing and GIS techniques: contribution from the analytic hierarchy process. *Arabian Journal of Geosciences, 4*(3-4), 463-473.

653. Yu, X. J., & Ng, C. N. (2007). Spatial and temporal dynamics of urban sprawl along two urban-rural transects: A case study of Guangzhou, China. *Landscape and Urban Planning, 79*(1), 96-109.

654. Zaidi, A., & Zafar, S. (2018, May). Karachi: An Expanding City with Rising Disasters. In *World Environmental and Water Resources Congress 2018: Watershed Management, Irrigation and Drainage, and Water Resources Planning and Management* (pp. 337-342). Reston, VA: American Society of Civil Engineers.

655. Zaidi, S. H. (1990). Noise levels in Karachi on a transporters strike day. *J Pak Med Assoc, 40,* 299-300.

656. Zaidi, S.H. (1996). Noise Levels in Karachi on the Rise, Daily Leader, May 08, Karachi.

657. Zhang, B. (2004). Study on Urban Growth Management in China. Beijing: Xinhua Press. 56–57.

658. Zhang, K. H. (2002). What explains China's rising urbanization in the reform era? *Urban Studies, 39*(12), 2301-2315.

659. Zhang, T. (2002). Urban development and a socialist pro-growth coalition in Shanghai. *Urban Affairs Review, 37*(4), 475-499.

660. Zhang, X., Chen, J., Tan, M., & Sun, Y. (2007). Assessing the impact of urban sprawl on soil resources of Nanjing city using satellite images and digital soil databases. *Catena, 69*(1), 16-30.

661. Zhang, Y., & Wildemuth, B. M. (2009). Unstructured interviews. *Applications of social research methods to questions in information and library science*, 222-231.

662. Zohry, A. (2009). The development impact of internal migration: Findings from Egypt. *International Union for the Scientific Study of Population.*

663. Zubair, O. A., Ojigi, L. M., & Mbih, R. A. (2015). Urbanization: A catalyst for the emergence of squatter settlements and squalor in the vicinities of the federal capital city of Nigeria. *Journal of Sustainable Development, 8*(2), 134.

664. Życzkowski, K. (2003). Rényi extrapolation of Shannon entropy. *Open Systems & Information Dynamics, 10*(03), 297-310.

Annexure A

Interviewees' List

Id	Participants	Method of Data Collection
IDI-01-M	Male	In depth interview
IDI-02-M	Male	In depth interview
IDI-03-M	Male	In depth interview
IDI-04-M	Male	In depth interview
IDI-05-M	Male	In depth interview
IDI-06-M	Male	In depth interview
IDI-07-M	Male	In depth interview
IDI-08-M	Male	In depth interview
IDI-09-M	Male	In depth interview
IDI-10-M	Male	In depth interview

Annexure B

Interview Protocol

The estimated time of a one-to-one interview is (1 hour). Experts, officials, and people with relevant expertise, having more than 8 years of experience and requisite skills, were interviewed. The ethical considerations were part of the interview. The responses were recorded, and notes were taken.

Consent Form

Name of the Participant

....

Department/Organization

....

Dissertation Topic ....

1) I agree with the instructions given by the interviewer
2) The aim of the responses will just be used for thesis purposes
3) I agree and permit the interviewer to record my interview
4) I have no issues in giving the interview
5) Choose (A) or (B)
a) You can disclose my information
b) Please use pseudo names and don't disclose my personal information
6) Please share your experience regarding the below questions
7) I agree with the following instructions and will share all my experiences according to the questions asked by the interviewer.

....

Signature of the Participant

Dated: ....

The time when the interview starts: ....

The time when the interview ends: ....

Q1: Describe urban sprawling.

....

Q2: How do you see urban sprawling in Karachi? Illustrate with an example.

....

Q3: What do you think are the major effects of urban sprawling in Karachi?

....

Q4: What are the reasons for the city's expansion?

....

Q5: How can the expansion (reasons) you justified be controlled?

....

Q6: How can infrastructure issues be responsible for the city's expansion?

....

Q7: How can these issues be tackled? Answer according to your own understanding.

....

Q8: According to your understanding, what mechanism do you think should be introduced to control urban sprawling?

....

Q9: Who can be held accountable for urban mess in Karachi?

....

Q10: How can urban sprawling affect economic inequality and hardship in Pakistan?

....

Q11: How can urban development plans be established by government sectors to maintain quality standards?

....

Q12: What challenges do you think the city is facing due to urban sprawling? How do you think these challenges can be met? Explain with an example.

....

Thank you very much for your participation and kind consideration.

Annexure C

Assessment of livability within Karachi Metropolitan Area (KMA) – A Household Reaction Survey:
I am Akhtar Hussain, a doctoral student from the Department of Social Sciences, SZABIST Karachi. Currently, I'm doing a household survey on residents' reactions to existing livability, infrastructure facilities, and income within the Karachi Metropolitan Area (KMA). It's a part of my doctoral thesis, and the data will be used for academic purposes only. Being a resident from the respective Municipality/Municipal Corporation area within KMA, you just need to tick mark once or multiple if needed. Thank you for your cooperation.

Section A

Name: --
Town/District/Municipality/Municipal Corporation where presently you are residing/living: --

- Age Group

a) 18-25
b) 26-35
c) 36-45
d) 46-55
e) More than 55

- Sex

a) Male
b) Female
c) Family Size

- Are you the head of household? Yes or no. If no, what is your relationship with the household?

Relation: ------------------------------------

- Education Level

a) Below 10th
b) 10th (Secondary)
c) 12th (Higher Secondary)
d) Graduate
e) Post-graduate & others
f) Illiterate

- Employment Status

a) Employed
b) Self-employed
c) Unemployed
d) Retired
e) Others

- How long have you been a resident of Karachi?

a) Less than 10 years
b) 10-20 years
c) 20-30 years
d) 30+ years

- Are you satisfied with the urban services of the city?

a) Very much dissatisfied
b) Dissatisfied
c) Neutral
d) Satisfied
e) Very much satisfied

- Do you think the level of development where you live has changed in the last 5 years?

a) Improved
b) Declined

c) Unchanged

➢ What is the biggest problem in Karachi?

a) Transportation
b) Water/sanitation
c) Solid waste/*kachra*
d) Owning house
e) Law and order
f) Utilities
g) Other ....

Section B

Citizen's Reaction about Infrastructure-Related Services

Urban Public Transportation

➢ Do you use public transport?

a) Most of the time
b) Occasionally
c) Sometimes
d) Always
e) Never

➢ Do you travel to your workstation on public transport?

a) Most of the time
b) Occasionally
c) Sometimes
d) Always
e) Never

➢ How would you rate your experience of the bus service in Karachi?

a) Very dissatisfied
b) Dissatisfied
c) Neutral

d) Satisfied
e) Very much satisfied

- Do you use your own transportation for travel purposes?

a) Most of the time
b) Occasionally
c) Sometimes
d) Always
e) Never

- How do you see the condition of the buses in Karachi?

a) Good
b) Bad
c) Worse
d) Out-dated

- Did you reach the destination on time using the bus service in Karachi?

a) Most of the time
b) Occasionally
c) Sometimes
d) Always
e) Never

- Do you own a motorbike/car?

a) Yes
b) No

- Are you often caught in the traffic jams?

a) Most of the time
b) Occasionally
c) Sometimes
d) Always
e) Never

- Which mode of public transportation do you need and would you use if provided?

a) Rapid bus transit
b) Mass transit
c) Tram
d) Other ....

Urban Water-Related Services

➢ Do you have a tap water supply at your dwelling?
a) Yes, I do have
b) No, I don't have
c) It doesn't operate
d) It is disconnected

➢ Do you get a regular supply of tap water?
a) Everyday
b) A few days in a week
c) A few days in a month
d) Very rarely

➢ Are you satisfied with the quality of the water?
a) Dissatisfied
b) Very dissatisfied
c) Neutral
d) Satisfied
e) Very satisfied

➢ Do you use tap water for drinking purposes?
a) Yes, I do
b) No, it's in bad quality
c) It has a bad odor
d) It has a bad color

➢ Do you use tanker services to provide water?
a) Yes
b) No

If yes, how many tankers per month ....

- Does the cost of tanker water affect your monthly budget?

a) Yes, it eats my income
b) It's manageable
c) It's necessary
d) I don't have other options

- Do you think water tanker mafia charges high prices?

a) Yes, they operate like a mafia
b) They charge reasonably
c) They have limited options

- How much do you pay per month for tanker water?

....

Urban Garbage Collection and Disposal

- Do you live in a clean neighborhood?

a) Yes
b) No

- If yes, how do you rate your neighborhood?

a) It's clean most of the time
b) It's cleaned very rarely
c) It's always dirty

- Does KMC/DMC/CANNT regularly clear the disposal from your town or neighborhood?

a) Yes
b) No

- How do you rate the services of KMC/DMC/CANNT?

a) They fulfill their responsibilities
b) They don't fulfill their responsibilities
c) They are incompetent

- How do you dispose of your private household garbage?

a) It's disposed of in the open area of the street
b) It's disposed of through vendor
c) We make efforts to recycle

- Do you dispose of your garbage in designated places by local authorities?

a) We always do that
b) We don't follow strict discipline
c) We don't have designated places

- Is the designated place for garbage cleaned regularly?

a) Yes
b) No

- Your neighbors always put garbage in the designated places.

a) Very dissatisfied
b) Dissatisfied
c) Neutral
d) Satisfied
e) Very satisfied

Urban Sewerage Services

- Is your town area sewerage system underground?

a) Yes
b) No
c) I don't know

- Are the drains cleaned regularly?

a) It's drained regularly
b) It's never drained
c) It's drained very rarely

- Do you face overflow of the drains in your surroundings?

a) Yes, most of the time
b) Not at all
c) Very rarely

- How many times do you see the overflow of the drains in a month?

a) Plenty of time
b) A few times in a month
c) Never see

- Are you satisfied with the quality of your drains in neighborhoods?

a) Yes
b) No

- Do you face the situation when water and sewerage lines get mixed?

a) Yes, I do experience
b) No, I never witnessed it
c) Very rarely
d) I don't know

- Do you complain to the respective authorities for the resolution of sewerage issues?

a) Yes, I do complain
b) No, it's useless
c) They are not bothered

Urban Housing Scenario

- What is the type of your house?

a) Townhouse
b) Bungalow
c) Flat
d) Squatter settlement

e) Slums

- Do you live in a combined family?

a) Yes, I live in a combined family
b) No, I live in a nuclear family

- Which type of family system would you prefer?

a) Joint family system
b) Nuclear family system

- Is this your own house?

a) I own it
b) It's rented

- Do you own any flat/house/plot in booking?

a) Yes
b) No

- What is the reason for not owning a house/apartment/plot?

a) Land is expensive
b) Houses are expensive
c) I can't afford it.

- Would you be interested in low-cost housing schemes?

a) Yes, very much
b) It's necessary
c) Not interested

- How would you describe your locality?

a) It's elite & rich
b) It's a mixed neighborhood
c) It's homogeneous

Urban Income/Expenditure Levels

➤ Are you satisfied with the disposable income of your household?

a) Yes, I am satisfied
b) No, I am not satisfied

➤ Do you easily meet your family's expenses?

a) Yes, easily
b) No, on tight budget
c) It's very expensive
d) I can't meet them

➤ Which of the following assets do you own?

a) Car
b) Bike
c) House
d) Plot
e) Nothing

➤ Do you face an overdraft situation in your finances?

a) Always
b) Very rare
c) Never

➤ Can you mention the biggest household expense?

a) Food expense
b) Utilities
c) Transportation
d) Schooling
e) Other

➤ Do you save something after meeting expenses?

a) Yes, I do save
b) I can't save
c) Sometimes

- Do you feel financially secure?

a) Yes
b) No
c) Just ok

- What is your monthly income range?

....

- What is your monthly expense range?

....

- Are you satisfied with the city's economic situation?

a) Yes
b) No

Other Miscellaneous Questions

- Do you think the law and order situation in the city has improved in recent years?

a) It has improved considerably
b) It is just better
c) It is worsened

- Have you experienced street crime in the city?

a) Yes, on a regular basis
b) Very often
c) Never

- What is the reason for an increase in the overall rate of crime?

a) Economic issues
b) Poverty
c) Failure of law enforcement agencies
d) Other

- Are you satisfied with your experience of public hospitals?

a) They are pathetic
b) They are good
c) I never used public hospitals
d) Missing facilities

➢ Do you use public schools for the educational purpose of your children?

a) Yes
b) No

➢ If yes, how would you describe your experience?

a) They are pathetic
b) They are good
c) Missing facilities

➢ Do you have a regular supply of the K-ELECTRIC?

a) Yes, it's zero load shedding
b) 2-5 hours load shedding
c) More than 5 hours
d) No supply

➢ Do you have a regular supply of the SSGC?

a) Yes
b) No
c) No connection

➢ Are you satisfied with the local government institutions of Karachi?

a) Yes
b) No

➢ How would you rate the overall living experience in Karachi?

a) It's nice and livable
b) It's getting messy and unorganized
c) It's shabby and dirty

d) It's worsening and becoming unlivable

- Any comments or suggestions about this survey

……………………………………………………………………………………

Thank you very much for your participation

Dated: ………………………………………

District: ……………………………………

Town: ………………………………………

Timings: …………………………………

Enumerator's Name: ……………………

Enumerator's Signature: ………………

Remarks: …………………………………

9 788119 524310

Printed at Repro India Ltd.